ISBN 978-0-260-60981-6
PIBN 11119602

1 MONTH OF
FREE
READING

at

www.ForgottenBooks.com

By purchasing this book you are eligible for one month membership to ForgottenBooks.com, giving you unlimited access to our entire collection of over 1,000,000 titles via our web site and mobile apps.

To claim your free month visit:

www.forgottenbooks.com/free1119602

English
Français
Deutsche
Italiano
Español
Português

www.forgottenbooks.com

Mythology Photography **Fiction**
Fishing Christianity **Art** Cooking
Essays Buddhism Freemasonry
Medicine **Biology** Music **Ancient
Egypt** Evolution Carpentry Physics
Dance Geology **Mathematics** Fitness
Shakespeare **Folklore** Yoga Marketing
Confidence Immortality Biographies
Poetry **Psychology** Witchcraft
Electronics Chemistry History **Law**
Accounting **Philosophy** Anthropology
Alchemy Drama Quantum Mechanics
Atheism Sexual Health **Ancient History**
Entrepreneurship Languages Sport
Paleontology Needlework Islam
Metaphysics Investment Archaeology
Parenting Statistics Criminology
Motivational

IOWA STATE TEACHERS COLLEGE

COURSES OF STUDY

AND

PROGRAM OF RECITATIONS
UNIVERSITY OF ILLINOIS

FOR SCHOOL YEAR 1~~910-1911~~.
PRESIDENT'S OFFICE

BULLETIN

OF THE

IOWA STATE TEACHERS COLLEGE

CEDAR FALLS, IOWA

JULY 1910
Vol. XI. No. 2

NOTE: The spelling used in this Bulletin conforms to that authorized by the Simplified Spelling Board, and exhibits the little modifications that the shortend new forms make in the appearance of the printed page.

CALENDAR FOR YEAR 1910-1911.

Fall term opens Tuesday, August 30, 1910.
Winter term opens Tuesday, November 29, 1910.
Spring term opens Tuesday, March 14, 1911.
Summer term opens Saturday, June 10, 1911.

IOWA STATE TEACHERS COLLEGE.

THE COURSE OF STUDY.

Requirements for Admission.

Applicants for unconditional admission to the College Course or the Junior College Courses, hereafter printed in detail, must be at least sixteen years of age and must present satisfactory records from accredited secondary schools showing a total of fifteen units of work in accordance with the standards approved by the Iowa State Board of Education. The term unit as here used signifies a year's work where the class hours are forty-five minutes, the number of class hours per week being not less than five.

Outline Of The College Course Giving Distribution Of Work And Directions Concerning The Opportunities Offerd.

THE COLLEGE COURSE.

Degree: Bachelor of Arts in Education.

First Grade State Certificate Standard.

Entrance Requirements: Four Years Accredited High School..

Freshman Year.

A	B	C
1. Electiv.	1. Electiv.	1. Electiv.
2. Electiv.	2. Electiv.	2. Electiv.
3. Rhetoric.	3. Education I.	3. Education II.

Sophomore Year.

A	B	C
1. Electiv.	1. Electiv.	1. Electiv.
2. Electiv.	2. Electiv.	2. Electiv.
3. Education III.	3. Education IV.	3. Prac. Teaching.

Junior Year.

A	B	C
1. Electiv.	1. Electiv.	1. Electiv.
2. Electiv.	2. Electiv.	2. Electiv.
3. Prac. Teaching.	3. Education V.	3. Education VI.

Senior Year.

A	B	C
1. Electiv.	1. Electiv.	1. Electiv.
2. Electiv.	2. Electiv.	2. Electiv.
3. Prac. Teaching.	3. Electiv.	3. Electiv.

Notes.—1. Unless Solid Geometry and two years of foren language are included in the credits filed from the secondary school, these must be taken as part of the College Course.

2. Students who complete the full college course shall receive the degree of Bachelor of Arts in Education and a First Grade State Certificate. Those who complete twenty-seven full college credits shall be entitled to the diploma of Master of Didactics, but shall not receive a State Certificate unless they have met all the requirements for such certificate demanded by the State Board of Examiners.

On the completion of eighteen college credits, students may receive the diploma of Bachelor of Didactics and a Second Grade State Certificate, provided the studies pursued by them in the secondary school and the Teachers College include all the state certificate constants as designated by the State Board of Examiners. In addition to the constants enumerated in the Freshman and Sophomore years, all candidates for either the Bachelor of Didactics diploma or the Master of Didactics diploma must elect one additional term in each of the following subjects: English, History, Mathematics, Advanced Economics or American Government, Physics, and Practis Teaching. In planning electivs, students should notis that Trigonometry is a prerequisit to courses in college Physics.

METHOD OF CHOOSING ELECTIVS.

Majors.—It is necessary for the student who takes the College Course to select one major study with some one department. A major consists of at least two full years of work, thus covering six term credits. The different majors that are offerd are in the following lines. After the one major is decided the student is under the direction of the department in which the major belongs.

1. English and Public Speaking.
2. Mathematics.
3. Mathematics and Physics.
4. History and Political Science.
5. Latin.
6. German.
7. Greek.
8. Physical Science.
9. Natural Science.
10. General Science.
11. Any other arrangement of majors approved by the Faculty.

Maximum Credits of One Kind.—The largest number of term credits that is permitted from any one department shall be twelv. This is limited in order to keep a fair balance and insure broad general scholarship as well as specialization in some one line.

Other Studies.—All other electiv studies that are to obtain credit upon the College course must be selected from the other departments and must all be pure College courses.

In addition there is allowd each term an art study such as music, manual training, drawing, cooking, penmanship or a lecture course as an extra hour of work, but such studies do not substitute for any of the thirty-six term credits required for graduation.

It is advised that a term of vocal music be placed on the schedule of each student the first term enrold in order to get redy for other music work that may be desired.

DEPARTMENT SUBJECTS IN THE COLLEGE COURSE.

This tabular arrangement gives the entire program of studies with the nomenclature adopted by the Faculty for the College Course.

The numbers by which the courses in the different departments are to be designated are given below:

Professional.

Required Work—

    I.   First Term Psychology.
    II. Second Term Psychology.
  III. School Management.
  IV. History of Education.
    V. Philosophy of Education.
  VI. American Education.

Electiv Courses—

  VII. Experimental Psychology.
VIII. School Supervision.
  IX. Great Educators.

English.

    I. Rhetoric.
    II. English Literature.
  III. Shakespeare.
  IV. Epic Poetry in English.

    V. The English Romantic Movement.
   VI. The Development of the English Drama.
  VII. The History of the English Language and
         Anglo Saxon.
 VIII. Anglo Saxon and Middle English.
   IX. Literary Criticism.
    X. The Development of the English Novel.
   XI. English of the Nineteenth Century.
  XII. Theme Writing and Story Telling.
 XIII. Teachers' English.
 XIV. American Literature.

Public Speaking.

     I. Elocution I.
    II. Elocution II.
   III. Applied Drama.
IV., V., VI. Repertoire I., II., and III.
   VII. Principles of Expression.
  VIII. Argumentation.
   IX. Oratory.

Latin and Greek.

Latin—

      I. Cicero (Cato Major) and Livy.
     II. Livy.
    III. Horace (Epodes and Odes).
  IV.-XII. Roman Life.
 XIII.-XV. Teachers' Latin.
XVI.-XVIII. Elementary Latin for High School Gradu-
         ates.
 XIX.-XXI. Vergil's Aeneid.

Note—Only Courses I. to XV., inclusiv, can be counted toward a Latin Major.

Greek.

  I., II. Lessons.
   III. Anabasis.
   IV. Plato.
 V., VI. Homer.

German and French.

German—

      I. Lessons—Grammar.
     II. Lessons—Grammar.
   III. Immensee and Hoeher als die Kirche.
   IV. Die Journalisten.
     V. Wilhelm Tell.
   VI. German Prose Composition.
  VII. Emilia Galotti and Lyrics and Ballads.
VIII. Nathan der Weise.
   IX. Iphigenie auf Tauris and Die Braut von Messina.

French.

      I. Lessons—Grammar and Pronunciation.
     II. Lessons, with reading easy French.
   III. L'Abbe Constantin, Le Voyage de Monsieur Perrichon.

Geometry and Surveying.

      I. Solid Geometry. (Freshman Year).
     II. Surveying.

Mathematics.

      I. Higher Algebra I.
     II. Higher Algebra II.
   III. Trigonometry.
   IV. History and Teaching of Mathematics.
     V. Analytical Geometry.
   VI. Differential Calculus.
  VII. Integral Calculus.

Chemistry.

      I. General Inorganic.
     II. General Inorganic.
   III. Qualitativ Analysis.
   IV. Qualitativ Analysis.
     V. Quantitativ Analysis.
   VI. Quantitativ Analysis.

VII. Special Methods in Quantitativ Analysis.
VIII. Household Chemistry.
IX. Household Chemistry.
X. Food Analysis.

Physics.

I. Mechanics of Solid and Fluids.
II. Sound and Light.
III. Heat, Electricty, and Magnetism.
IV. Teachers' Special Course.
V. Sound.

Natural Science.

I. Physiology I.
II. Botany I.
III. Hygiene and Sanitation.
IV., V. Zoology I. and II.
VI. Physiography I.
VII., VIII. Geology I., II.
IX. Mineralogy.
X. Astronomy.
XI. Commercial Geography of North America.
XII. Commercial Geography of Europe.
XIII. Influences of Geography upon American History.

Major—

Zoology I.
Physiography I.
Geology I.
Physiology I.
Botany I.
Hygiene and Santitation.

History

I. American History.
II. English History.
III. Greek History.

IV.   Roman History.
V.   Medieval History.
VI.   Modern History.
VII.   Eighteenth Century History.
VIII.   Nineteenth Century History.
IX.   Method History or Teachers' History.

Economics—

I.   Theory.
II.   Problems.
III.   English Industrial History.
IV.   American Industrial History.
V.   Commercial History of Europe.
VI.   Money and Banking.
VII.   Labor and Labor Unions.

Government.—

I.   American Government.
II.   American Constitutional History I.
III.   American Constitutional History II.
IV.   English Government.
V.   Modern European Governments.
VI.   International Law.
VII.   Constitutional Law.

Art.

I.   History of Architecture and Sculpture.
II.   History of Painting.

Manual Arts.

I., II.   Manual Training Methods.
III.   Organization and Economics of Manual Training.

Physical Education.—

I., II.   Anatomy.

THE PROFESSIONAL COURSE OF STUDY FOR COLLEGE GRADUATES.

The Iowa State Teachers College has developt professional courses for college graduates that deserv special recognition for their practical features and for their large professional helpfulness. College graduates of decided success in teaching can complete one of these courses by attending three successiv summer terms and doing special assignd work during the interim. Before graduation they will need to establish proofs of their success being excellent and positiv. Where practis teaching is omitted with the consent of the department, other professional credits may be substituted on arrangement with the department. Those not having this standard of success are develop and traind by the Practis Teaching department, which is in activ work during the fall, winter and spring terms of each school year. For inexperienced teachers, the regular sessions are better adapted, as the training schools are then completely in session.

I. Professional Course in Education.

First Term.

1. Advanced Psychology.
2. School Management.
3. History of Education.

Second Term.

1. Philosophy of Education.
2. American Education.
3. Practis Teaching.

Third Term.

1. Experimental Psychology.
2. Great Educators.
3. Practis Teaching.

College graduates who complete this course will be entitled to receive the degree of Bachelor of Arts in Education and a First Grade State Certificate.

II. Professional Course with Electivs.

1. Education ....3 credits
2. Training School Work ....2 credits
3. Scholastic Studies ....4 credits
   ___
   Total required ....9 credits

Graduates of approved colleges can complete this course in one year, and will receive the diploma of Master of Didactics and a First Grade State Certificate, provided they meet all the requirements demanded by the State Board of Educational Examiners.

Observations on These Courses.

1. Some branches of the above work can be personal, individual studies, laboratory and library in character, on lines outlined by the Professional department. These studies are to be carefully made and results submitted to the department for examination, criticism and instruction. The library is so strong in Pedagogy that this work is of great and lasting professional value.

2. For entrance upon this course a complete detail of all the work taken at the college must be filed.

3. Substitutions will be granted for efficient pedagogical work taken at a college with a strong professional department. Great liberty will be allowd to such grade of students so as to enable them to prepare both wisely and well for the best public servis in any special line of school work, but in every case a year's attendance at this college is required. Such students are excused from orations and literary society work if they apply to the Faculty for such release.

4. College graduates who wish Primary or Kindergarten training will be given a year's work on application and can graduate at the end of that time of residence, provided the work done is creditable.

5. Any college graduate interested in this course is requested to write for further information to the President of the Iowa State Teachers College or to C. P. Colgrove.

JUNIOR COLLEGE COURSES.

SPECIAL TEACHER PREPARATION.

Standards Required and Honors Conferd.

Special State Certificates.—For the completion of these courses the State Board of Educational Examiners grants a five year special state certificate, said certificate authorizing the graduate to teach such branches in the public schools.

The Diploma Conferd.—The junior college courses each cover two years of strong work in scholastic, general professional and special professional lines. They are the equivalent in standard of excellence with other college courses of similar length and they give special attention to some one line of definit training. For the completion of these two years of study and training, a Special Teacher Diploma is awarded.

For the completion of an additional year of study, a Director's or Supervisor's Diploma as a special teacher is awarded as an additional recommendation of qualification and training for executiv work along these specialties of teaching. When a three-year course is printed, the third year is the supervisors' or directors' course.

In some particular departments where students complete the full line of special professional work required, such as music and art, department certificates may be obtaind by such persons as do not desire to complete the scholastic and the general professional work required for a diploma.

In all junior college courses the electiv studies must be chosen from the list of branches and term's work designated as of full college grade. These elections must be made by consulting the heds of the departments involvd in order to avoid all mistakes.

College graduates of standard institutions are granted a one year course in any of these special lines if their former work permits it to be done.

THE PRIMARY TEACHERS' COURSE.

· First Year.

A	B	C
1. Prim'y Methods	1. Prim'y Methods	1. Prim'y Methods
2. Psychology.	2. Elocution.	2. Botany.
3. Pri. Handwork	3. Psychology.	3. Obs. in Training
4. Rhetoric.	4. Vocal Music.	School.
		4. Vocal Music.

Physical Training, five hours a week.
Literary Society Work.

Second Year.

A	B	C
1. Sch. Manage't.	1. Hist. of Educ'n	1. Kg. Theory & Ob
2. Drawing.	2. Drawing.	2. Drawing.
3. Zoology.	3. Eng. Literature.	3. Electiv.
4. Criticism and Practis.	4. Criticism and Practis.	4. Criticism and Practis.

Literary Society Work.

THE KINDERGARTNERS' COURSE.

First Year.

A	B	C
1. Kg. Theory.	1. Kg. Theory.	1. Kg Practis.
2. Psychology.	2. Psychology.	2. El. Handwork.
3. Rhetoric.	3. Vocal Music.	3. Vocal Music.
4. Drawing.	4. Drawing.	4. Nature Study.

Physical Training.
Literary Society Work.

Second Year.

A	B	C
1. Kg. Theory.	1. Kg. Theory.	1. Kg. Theory.
2. Kg. Practis.	2. Kg. Practis.	2. Sch. Managem't
3. Elocution.	3. Hist. of Educ'n.	3. Primary Theory
4. Electiv.	4. Electiv.	4. Electiv.
	Physical Training.	
	Literary Society Work.	

Supervisor Year.

A	B	C
1. Kg. Theory.	1. Kg. Theory.	1. Psychology.
2. Phil. of Educ'n	2. Sch. Supervis'n	2. Kg. Practis.
3. Harmony.	3. Public Speak'g	3. Hist. of Paint'g
4. Electiv.	4. Electiv.	4. Electiv.
	Literary Society Work.	

THE PUBLIC SCHOOL MUSIC TEACHERS' COURSE.

First Year.

A	B	C
1. Psychology.	1. Eng. Literature	1. Nature Study.
2. Rhetoric.	2. Psychology.	2. Voice.
3. 3d term Music.	3. 4th term Music	3. 6th term Music
Sightsinging (3)	Sightsinging &	Methods (2)
Ele. Harm'y (2)	Methods (3)	Harmony (2)
4. Voice.	Hist. of Mus. (2)	Hist. of Mus. (1)
	4. 5th term Music	4. 5th term Music
	Harmony (2)	Ear Train. (2)
	5. Voice.	Adv. Sight-
		singing (1)
		5. Piano.

Physical Training.
Literary Society Work.

Second Year.

A	B	C
1. Sound.	1. History.	1. Hist. of Educa'n
2. Elocution.	2. Sch. Manage't	2. Voice.
3. 7th term Music	3. 8th term Music	3. 9th term Music
Hist of Mus. (2)	Musical	Supervision (2)
Harmony (2)	Appreciat'n (2)	Harmony (2)
Conducting (1)	Harmony (2)	Theory of
4. Observation	Child Voice (1)	Music (1)
(half credit.)	4. Prac. Teaching.	4. Prac. Teaching.
	Physical Training.	
	Literary Society Work.	

The figure in parenthesis indicates the number of recitation hours per week, when less than five hours a week are given.

Two years of voice are required (one lesson per week.)

One year of piano is required (one lesson per week.)

Students completing all the music work required in the above course and the practis teaching, in addition to one term of psychology, one term of school management, one term of elocution, and two electivs in English, may be granted a certificate from the department.

THE DRAWING TEACHERS' COURSE.

First Year.

A	B	C
1. Cast Drawing.	1. Cast Drawing.	1. Hist. of Paint'g.
2. Hist. (Greek)	2. Medieval Hist.	2. Pscyhology.
3. Elocution	3. Psychology.	3. Phys. Sci. Elect.
4. Rhetoric.	4. Hist. of Arch.	4. Electiv.
	& Sculpture	
	Physical Training.	
	Literary Society Work.	

Second Year.

A	B	C
1. Still Life.	1. Perspectiv.	1. Superv'n in Art
2. Zoology.	2. El. Handwork.	2. Mathematics.
3. Pol. Sci. Elec'v	3. Eng Literature	3. Hist of Educa'n
4. Sch. Manage't	4. Prac. Teaching	4. Prac. Teaching
	Physical Training.	
	Literary Society Work.	

Third Year.

A	B	C
1. Water Color.	1. Mech. Drawing	1. Design
2. Profes'l Elec'v	2. Geology.	2. Chemistry.
3. Physiography.	3. Phil. of Educ'n	3. Botany.
4. El. of Lit. Crit.	4. Sheet Met. W'k	4. Electiv.
	Literary Society Work.	

THE MANUAL TRAINING TEACHERS' COURSE.

First Year.

A	B	C
1. Rhetoric.	1. Higher Alg'a I.	1. Eng. Literature
2. Psychology.	2. Psychology.	2. Sch. Manage't.
3. Com. Geog. of N. A.	3. Prim. Handw'k	3. Bench Work.
	4. 2d Drawing.	4. Design.
4. 1st Drawing.	5. Mech. Drawing.	5. Mech. Drawing.
	Physical Training.	
	Literary Society Work.	

Second Year.

A	B	C
1. Trigonometry.	1. Hist. of Educ'n	1. XIX. Cent. Hist
2. Man. Training Methods I.	2. Man. Training Methods II.	2. Physics I.
		3. Bench Work.
3. Bench Work.	3. Bench Work.	4. Mech. Drawi'g
4. Sheet M't W'k	4. Special Electiv.	5. Prac. Teaching.
5. Ele. Handwork	5. Prac. Teaching.	
	Physical Training.	
	Literary Society Work.	

Third Year.

A	B	C
1. Profes'l Electiv	1. Phil. of Educ'n	1. Org. & Econ. of
2. Elocution	2. Chemistry I.	Man. Training.
3. Bench Work.	3. Special Electiv	2. Chemistry II.
4. Electiv.	4. Indus. History.	3. Nat. Sci. Elec'v
		4. Special Electiv

Literary Society Work.

THE DOMESTIC SCIENCE TEACHERS' COURSE.

First Year.

A	B	C
1. Foods, comp & Dietary Uses.	1. Foods, comp & Dietary Uses.	1. Foods, comp & Dietary Uses.
2. Cookery.	2. Cookery.	2. Cookery.
3. Sewing.	3. Sewing.	3. Waitress Work.
4. Inorg. Chem.	4. Inorg. Chem.	4. Qual. Analysis.
5. Rhetoric.	5. Sanitation.	5. Sewing.
		6. Methods in Dom Science.
		7. Psychology.

Physical Training.
Literary Society Work.

Second Year.

A	B	C
1. Cookery.	1. Cookery.	1. Cookery.
2. House'd Chem.	2. House'd Archi-	2. Food Analysis.
3. Adv. Physiol'y	tecture.	3. Hist. of Educ'n
4. Prac. Teaching.	3. House'd Chem.	4. Sch. Managem't
	4. Psychology.	5. Prac. Teaching.
	5. Prac. Teaching.	

Physical Training.
Literary Society Work.

NOTE.—This course is of a kind that it is practically necessary to begin the same at the opening of the fall term and continue it regularly for the time requird.

THE PHYSICAL EDUCATION TEACHERS' COURSE.

First Year.

A	B	C
1. Electiv (Math.)	1. Chemistry I.	1. Chemistry II.
2. Electiv (Hist.)	2. Elocution.	2. Electiv. (Eng.)
3. Rhetoric.	3. Psychology.	3. Psychology.

Physical Training.
Literary Society Work.

Second Year.

A	B	C
1. Gym. Pedagogy	1. Theory and Sys-	1. Hist. of Physic'l
2. Anatomy I.	tems of Ph'y Ed.	Training.
3. Sch Managem't	2. Anatomy II.	2. Adv. Hygiene
	3. Hist of Educa'n	3. Elec. (Pol. Sci.).

Physical Training.
Literary Society Work.

Third Year.

A	B	C
1. Anthropom'y &	1. Prac.Teaching.	1. Physiology of
Phys. Diagno's	2. Elec. (Nat.Sci.)	Exercise.
2. Adv. Physiol'y	3. Phil. of Educ'n.	2. Electiv.
3. Electiv.		3. Genetic Psych.
		4. Med. Gymnast's
		and Massage.

Physical Training.
Literary Society Work.

Special Course for College Graduates.

A	B	C
1. Gym. Pedago'y	1. Theory and Sys-	1. Hist. of Phys. Tr
2. Anatomy I.	tems of Ph'l Ed.	2. Hygiene.
3. Adv. Physiol'y	2. Anatomy II.	3. Physiology of
4. Anthropom'y &	3. Electiv.	Exercise.
Phys. Diagnosis	4. Prac. Teaching	4. Medical Gym. &
		Massage.

Physical Training.

TEACHERS' CERTIFICATE COURSES.

Courses Offerd in Subjects Required by the State Board of Educational Examiners.

I. The Uniform County Certificate Course.

The Teachers College maintains classes every term for the accommodation of students who wish to prepare for the examination required for county and state certificates.

Conditions of Admission—Plans of Management.

1. Students who possess third grade uniform county certificates, whether in force or not, may enter without formal examination on this credential of scholarship, but they will be required to take all branches on the certificate that are recorded as below seventy-five per cent in the two term classes regularly provided. Students who have completed eighth grade work in city schools, or those having country school diplomas, who are at least sixteen years of age, are admitted to the course but are assignd to classes where two terms of work is required in arithmetic, grammar, U. S. history, geography, civics, and vocal music. Students without credentials of any kind or who do not meet these minimum standards are given work in the Secondary or High School maintaind by the College, unless they establish their qualifications as conforming to said standards by taking an examination equivalent to that required for third grade county certificate.

Students who possess second grade county certificates are admitted to study such subjects as are needed to prepare them for first grade certificate standard.

Uniform County Certificate Course.

First Year.

A	B	C
1. Arithmetic.	1. Geography.	1. U. S. History.
2. Eng. Grammar.	2. Algebra.	2. Algebra.
3. Physiology.	3. Didactics.	3. Reading.
4.Orthography.	4. Penmanship.	4. Vocal Music.
	Physical Training.	

Second Year.

A	B	C
1. Eng. Composi'n	1. Eng. Electiv	1. Civics.
2. Physics.	2. Physics.	2. Methods.
3. Physiography.	3. El. Economics.	3. Gen History.
4. Electiv.	4. Electiv.	4. Electiv.
	Physical Training.	

NOTE.—The electiv terms work here authorized are to be chosen from the State Certificate course.

II.   The State Certificate Course.

Conditions of Admission and Plans of Management Explaind.

1.   Students who have completed the county certificate teachers' course or who are holders of the first grade uniform county teachers' certificate are granted admission to this course.

2.   Students who have completed unaccredited high school courses of at least two years will receive credit for entrance requirements to this course in proportion to the quality and quantity of work proven by their certificates furnisht by the high school from which they graduated, such credit to become permanent provided the work done in the College justifies such after recognition. Students presenting additional work earnd in other schools will have their status decided by a committee of the Faculty.

3.   Students having scholarship equivalent to first

grade uniform county certificate or who have graduated from unaccredited high schools of more than two years, are admitted on equivalent three year courses to prepare as teachers in kindergarten, primary, music or other special teacher work.

State Certificate Course.

Granting an Elementary Teacher Diploma and a Second Grade State Certificate.

First Year.

A	B	C
1. Algebra. *	1. Plane Geomet'y	1. Plane Geomet'y
2. Physics. *	2. Bookkeeping.	2. Vocal Music.
3. Gen. History. *	3. Elocution.	3. Prin of Educa'n
4. Electiv.	4. Electiv.	4. Electiv.
	Physical Training.	

Second Year.

A	B	C
1. Drawing.	1. Drawing.	1. Math Electiv.
2. Psychology.	2. Psychology.	2. Sch. Managem't
3. Solid Geometry	3. Sanitation.	3. Gen. Botany.
4. Electiv.	4. Electiv.	4. Electiv.
	Physical Training.	

• Literary Society Work.

Third Year.

A	B	C
1. Rhetoric.	1. Eng. Electiv.	1. Science Electiv.
2. Econ. Electiv	2. Govt. Electiv.	2. Hist. Electiv.
3. Hist. of Edu'n.	3. Prac. Teaching.	3. Prac. Teaching.
4. Electiv.	4. Electiv.	4. Electiv.

Literary Society Work.

*Two terms work if elementary teachers course was not completed at this College or in an equivalent school.

NOTES.—The electiv terms of work here provided are intended for the study of Latin or German. Substitutes for these foren languages may be granted in other departments where the student does not purpose to later become a candidate for the diploma Bachelor of Didactics.

A term's work in Teachers' Arithmetic or Teachers' Grammar may be taken during the course if there are sufficient students desiring such special study.

THE SPECIAL COMMERCIAL TEACHERS' COURSE.

Granting a Department Certificate.
First Year.

A	B	C
1. Penmanship.	1. Penmanship.	1. Penmanship.
2. Bookkeeping.	2. 2d Bookkeeping.	2. 3d Bookkeeping.
3. Arithmetic.	3. Com. Geography.	3. Com. Geography.
4. Grammar.	4. Eng. Comp.	4. Rhetoric.

Physical Training.
Rhetoricals or Literary Society Work.

SPECIAL MUSIC TEACHER COURSES.

Cónditions of Admission.—Students are admitted to these music courses on liberal terms as to preparatory training and are encouraged to begin early enough to develop the skill and capability for professional artistic success that are so notably demanded in teachers of these kinds.

To become a candidate for graduation, the student must have attaind to the scholastic qualifications required of secondary schools for full college entrance. These scholastic conditions may be acquired in any good secondary school or may be accomplisht in the certificate courses at the College.

Conditions of Graduation.—A special Teacher Diploma will be awarded to such persons as complete satisfactorily any one of the courses here outlined, but as skill and capability as musicians are also essential qualities to be attaind, the exact time necessary to complete any one of these courses can not be stated in school years. The candidate must have sufficient proficiency in the special line chosen to secure the recommendation of the professors in charge of the work to become an applicant for graduation. The courses as here mapt out, outside of the attainment in capability as a musician, can be satisfactorily completed in three years.

THE PIANO COURSE.

Piano lessons must be continued thru the entire period of study, two lessons a week. A second study—voice or orchestral instrument—must also be carried, with either one or two lessons a week, each term except the last year.

Other required work will be:

First Year.

A	B.	C
Elem'ts of Music 5	Elem'ts of Music 5	German 5
German 5	German 5	Music History 1
Music History 2.		Ear Training 2

Second Year.

A	B	C
Harmony 2	Harmony 2	Harmony 2
Music History 2	Eng. Literature 5	Psychology 5
Sound 5		

Third Year.

A	B	C
Harmony 2	Harmony 2	Harm. Analysis 2.
Psychology 5	Medieval Hist. 5	Modern History 5

Piano—9 terms, twice a week (at least.)

Second Study—6 terms, once or twice a week (at least.)

The figures after the subjects indicate the number of recitation periods per week.

THE VIOLIN COURSE.

Violin lessons must be continued thru the entire period of study—two lessons per week. The piano work must be carried for two years successfully with at least one lesson a week. Attendance at two orchestra rehearsals and one class in ensemble playing is also required each week.

First Year.

A	B	C
Elem'ts of Music 5	Elem'ts of Music 5	Musical History 1
German 5	German 5	German 5
Musical History 2		Ear Training 2

Second Year.

A	B	C
Harmony 2	Harmony 2	Harmony 2
Musical History 2	Eng. Literature 5	Psychology 5
Sound 5		

Third Year.

A	B	C
Harmony 2	Harmony 2	Harm. Analy's 2
Psychology 5	Medieval Hist. 5	Modern History 5

The figures after the subjects indicate the number of recitation periods per week.

THE VOICE COURSE.

Three years of voice lessons (two a week), and two years piano lessons (one a week), will be required.

First Year.

A	B	C
Elem'ts of Music 5	Elem'ts of Music 5	German 5
German 5	German 5	Elem'ts of Music 5
Music History 2	Theory of Phys. Training 5	Ear Training 2

Second Year.

A	B	C
Harmony 2	Harmony 2	Harmony 2
Music Hist. 2	Eng. Literature 5	Psychology 5
Sound 5		

Third Year.

A	B	C
Harmony 2	Harmony 2	Harm. Analy's 2
Psychology 5	French 5	French 5
French 5	Medieval Hist. 5	Modern History 5

The figures after the subjects indicate the number of recitation periods per week.

PROGRAM OF RECITATIONS.

Explanatory Note.

This program of recitations is printed for the full school year, presenting the work for the Fall, Winter and Spring Terms. The work is organized on the basis of the past year and may be expanded if numbers enrold should demand it.

The nomenclature used gives in order: 1. The College Course. 2. The Junior College Courses. 3. The Teachers' Certificate Courses, for each term. The subject of study is given in the terminology adopted by the departments, complete explanation being given in the Catalog and Circular for 1910. The name of the teacher is given following each subject assignd for the term and the Arabic numeral following the teacher's name gives the hour at which the recitation will occur.

The following are the hours of work in the school for the year:

First Hour—8:00 to 8:55.
Second Hour—8:55 to 9:50.
Assembly—9:50 to 10:20.
Third Hour—10:20 to 11:15.
Fourth Hour—11:15 to 12:10.
Fifth Hour—1:30 to 2:25.
Sixth Hour—2:25 to 3:20.
Seventh Hour—3:20 to 4:15.

Of these the first to fifth, inclusiv, are regarded as regular class hours.

Students' Offis Hours.—Students having business

with the President's offis will receive attention from 7:30 to 9:50 a. m. and 1:00 to 2:00 p. m. Please note this and do not come other business hours except in emergencies that are unusual.

Library Hours.—School days, 7:30 a. m. to 5:00 p. m. Saturdays, 8:00 a. m. to 12:00 m.

Literary Societies.—Fridays, 2:25 p. m. Saturdays, 7:00 p. m.

Faculty Meetings.—Mondays, 2:25 p. m.

ASSIGNMENT FOR REHEARSALS OF MUSICAL SOCIETIES.

Choral Society—Thursdays, 2:25 p. m.

Cecilians—Wednesdays, 2:25 p. m.

Euterpeans—Tuesdays, 2:25 p. m.

Young Ladies' Glee Club—Mondays, 2:25 p. m.

Minnesingers—Wednesdays, 2:25 p. m.

Troubadours—Tuesdays, 2:25 p. m.

Orchestra—Mondays and Thursdays, 3:30 p. m.

Band—Tuesdays and Fridays, 3:30 p. m.

Ensemble Class—Wednesdays, 3:00 p. m.

Junior Band—Wednesdays, 3:30 p. m.

FALL TERM.

College Course.

Professional Instruction in Education.—I. 1st Psychology, Mr. Samson 1; Mr. Dick 4. II. 2nd Psychology, Mr. Samson 2. III. School Management, Mr. Colgrove 2; Mr. Dick 1-3. IV. History of Education, Mr. Walters 2. IX. Great Educators, Mr. Walters 1.

Training in Teaching.—Illustrativ Teaching, Mr. Bender (Tuesday, Wednesday, Thursday) 3-5-6.

English Language and Literature.—I. Rhetoric, Mr. Lynch 1-5; Mr. Gist 4-5; Miss Lambert 2; Miss Gregg 5; Miss Hearst 4; Miss Lodge 1-3. II. (a) English Literature, Mr. Lynch 3; Miss Lambert 4. III. Shakespeare, Mr. Gist 2. XI. English Literature of the 19th Century, Miss Lambert 1.

Elocution and Public Speaking.—I. Elocution I., Miss Martin 2-3. IV. Repertoire I., Miss Martin 4. VIII. Argumentation, Mr. Barnes 2; IX. Oratory I., Mr. Barnes 3.

Latin and Greek.—(1) **Latin.** I. Cicero (Cato Major) and Livy, Mr. Merchant 2. X. Tacitus and Pliny, Mr. Merchant 1. XIII. Teachers' Latin, Mr. Merchant 1 (Mon., Fri.) and 6 (Tues., Wed., Thurs.) XVI. Elementary Latin: Introductory Work 5, or Cicero 3, Mr. Merchant. XIX. Vergil (Aeneid, First term), Miss Call 2. (2) **Greek.** I. Lessons, Miss Call 4. IV. Xenophon, Miss Call 5.

German and French.—(1) **German.** I. Grammar, Mr. Knoepfler 4. II. Grammar, Miss Lorenz 5. III. Immensee and Hoeher als die Kirche, Miss Lorenz 1. IV. Die Journalisten, Miss Lorenz 3. V. Wilhelm Tell or Maria Stuart or Die Jungfrau von Orleans, Miss Lorenz 2. VI. Prose Composition, Mr. Knoepfler 1. VII. Emilia Galotti and German Lyrics and Ballads, Mr. Knoepfler 3. (2) **French.** I. Lessons, Mr. Knoepfler 2.

Mathematics.—I. Higher Algebra I., Miss Seals 2. III. Trigonometry, Mr. Cory 1. V. Analytical Geometry, Mr. Condit 1.

Chemistry.—I. Inorganic, Mr. Getchell 3. II. Inorganic, Mr. Page 2. III. IV. Qualitativ Analysis, Mr. Getchell 1-5. V. VI. Quantitativ Analysis, Mr. Getchell 5-6.

Physics.—I. Mechanics of Solids and Fluids, Mr. Begeman 3. V. Sound, Mr. Begeman 5.

Natural Science.—I. Physiology I., Mr. Newton 3. IV. Zoology I., Mr. Arey 1. VI. Physiography I., Mr. Cable 2. XI. Commercial Geography of North America, Miss Aitchison 1.

History.—I. American, Miss Riggs 4. III. Greek, Miss Rice 1. VI. Modern, Miss Riggs 3.

Economics.—I. Economic Theory, Mr. McKitrick 2. V. Commercial History of Europe, Mr. McKitrick 4.

Government.—I. American Government, Mr. Meyerholz 4. II. American Constitutional History I., Mr. Meyerholz 5. VII. Constitutional Law, Mr. Meyerholz 3.

The Manual Arts.—I. Manual Training Methods I., Mr. Bailey 2.

Physical Education.—I. Anatomy I., Mr. Seymour 3.

JUNIOR COLLEGE COURSES.

Professional Instruction in Education.—1st Psychology, Mr. Colgrove 1-3-5. History of Education, Mr. Walters 3-4. 1st Primary Methods, Miss McGovern 2-3-4. 2nd Primary Methods, Miss McGovern 1.

Training in Teaching.—Primary Criticism, Miss Hatcher 6. Kindergarten Theory (Junior) Miss Ward 4. Kindergarten Theory (Senior) Miss Ward and Miss Dowdell 4. Kindergarten Practis, Miss Dowdell 2-3.

Chemistry.—1st Inorganic Chemistry, Mr. Page 1. Household Chemistry, Mr. Page 4.

Physics.—Sound, Mr. Begeman 5.

Natural Science.—Zoology, Mr. Arey 3-4-5.

Art.—Water Color, Miss Thornton 1. 1st Primary Drawing, Miss Thornton 2-3-4. Cast Drawing, Miss Patt 2. 1st Kindergarten Drawing, Miss Patt 3. Still Life, Miss Patt 4. Perspectiv, Miss Patt 1.

Vocal Music.—1st Vocal Music, Mr. Fullerton 3;

Miss Dickey 1; Miss Stenwall 5; Mr. Hays 4. 2nd Vocal Music, Mr. Fullerton 1; Miss Stenwall 4; Mr. Hays 2 3rd Music, (a) Harmony (Tuesday, Thursday), Mr. Fullerton; (b) Sightsinging (Monday, Wednesday, Friday), Mr. Fullerton 2. 4th Music, (a) History (Monday, Thursday), Miss Childs; (b) Sightsinging (Tuesday, Wednesday, Friday), Miss Stenwall 3. 7th Music, (a) History (Monday, Wednesday), Miss Childs; (b) Harmony (Tuesday, Friday), Mr. Merrill; (c) Conducting (Thursday), Mr. Fullerton 4. Practis Teaching for Music Students, Miss Dickey 3; Miss Stenwall 2.

Physical Education.—Anatomy I., Mr. Seymour 3. Gymnastic Pedagogy, Mr. Seymour 4. Anthropometry and Physical Diagnosis, Mr. Seymour 5. Primary Physical Training, 3-4.

The Manual Arts.—Manual Training Methods I., Mr. Bailey 2. 1st Mechanical Drawing, Mr. Bailey 3. Advanced Mechanical Drawing, Mr. Bailey 5. 1st Bench Work, Mr. Bailey 1. Advanced Bench Work, Mr. Brown 3-5. Woodturning, Mr. Brown 3-5. Primary Handwork, Mrs. McMahon 1-3-5. 1st Sewing, Mrs. McMahon 2. Elementary Handwork, Mr. Brown 4.

Home Economics.—Domestic Science. (1) 1st Year Training Class. Foods; Composition and Dietary Uses, Miss Townsend (Monday, Wednesday) 1:30 to 2:25. Cookery, Miss Townsend (Monday, Wednesday), 2:25 to 5:00. (2) 2nd Year Training Class. Cookery, Miss Townsend (Tuesday, Thursday) 3:15 to 5:30. Practis Teaching in Cookery (Tuesday, Thursday), 1:00 to 3:15.

COUNTY AND STATE CERTIFICATE COURSE.

Professional Instruction in Education.—1st Psychology, Mr. Samson 3. 2nd Psychology, Mr. Samson 5. School Management, Mr. Colgrove 2; Mr. Dick 1-3. History of Education, Mr. Walters 3-4. Principles of Education, Mr. Dick 2. Methods, Miss Buck 2-3. Didactics, Miss Buck 1-5.

English Language and Literature.—Rhetoric, Mr. Lynch 1-5 Mr. Gist 4-5; Miss Lambert 2; Miss Gregg 5; Miss Hearst 4; Miss Lodge 1-3. American Literature, Miss Baker 2. 1st English Classics Miss Oliver 4. 2nd English Classics, Miss Hearst 5. Complete English Composition, Miss Lodge 4. Complete English Grammar, Miss Gregg 2-3-4. 1st half English Composition, Miss Baker 5. 2nd half English Composition, Miss Baker 3. 1st half English Grammar, Miss Baker 4; Miss Hearst 1. 2nd English Grammar, Miss Hearst 2. Orthography, Miss Oliver 1-2.

Elocution and Public Speaking.—Elocution, Miss Falkler 2-4. Reading, Miss Falkler 1-3.

Latin and Greek.—Latin. 1st Latin Lessons, Miss Call 1. 2nd Caesar, Miss Call 3.

Geometry and Surveying.—Beginning Geomtery, Mr. Wright 2-3. Middle Geometry, Mr. Wright 4. Solid Geometry, Mr. Wright 5.

Mathematics.—1st Algebra, Miss Seals 4-5. 2nd Algebra, Miss Seals 3. 3rd Algebra, Mr. Condit 2. Two term Algebra, Mr. Condit 5. Complete Arithmetic, Mr. Condit 3; Mr. Cory 2-4. 1st half Arithmetic, Miss Lambert 2-3-4. 2nd half Arithmetic, Miss Lambert 5.

Physics.—1st Physics, Mr. Hersey 1-4; ———— 2-3. 2nd Physics, Mr. Hersey 2; ———— 5.

Natural Science.—General Botany, Mr. Newton 5. Physiology, Mr. Newton 1-2. Physiography, Mr. Cable 1-3. Complete Geography, Mr. Cable 5. 1st half Geography, Miss Aitchison 2-4. 2nd half Geography, Miss Aitchison 3.

History.—1st General History, Miss Rice 3. 2nd General History, Miss Riggs 2. Complete U. S. History, Miss Riggs 5. 1st half U. S. History, Miss Rice 4; Mr. Peterson 1. 2nd half U. S. History, Miss Rice 5.

Economics.—Economics, Mr. McKitrick 5. Elementary Economics, Mr. McKitrick 3; Mr. Peterson 4.

Government.—Iowa and U. S. Civics (Review), Mr. Meyerholz 2. Iowa History and Civics, Mr. Peterson 2 U. S. Civics, Mr. Peterson 3.

Art.—1st Drawing, Miss Patt 4. 2nd Drawing, Miss Patt 1.

Commercial Education.—1st Penmanship, Mr. Cummins 1-2. Advanced Penmanship, Mr. Cummins 4. 1st Bookkeeping, Mr. Cummins 3.

Vocal Music.—1st Vocal Music, Mr. Fullerton 3; Miss Dickey 1; Miss Stenwall 5; Mr. Hays 4. 2nd Vocal Music, Mr. Fullerton 1; Miss Stenwall 4; Mr. Hays 2.

Home Economics.—Domestic Science. 1st Cookery, Miss Townsend (Tuesday, Thursday), 1:00 to 3:15.

WINTER TERM.

College Course.

Professional Instruction In Education.—I. 1st Psychology, Mr. Samson 1. II. 2nd Psychology, Mr. Samson 2; Mr. Dick 1. III. School Management, Mr. Colgrove 2; Mr. Dick 1-4. IV. History of Education, Mr. Walters 4. V. Philosophy of Education, Mr. Walters 2. VI. American Education, Mr. Seerley 1.

English Language and Literature.—I. Rhetoric, Mr. Lynch 5; Mr. Gist 1-4; Miss Lodge 2-4. II. (a) English Literature, Mr. Lynch 2; (b) English Literature, Miss Lambert 3; IV. Epic Poetry in English, Mr. Lynch 3. VII. Anglo Saxon and The History of the English Language, Mr. Gist 2. XIV. American Literature, Miss Lambert 1.

Elocution and Public Speaking.—II. Elocution II., Miss Martin 3. III. Applied Drama, Miss Martin 4. V. Repertoire II., Miss Martin 2. IX. Oratory I, Mr. Barnes 1; Oratory II., Mr. Barnes 3.

Latin and Greek.—(1) **Latin. II.** Livy, Mr. Merchant 2. XI.. Pliny and Martial, Mr. Merchant 1. XIV. Teachers' Latin, Mr. Merchant 1 (Monday, Friday) and 6 (Tuesday, Wednesday, Thursday). XVII. Elementary Latin: Caesar 5, or Cicero 3, Mr. Merchant. XX. Vergil (Aeneid, Second term), Miss Call 2. (2) **Greek.** II. Lessons, Miss Call 4.

German and French.—(1) **German.** I. Grammar, Miss Lorenz 1. II. Grammar, Mr. Knoepfler 4. III. Immensee and Hoeher als die Kirche, Miss Lorenz 5. IV. Die Journalisten, Miss Lorenz 2. V. Wilhelm Tell or Maria Stuart or Die Jungfrau von Orleans, Miss Lorenz 3. VI. Prose Composition, Mr. Knoepfler 1. VIII. Nathan der Weise, Mr. Knoepfler 3. (2) **French.** II. Lessons, Mr. Knoepfler 2.

Mathematics.—I. Higher Algebra 1., Miss Seals 2. III. Trigonometry, Mr. Condit 3. VI. Differential Calculus, Mr. Condit 1.

Chemistry.—I. Inorganic, Mr. Page 2. II. Inorganic, Mr. Getchell 3. III., IV. Qualitativ Analysis, Mr. Getchell 1-2. V., VI., Quantitativ Analysis, Mr. Getchell 5-6. VIII. Assaying, Mr. Page 5-6.

Physics.—I. Mechanics of Solids and Fluids, Mr. Begeman 4. II. Sound and Light, Mr. Begeman 3.

Natural Science.—III. Hygiene and Sanitation, Mr. Newton 4-5. VII. Geology I., Mr. Arey 3. IX. Mineralogy, Mr. Arey 4. XI. Commercial Geography of North America, Miss Aitchison 5. XIII. Influences of Geography upon American History, Mr. Cable 4.

History.—IV. Roman, Miss Rice 2. V. Medieval, Miss Riggs 1. VII. 18th Century, Miss Riggs 2.

Economics.—III. English Industrial History, Mr. McKitrick 1. VI. Money and Banking, Mr. Mc Kitrick 3.

Government.—III. American Constitutional History II., Mr. Meyerholz 4. IV. English Government, Mr. Meyerholz 2. VI. International Law, Mr. Meyerholz 3.

Art.—I. History of Architecture and Sculpture, Miss Thornton 2.

The Manual Arts.—II. Manual Training Methods II., Mr. Bailey 2.

Physical Education.—II. Anatomy II., Mr. Seymour 3.

Junior College Courses.

Professional Instruction in Education.—1st Psychology, Mr. Dick 5. 2nd Psychology, Mr. Colgrove 1-3-5. History of Education, Mr. Walters 1-3. 1st Primary Methods, Miss McGovern 5. 2nd Primary Methods, Miss McGovern 2-3-4.

Training in Teaching.—Primary Criticism, Miss Hatcher 6. Kindergarten Theory (Junior), Miss Ward and Miss Dowdell 4. Kindergarten Theory (Senior) Miss Ward 4. Kindergarten Practis, Miss Dowdell 2-3.

English Language and Literature.—English Literature, Miss Lambert 5.

Chemistry.—2nd Inorganic, Mr. Page 1. Household Chemistry, Mr. Page 4.

Natural Science.—Structrual Botany, Mr. Arey 1-2.

Art.—History of Architecture and Sculpture, Miss Thornton 2. Cast Drawing, Miss Patt 5. Still Life, Miss Thornton 1-3. Perspectiv, Miss Patt 3-4. 2nd Primary Drawing, Miss Thornton 1-4. 2nd Kindergarten Drawing, Miss Patt 1.

Vocal Music—1st Vocal Music, Mr. Fullerton 3; Miss Stenwall 1; Mr. Hays 2-5. 2nd Vocal Music, Miss Stenwall 3; Miss Dickey 1. 3rd Music, Mr. Fullerton 1; 4th Music, (a) History (Monday, Thursday), Miss Childs; (b) Sightsinging (Tuesday, Wednesday, Friday), Miss Stenwall 4. 5th Music, (a) Ear Training (Monday, Wednesday), Mr. Fullerton; (b) Harmony (Tuesday, Friday), Mr. Merrill; (c) Conducting (Thursday), Mr.

Fullerton 2. 8th Music, (a) Appreciation, (Monday, Thursday), Mr. Fullerton; (b) Harmony (Tuesday, Friday), Mr. Merrill; (c) Child Voice (Wednesday), Miss Stenwall 4. Practis Teaching for Music Students, Miss Dickey 3; Miss Stenwall 2.

Physical Education.—Anatomy II., Mr. Seymour 3. Theory and Systems of Physical Education, Mr. Seymour 5. 2nd Primary Physical Training 3-4.

The Manual Arts.—Manual Training Methods II., Mr. Bailey 2. 1st Bench Work, Mr. Bailey 4. Advanced Bench Work, Mr. Brown 2-5. 1st Mechanical Drawing, Mr. Brown 3. Advanced Mechanical Drawing, Mr. Bailey 5. Sheet Metal Work, Mr. Bailey 3. Woodturning, Mr. Brown 2-5. Elementary Handwork, Mr. Brown 1. Primary Handwork, Mrs. McMahon 1-2-5. 2nd Sewing, Mrs. McMahon 2.

Home Economics.—Domestic Science. (1) 1st Year Training Class. Foods: Composition and Dietary Uses, Miss Townsend (Monday, Wednesday), 1:30 to 2:25. Cookery, Miss Townsend (Monday, Wednesday), 2:25 to 5:00. (2) 2nd Year Training Class. Household Architecture, Miss Townsend (Tuesday), 3:30; (Friday) 1:30 to 2:25. Cookery, Miss Townsend (Thursday), 3:15 to 6:00. Practis Teaching in Cookery (Tuesday, Thursday), 1:00 to 3:15.

County and State Certificate Courses.

Professional Instruction in Education.—1st Psychology, Mr. Samson 3. 2nd Psychology, Mr. Samson 5. School Management, Mr. Colgrove 2, Mr. Dick 1-4. History of Education, Mr. Walters 1-3. Principles of Education, Mr. Dick 2. Methods, Miss Buck 2-3. Didactics, Miss Buck 1-5.

English Language and Literature.—Rhetoric, Mr. Lynch 5; Mr. Gist 1-4; Miss Lodge 2-4. American Literature, Miss Baker 1. 1st English Classics, Miss Oliver 4. 2nd English Classics, Miss Hearst 5. Complete English Composition, Miss Lodge 1. Complete English Grammar, Miss Gregg 2- 3- 4- 5. 1st half English Composition, Miss

Baker 2. 2nd half English Composition, Miss Baker 5. 1st half English Grammar, Miss Hearst 2-3. 2nd half English Grammar, Miss Baker 3; Miss Hearst 4. Orthography, Miss Oliver 1-2.

Elocution and Public Speaking.—Elocution, Miss Falkler 2-3-5. Reading, Miss Falkler 1.

Latin and Greek.—Latin. 2nd Latin Lessons, Miss Call 1. 1st Cicero, Miss Call 3.

Geometry and Surveying.—Beginning Geometry, Mr. Wright 4. Middle Geometry, Mr. Wright 2-3. Solid Geometry, Mr. Wright 5.

Mathematics.—1st Algebra, Miss Lambert 2. 2nd Algebra, Miss Seals 3-4. 3rd Algebra, Miss Seals 5. Two term Algebra, Mr. Condit 5. Complete Arithmetic, Mr. Condit 2; Mr. Cory 4. 1st half Arithmetic, Mr. Cory 1-2-3. 2nd half Arithmetic, Miss Lambert 3-4-5.

Physics.—1st Physics, Mr. Hersey 1-4; ——————— 2. 2nd Physics, ——————— 3-5. 3rd Physics, Mr. Hersey 2.

Natural Science.—Hygiene and Sanitation, Mr. Newton 4-5. Physiology, Mr. Newton 2-3. Physiography, Mr. Cable 3-5. Complete Geography, Mr. Cable 1. 1st half Geography, Miss Aitchison 1-4. 2nd half Geography, Miss Aitchison 3.

History.—1st General History, Miss Rice 3. Complete U. S. History, Miss Riggs 3-4. 1st half U. S. History, Miss Rice 4; Mr. Peterson 3. 2nd Half U. S. History, Miss Rice 5.

Economics.—Economics, Mr. McKitrick 5. Elementary Economics, Mr. McKitrick 4; Mr. Peterson 5.

Government.—Iowa and U. S. Civics (Review), Mr. Meyerholz 1. Iowa History and Civics, Mr. Peterson 1. U. S. Civics, Mr. Peterson 2.

Art.—1st Drawing, Miss Thornton 1-3. 2nd Drawing, Miss Patt 3-4.

Commercial Education.—1st Penmanship, Mr. Cummins 3-5. Advanced Penmanship, Mr. Cummins 4. 1st Bookkeeping, Mr. Cummins 1. 2nd Bookkeeping, Mr. Cummins 2.

Vocal Music.—1st Vocal Music, Mr. Fullerton 3; Miss Stenwall 1; Mr. Hays 2-5. 2nd Vocal Music, Miss Stenwall 3; Miss Dickey 1.

Home Economics.— Domestic Science. 1st Cookery, Miss Townsend (Tuesday, Thursday), 1:00 to 3:15.

Lecture Courses.—Library Course for Teachers, Miss Biscoe 5.

SPRING TERM.

College Course.

Professional Instruction in Education.—I. 1st Psychology, Mr. Samson 2. II. 2nd Psychology, Mr. Samson 1. III. School Management, Mr. Colgrove 2-3; Mr. Dick 1-4. IV. History of Education, Mr. Walters 2. V. Philosophy of Education, Mr. Walters 4. VII. Experimental Psychology, Mr. Colgrove 4. VIII. School Supervision, Mr. Dick 2.

English Language and Literature.—I. Rhetoric, Mr. Lynch 2-5; Mr. Gist 1. II. (a) English Literature, Miss Hearst 1; (b) English Literature, Miss Lambert 2. III. Shakespeare, Mr. Gist 2. VI. Development of the English Drama, Miss Lambert 1. VIII. Anglo Saxon and Middle English, Mr. Gist 4. X. The Development of the English Novel, Miss Lodge 5. XIII. Teachers' English, Mr. Lynch 3. XIV. American Literature, Miss Lambert 4.

Elocution and Public Speaking.—II. Elocution II., Miss Martin 1. VII. Principles of Expression, Miss Martin 2. VIII. Argumentation, Mr. Barnes 2; IX. Oratory I., Mr. Barnes 3.

Latin and Greek.—(1) **Latin.** III. Horace, Mr. Merchant 2. XII. Juvenal, Mr. Merchant 1. XV. Teachers' Latin, Mr. Merchant 1 (Monday, Friday) and 6 (Tuesday, Wednesday, Thursday). XVIII. Elementary Latin: Cicero 5, or Vergil's Bucolics and Georgics 3, Mr. Merchant. XXI. Vergil (Aeneid, Third term), Miss Call 2. (2) **Greek.** III. Anabasis, Miss Call 4.

German and French.—(1) **German.** I. Grammar, Mr. Knoepfler 1. II. Grammar, Miss Lorenz 5. III. Immensee and Hoeher als die Kirche, Mr. Knoepfler 4. IV. Die Journalisten, Miss Lorenz 1. V. Wilhelm Tell or Maria Stuart or Die Jungfrau von Orleans, Miss Lorenz 2. VI. Prose Composition, Miss Lorenz 3. IX. Iphigenie auf Tauris and Die Braut von Messina, Mr. Knoepfler 3. (2) **French.** III. L'Abbe Constantin and Le Voyage de Monsieur Perrichon, Mr. Knoepfler 2.

Geometry and Surveying.—I. Solid Geometry, Mr. Wright 4. II. Surveying, Mr. Wright 3.

Mathematics.—II. Higher Algebra II., Mr. Condit 2. III. Trigonometry, Mr. Condit 1. IV. History and Teaching of Mathematics, Mr. Condit 5. VII. Integral Calculus, Mr. Condit 3.

Chemistry.—I. Inorganic, Mr. Page 3. II. Inorganic, Mr. Page 2. III. IV. Qualitativ Analysis, Mr. Getchell 3-4. V. VI. Quantitativ Analysis, Mr. Getchell 5-6. VII. Water Analysis, Mr. Getchell 5-6.

Physics.—I. Mechanics of Solids and Fluids, Mr. Begeman 4. III. Heat, Electricity and Magnetism, Mr. Begeman 1.

Natural Science.—II. Botany I., Mr. Newton 1-2 (Laboratory work, Tuesday, Friday, 3-5). V. Zoology II., Mr. Arey 4. VIII. Geology II., Mr. Arey 3. X. Astronomy, Mr. Cable 1. XI. Commercial Geography of North America, Miss Aitchison 3. XII. Commercial Geography of Europe, Miss Aitchison 2.

History.—II. English, Miss Rice 2. VI. Modern, Miss Riggs 2. VIII. 19th Century, Miss Riggs 1.

Economics.—I. Economics Theory, Mr. McKitrick 3.

Government.—I. American Government, Mr. Meyerholz 3. V. Modern European Governments, Mr. Meyerholz 2. English Constitutional History, Mr. Meyerholz 4.

Art.—II. History of Painting, Miss Thornton 1.

The Manual Arts.—III. Organization and Economics of Manual Training, Mr. Bailey 4.

Junior College Courses.

Professional Instruction in Education.—2nd Psychology, Mr. Colgrove 1. History of Education, Mr. Walters 1-3. 2nd Primary Methods, Miss McGovern 1· 3rd Primary Methods, Miss McGovern 2-3-4.

Training in Teaching.—Observation in Training School (Primary), Miss Hatcher 2-5. Primary Theory (for Kindergartners), Miss Hatcher 5. Primary Criticism, Miss Hatcher 6. Kindergarten Theory and Observation (for Primary Teachers), Miss Ward 2. Kindergarten Theory (Senior), Miss Ward 4. Kindergarten Practis, Miss Ward 2-3.

Chemistry.—Qualitativ Analysis, Mr. Getchell 1-2. Food Analysis, Mr. Page 4.

Natural Science.—Nature Study, Mr. Arey 2. Structural Botany, Mr. Arey 1.

Art.—History of Painting, Miss Thornton 1. Supervision in Art, Miss Thornton 4. Design, Miss Patt 3. Still Life, Miss Patt 2. Perspectiv, Miss Thornton 2; Miss Patt 1-4. 3rd Primary Drawing, Miss Thornton. 1-3.

Vocal Music.—1st Vocal Music, Miss Stenwall 1; Mr. Hays 3. 2nd Vocal Music, Miss Dickey 1; Miss Stenwall 3; Mr. Hays 2. 3rd Music, Mr. Fullerton 2. 4th Music, (a) History (Monday, Wednesday) Miss Childs; (b) Sightsinging (Tuesday, Thursday, Friday), Miss Stenwall 4. 5th Music, (a) Ear Training (Monday, Wednesday), Mr. Fullerton; (b) Harmony (Tuesday, Thursday), Mr. Merrill; (c) Conducting (Friday), Mr. Fullerton 1. 6th Music, (a) Methods (Monday, Wednesday), Mr. Fullerton and Miss Dickey; (b) Harmony (Tuesday, Friday), Mr. Merrill; (c) History (Thursday), Miss Childs 4. 9th Music, (a) Harmony (Monday, Thursday), Mr. Merrill; (b) Supervision (Tuesday, Wednesday), Mr. Fullerton and Miss Dickey; (c) Theory (Friday), Mr. Fullerton 4. Practis Teaching for Music Students, Miss Dickey 3; Miss Stenwall 2.

Physical Education.—Physiology of Exercise, Mr. Seymour 3. Advanced Hygiene, Mr. Seymour 4. History of Physical Education, Mr. Seymour 5. ⸱3rd Primary Physical Training, 3-5.

The Manual Arts.—Organization and Economics of Manual Training, Mr. Bailey 4. 1st Bench Work, Mr. Bailey 2. Advanced Bench Work, Mr. Brown 4-5. 1st Mechanical Drawing, Mr. Brown 3. Advanced Mechanical Drawing, Mr. Bailey 5. Sheet Metal Work, Mr. Bailey 3. Woodturning, Mr. Brown 4. Elementary Handwork, Mr. Brown 1. Primary Handwork, Mrs. McMahon 3-5. 3rd Sewing, Mrs. McMahon 2.

Home Economics.—Domestic Science. (1) 1st Year Training Class. Foods: Composition and Dietary Uses, Miss Townsend (Monday, Wednesday) 1:30 to 2:25. Cookery, Miss Townsend (Monday, Wednesday) 2:25 to 5:00. Waitress Work, Miss Townsend (Tuesday, Thursday, Friday) 11:15 to 12:10. Methods in Domestic Science, Miss Townsend (Wednesday) 11:15 to 12:10. (2) 2nd Year Training Class. Cookery, Miss Townsend (Tuesday) 3:30 to 5:00. Practis Teaching in Cookery (Tuesday, Thursday) 1:00 to 3:15.

County and State Certificate Courses.

Professional Instruction in Education.—1st Psychology, Mr. Samson 3. 2nd Psychology, Mr. Samson 5. School Management, Mr. Colgrove 2-3; Mr. Dick 1-4. History of Education, Mr. Walters, 1-3. Principles of

Education, Mr. Dick 3. Methods, Miss Buck 3-5. Didactics, Miss Buck 2-4.

English Language and Literature.—Rhetoric, Mr. Lynch 2-5; Mr. Gist 1. American Literature, Miss Gregg 5. 1st English Classics, Miss Oliver 4. 2nd English Classics, Miss Hearst 5. Complete English Composition, Miss Lodge 2. Complete English Grammar, Miss Gregg 2-3-4. 1st half English Composition, Miss Baker 2. 2nd half English Composition, Miss Lodge 4. 1st half English Grammar, Miss Hearst 2-4. 2nd half English Grammar, Miss Baker 3-5. Orthography, Miss Oliver 1-2.

Elocution and Public Speaking.—Elocution, Miss Falkler 1-3-4. Reading, Miss Falkler 2.

Latin and Greek.—Latin. 1st Caesar, Miss Call 1. 2nd Cicero, Miss Call 3.

Geometry and Surveying.—Middle Geometry, Mr. Wright 2. Solid Geometry, Mr. Wright 5.

Mathematics.—1st Algebra, Miss Seals 2. 2nd Algebra, Miss Lambert 5. 3rd Algebra, Miss Seals 4-5. Two term Algebra, Miss Seals 3. Complete Arithmetic, Mr. Cory 1; Miss Lambert 2. 1st half Arithmetic, Miss Lambert 3-4. 2nd half Arithmetic, Mr. Cory 3-4. Teachers' Arithmetic, Mr. Cory 2.

Physics.—1st Physics, Mr. Hersey 2-3. 2nd Physics, Mr. Hersey 5; ———— 1. 3rd Physics, ———— 3-5.

Natural Science.—General Botany, Mr. Newton 1-2. Physiology, Mr. Newton 4. Physiography, Mr. Cable 2-5. Complete Geography, Mr. Cable 3. 1st half Geography, Miss Aitchison 4. 2nd half Geography, Miss Aitchison 1.

History.—1st General History, Miss Rice 4. 2nd General History, Miss Riggs 3. Complete U. S. History, Miss Riggs 4. 1st half U. S. History, Miss Rice 3; Mr. Peterson 5. 2nd half U. S. History, Miss Rice 1.

Economics.—Economics, Mr. McKitrick 1. Elementary Economics, Mr. McKitrick 4; Mr. Peterson 3.

Government.—Iowa and U. S. Civics (Review), Mr. Meyerholz 1. Iowa History and Civics, Mr. Peterson 1. U. S. Civics, Mr. Peterson 2.

Art.—1st Drawing, Miss Patt 2. 2nd Drawing, Miss Thornton 2; Miss Patt 1-4.

Commercial Education.—1st Penmanship, Mr. Cummins 1-3. Advanced Penmanship, Mr. Cummins 4. 1st Bookkeeping, Mr. Cummins 2. 2nd Bookkeeping, Mr. Cummins 1. 3rd Bookkeeping, Mr. Cummins 3.

Vocal Music.—1st Vocal Music, Miss Stenwall 1; Mr. Hays 3. 2nd Vocal Music, Miss Dickey 1; Miss Stenwall 3; Mr. Hays 2.

Home Economics.—Domestic Science. 1st Cookery, Miss Townsend (Tuesday, Thursday), 1:00 to 3:15.

UNIVERSITY OF ILLINOIS

PRESIDENT'S OFFICE

BULLETIN

OF THE

IOWA STATE TEACHERS
COLLEGE.

CEDAR FALLS, IOWA

COURSES OF STUDIES

AND

PROGRAM OF RECITATIONS

For the School Year,
1911-1912

Vol. XII. No. 1.
JUNE, 1911

Issued Quarterly. Publisht by the State Teachers College. Enterd at the Postoffis at Cedar Falls, Iowa, as Second Class Matter

Vol. XII.   JUNE, 1911   No. 1

BULLETIN

OF THE

IOWA STATE TEACHERS COLLEGE
CEDAR FALLS, IOWA

COURSES OF STUDY

AND

PROGRAM OF RECITATIONS
FOR SCHOOL YEAR 1911-1912.

NOTE: The spelling used in this Bulletin conforms to that authorized by the Simplified Spelling Board, and exhibits the little modifications that the shortend new forms make in the appearance of the printed page.

CALENDAR FOR YEAR 1911-1912.

Fall term opens Tuesday, September 5, 1911.

Winter term opens Tuesday, December 5, 1911.

Spring term opens Tuesday, March 19, 1912.

Summer term opens Saturday, June 15, 1912.

IOWA STATE TEACHERS COLLEGE
CEDAR FALLS, IOWA

STATE BOARD OF EDUCATION

OFFICERS OF THE BOARD

James H. Trewin, Cedar Rapids, President.
D. A. Emery, Des Moines, Secretary.

MEMBERS OF THE BOARD

P. K. Holbrook, Onawa.
C. R. Brenton, Dallas Center. } Term expires July 1, 1913.
D. D. Murphy, Elkader.

James H. Trewin, Cedar Rapids.
Roger Leavitt, Cedar Falls. } Term expires July 1,
E. P. Schoentgen, Council Bluffs. 1915.

A. B. Funk, Spirit Lake.
George T. Baker, Davenport. } Term expires July 1, 1917.
T. D. Foster, Ottumwa.

FINANCE COMMITTEE
Offis, Des Moines.

W. R. Boyd, Cedar Rapids, Chairman.
D. A. Emery, Des Moines, Secretary.
Thomas Lambert, Sabula.

FACULTY COMMITTEE

James H. Trewin, A. B. Funk, D. D. Murphy.

BILDING COMMITTEE

P. K. Holbrook, E. P. Schoentgen, George T. Baker.

BUSINESS COMMITTEE

T. D. Foster, C. R. Brenton, Roger Leavitt.

INSPECTOR OF HIGH SCHOOLS

Forest C. Ensign, M. Di., 1895, I. S. T. C; Ph. B., 1897; M. A., 1900, Iowa, Iowa City.

IOWA STATE TEACHERS COLLEGE

FACULTY—COLLEGE YEAR, 1911—1912.

Note— Each department is arranged as to seniority of entering the faculty, excepting the Hed Professor.

HOMER H. SEERLEY, B. Ph., 1873; B. Di., 1875; M. A.,1876, Iowa; LL. D., 1898, Penn; LL. D., 1901, Iowa. President, 1886.

CLASSIFICATION AS TO DEPARTMENTS.

PROFESSIONAL INSTRUCTION IN EDUCATION.

CHAUNCEY P. COLGROVE, B. A., 1881; M. A., 1884; D. Sc., 1908, Upper Iowa; M. A., 1896, Chicago. Professor and Hed of the Department, Acting President in case of the absence or disability of the President, 1896.

ANNA E. McGOVERN, B. Di., 1879; B. S., 1880, I. S .T. C. Professor of Primary Instruction, 1880.

HOMER H. SEERLEY, B. Ph., 1873; B. Di., 1875; M. A., 1876, Iowa; LL. D., 1898, Penn; LL. D., 1901, Iowa. Professor, 1886.

GEORGE W. SAMSON, B. S., 1878; M. S., 1881, Simpson. Professor of Psychology, 1894.

G. W. WALTERS, B. S., 1879; M. S., 1882, Iowa Wesleyan. Professor of History of Education, Philosophy of Education, 1895.

EDITH C. BUCK, B. A., 1882; M. A., 1885, Grinnell College. Professor of Elementary Instruction, 1896.

GEORGE S. DICK, B. Di., 1887; B. S., 1888, I. S. T. C.; B. Ph., 1897, Cornell College. Professor, 1906. Registrar and Examiner, 1911.

GEORGE H. MOUNT, B. A., 1903, Parsons; M. Di., 1905, I. S. T. C.; M. A., 1908; Ph. D., 1910, Iowa. Professor, 1911.

TRAINING IN TEACHING.

WILBUR H. BENDER, B. Di., 1886; M. Di., 1890, I. S. T. C.;

B. Ph., 1895, Iowa. Director of the Department, Supervisor of Training, 1897.

BRUCE FRANCIS, M. Di., 1891, I. S. T. C.; Ph. B., 1896, Iowa. Assistant Director, 1911.

FLORENCE E. WARD, Graduate Chicago Kindergarten College, 1903. Supervisor of Kindergarten Training, 1906.

MATTIE LOUISE HATCHER, Ph. B., Ed. B., 1909, Chicago. Supervisor of Primary Training, 1909.

Critic Teachers—

ELIZABETH HUGHES, B. Ph., 1886, Eastern Iowa Normal School; M. Di., 1889; B. A., 1908, I. S. T. C. Geography and History, Grammar and Secondary Grades, 1898.

IDA FESENBECK, B. Di., 1893; M. Di., 1894, I. S. T. C.; B. A., 1900, Iowa; Student Radcliffe College (Harvard), 1900—01. Reading, Literature and German, Grammar and Secondary Grades, 1901.

EVA LUSE, B. Di., 1901; M. Di., 1904, I. S. T. C.; B. A., 1906; M. A., 1910, Iowa. Language, Composition and Latin, Grammar and Secondary Grades, 1906.

MAE CRESSWELL, B. Di., 1902; B. A., 1908, I. S. T. C. Mathematics and Science, Grammar and Secondary Grades, 1908.

RUTH E. DOWDELL, Graduate Chicago Kindergarten College, 1908. Kindergarten, 1909.

ALICE GORDON, B. Di., 1906; M. Di., 1908, I. S. T. C. Primary Grades, 1906.

GERTRUDE DANDLIKER, Graduate Normal Department, Art Institute of Chicago, 1906. Drawing and Manual Training, 1909.

FLOE E. CORRELL, B. Di., 1904; M. Di., 1905, I. S. T. C.; B. A., 1909, Iowa. Preliminary Year, 1909.

AMY E. WEARNE, Graduate Stout Training School. Home Economics, 1911.

LULU M. STEVENS, Graduate Chicago Conservatory of Music. Music, 1911.

Critic Teachers in Training—

EMMA GAMBLE, Primary Teacher Diploma, 1910, I. S. T. C. Primary Grades, 1910.

EVA FALLGATTER, Primary Teacher Diploma, 1911, I. S. T. C. Primary Grades, 1910.

ALICE GRIER, B. Di., 1910, I. S. T. C. Grammar Grades, 1910.

KATHERINE NENNO, B. Di., 1910, I. S. T C. Grammar Grades, 1910.

GLEE MAECK, B. Di., 1909; M. Di., 1910, I. S. T. C. Grammar Grades, 1910—1911.

HANNAH GOSTRUP, B. Di., 1910, I. S. T. C. Grammar Grades, Fall Term, 1910.

MARY BARNUM. Grammar Grades, 1910.

GRACE McINTOSH, B. Di., 1907, I. S. T. C. Grammar Grades, November 30, 1910.

*CHRISTINE THOENE, B. Di., 1902; M. Di., 1910, I. S. T. C. Grammar Grades, 1909.

GRACE AITCHISON, M. Di., 1909, I. S. T. C. Grammar Grades, 1911.

MARGUERITE CADWALLADER, M. Di., 1911, I. S. T. C. Grammar Grades, 1911.

ENGLISH.

SAMUEL A. LYNCH, B. L., 1892; B. P., 1892, Missouri; M. A., 1900, Chicago. Professor and Hed of the Department, 1909.
Professors—

W. W. GIST, B. A., 1872; M. A., 1875; D. D., 1893, Ohio. Professor of English Language, 1900.

BERTHA MARTIN, Graduate Columbia College of Expression. Professor of Elocution and Dramatic Art, 1905.

JENNETTE CARPENTER, B. A., 1885; M. A., 1888, Cornell College. Graduate Student University of Chicago, 1893-94; Harvard Summer School, 1902-03; University of Berlin, 1910-11. Professor of Rhetoric and Literature, 1899.

LILLIAN V. LAMBERT, S. B., 1889; A. M., 1899, Penn College; Ph. B., 1895; Ph. M., 1906, Chicago; Graduate Work at Oxford, England, 1905; Graduate Work in English, Bryn Mawr, 1906-07. Professor of Rhetoric and Literature, 1907.

JOHN BARNES, A. B., 1904; A. M., 1905, Northwestern University; Graduate Cumnock School of Oratory, 1905. Professor of Public Speaking, 1910.
Assistant Professors—

EVA L. GREGG, B. A., 1910, I. S. T. C. English Grammar, 1895.
Resignd, June 6, 1911.

MARGARET E. OLIVER, B. A., 1885; M. A., 1888, Monmouth College; Graduate Columbia College of Expression, 1901. Orthography and English Classics, 1901.

MARY F. HEARST, B. Di., 1883; M. Di., 1892, I. S. T. C.; B. Ph., 1899; M. A., 1904, Iowa. English Grammar and English Classics, 1899.

LAURA FALKLER, Graduate Kansas City School of Oratory, 1895. Elocution, 1896.

Instructors—

MABEL J. LODGE, A. B., 1908, Chicago. English Composition and Rhetoric, 1909.

CLARA H. BAKER, B. A., 1900, Cornell College; M. A., 1910, Iowa. Substitute Instructor, Fall Term, 1910.

MRS. THEODORA C. B. DEAN, Graduate Columbia College of Expression, 1895. Elocution, Winter Term, 1910-11.

MARGARET WEIRICK, Ph. B., 1910, Chicago. Substitute Instructor, Winter.and Spring Terms, 1910-11.

LATIN AND GREEK.

FRANK IVAN MERCHANT, A. B., 1880, Shurtleff College; M. A., Ph. D., 1890, University of Berlin. Hed of the Department and Professor of Latin, 1907.

MYRA E. CALL, B. A., 1885; M. A., 1888, Iowa. Professor of Greek and Secondary Latin, 1895.

GERMAN AND FRENCH.

JOHN B. KNOEPFLER, Hed of Department and Professor, 1900.

CHARLOTTE M. LORENZ, B. A., 1902; M. A., 1904, Iowa. Instructor in German, 1908.

MATHEMATICS.

IRA S. CONDIT, B. A., 1886; M. A., 1889, Parsons College; Graduate Student, University of Chicago, Summer Sessions, 1906, 1908 and 1909. Hed of the Department and Professor, 1898.

D. SANDS WRIGHT, M. A., 1887, Penn College. Professor, 1876.

CHARLES S. CORY, M. Di., I. S. T. C., 1900; B. S., 1902, Iowa. Professor, 1907. Examiner of High School Records, 1909-11.

Assistant Professors—

*LAURA S. SEALS, B. S. D., Kirksville State Normal School, Missouri. 1898.

EMMA F. LAMBERT, B. Di., 1896; M. Di., 1897, I. S. T. C.; B. Ph., 1904, Iowa. 1901.

CHEMISTRY.

*ABBOTT C. PAGE, B. Ph., 1885, Yale. Hed of Department an: Professor, 1889.

PERRY A. BOND, M. S., Iowa. Assistant Professor, 1911.

ROBERT W. GETCHELL, B. A., I. S. T. C., 1911. Instructor, 1909.

GEORGE W. MUHLEMAN, B. S., 1899, Northwestern. Substitute Instructor, Winter and Spring Terms, 1910-11.

PHYSICS.

LOUIS BEGEMAN, B. S., 1889; M. S., 1897, Michigan; Ph. D., 1910, University of Chicago. Professor and Hed of the Department, 1899.

S. FREEMAN HERSEY, B. Ph., 1892, Beloit College. Professor, 1899.

WILLIAM H. KADESCH, B. S., 1906, Ohio Wesleyan; Ph. M., 1910, Chicago. Assistant Professor, 1910.

NATURAL SCIENCE.

MELVIN F. AREY, B. A., 1867; M. A., 1870, Bowdoin. Hed of the Department and Professor of Structural Botany, Mineralogy and Zoology, and Curator of the Museum of Natural History, 1890.

GEORGE W. NEWTON, B. Di., 1882, I. S. T. C.; B. A., 1887; M. A., 1890, Iowa; Graduate Student, Harvard, 1891. Professor of Biology, Physiology, Botany and Sanitation, 1896.

EMMETT J. CABLE, B. S., 1900; M. S., 1903, Cornell College; Graduate Student, University of Chicago, 1904. Professor of Geology and Geography, 1905.

ALISON E. AITCHISON, M. Di., 1903, I. S. T. C.; B. S., 1907, Iowa. Assistant Professor of Geography, 1903.

HISTORY.

SARA M. RIGGS, B. Di., 1885, I. S. T. C.; B. L., 1894, Michigan. Assistant in English, 1887-1891. Professor, 1895.

SARA F. RICE, M. A., 1890, Coe College. Professor, 1898.

*Granted leave of absence for the year.

GOVERNMENT.

CHARLES H. MEYERHOLZ, M. Di., 1898, I. S. T. C.; Ph. B., 1902; M. A., 1903, Iowa; A. M., 1905, Harvard; Ph. D., 1907, Leipsig. Professor, 1908.

HENRY J. PETERSON, A. B., 1905, St. Olaf College; M. A., 1907, Iowa. Graduate Student University of Chicago, 1909-10. Instructor, 1910.

ECONOMICS.

REUBEN McKITRICK, Graduate, State Normal School, Alva, Oklahoma, 1903; A. B., 1907, University of Oklahoma; Graduate Student, State University of Wisconsin, 1907-10. Professor, 1910.

ART.

HENRIETTA THORNTON, Student, Art Institute, Chicago; Academy of Fine Arts, Cincinnati; Pupil of George Smillie and Miss H. Revere Johnson, New York; Graduate Normal Art Course of Pratt Institute, 1892. Professor, 1895.

BERTHA L. PATT, Cummings School of Art, Des Moines; Art Students' League; Pupil of Charles W. Hawthorne, New York. Professor, 1895.

EFFIE SCHUNEMAN, Student, Pratt Institute. Instructor, 1911.

COMMERCIAL EDUCATION.

HARRY C. CUMMINS, Graduate Valder Business College, 1891; B. Di., 1898, I. S. T. C. Professor of Penmanship and Bookkeeping, 1898.

ROY V. COFFEY, Graduate, Michigan University. Instructor in Stenography and Typewriting, 1911.

MUSIC.

C. A. FULLERTON, B. Di., 1889; M. Di., 1890, I. S. T. C.; Student, University of Chicago, 1896-1897. Acting Director of the Department and Hed Professor of Public School Music and Director of Choral Society and of Glee Clubs, 1897.

*FRANCES M. DICKEY, B. Di., 1901, I. S. T. C.; Student, Teachers College (Columbia) 1909-10. Assistant Professor of Vocal Music, 1907.

*Resignd, July, 1911.

HULDA STENWALL, Student, Oberlin Conservatory, 1902-1904. Assistant Professor of Vocal Music, 1908.

*ROBERT FULLERTON, B. Di., 1894, M. Di., 1895, I. S. T. C.; Student, Oberlin Conservatory, 1897-1899; Pupil of James Sauvage, New York City, 1899, Albin Reed, Boston, 1900; Student, The New School of Vocal Science, Chicago, 1906-1908; Pupil of John Dennis Mehan, New York City, Vacations of 1908 and 1909. Instructor in Public School Music, 1894-96; 1902-05. Hed Professor of Voice, 1908.

ANNA GERTRUDE CHILDS, B. A., 1889; M. A., 1892, Grinnell College; Pupil of George Henschel, William Shakespeare, and George Ferguson. Professor of Voice and History of Music, 1901.

JOHN ROSS FRAMPTON, B. A., 1901; Mus. Bac., 1904; M. A., 1906, Oberlin; Colleag American Guild of Organists, 1909. Hed Professor of Organ and Piano and Instructor in Harmony, 1908.

LOWELL E. M. WELLES, Student, Oberlin Conservatory, Substitute Instructor of Voice, 1911—1912.

ELIZABETH F. BURNEY, Teacher of Public School Music Diploma, 1909, I. S. T. C. Instructor in Voice, 1909-11.

KATE KENNY, Mus. Bac., 1909, Oberlin. Instructor on Piano, 1910-1911.

W. E. HAYS, Instructor in Public School Music, 1909-1911.

GLEE MAECK, B. Di., 1909; M. Di., 1910, I. S. T. C. Instructor in Piano, 1911.

VIOLIN AND OTHER ORCHESTRAL INSTRUMENTS.

WINFRED MERRILL, Berlin: Violin, Professor Dr. Joseph Joachim and Professor Andreas Moser; Theory, Bernhard Ziehn. Professor, 1903.

ADOLPH KRAMER, Instructor.

PHYSICAL EDUCATION.

R. F. SEYMOUR, B. P. E., 1907, Y. M. C. A. Training School, Springfield, Mass. Hed of the Department and Physical Director, 1906.

JAMES OWEN PERRINE, B. A., 1909, Iowa. Instructor, January, 1911, to June, 1911.

*Granted leave of absence for the year.

MARGUERITE M. HUSSEY, Graduate Boston Normal School of Gymnastics, 1908. Assistant Physical Director, 1910.

HUMBERT F. PASINI, B. P. E., 1911, Y. M. C. A. Training School, Springfield, Mass. Instructor, 1911.

HELEN RUTH HALLINGBY, Director of Physical Training Diploma, 1909, I. S. T. C. Instructor, 1910.

MARY EVELYN SAMSON, A. B., 1909, Simpson College; Physical Training Director Diploma, 1910, I. S. T. C. Floor Instructor, 1910.

A. G. REID, Substitute Instructor, Fall Term, 1910.

*CLAYTON B. SIMMONS, B. A., 1904, Colgate; Director of Physical Training Diploma, 1907, I. S. T. C. Physical Director and Professor, 1906.

*Resignd, September 15, 1910.

MANUAL ARTS.

CHARLES H. BAILEY, B. S. in C. E., 1895, Iowa; Manual Training Diploma, 1903, Teachers College (Columbia); B. S., 1903, Columbia. Hed of the Department and Professor, 1905.

MRS. ALMA L. McMAHON, Graduate, Oshkosh, Wisconsin, Normal School, 1886; B. Ph., 1902, Wisconsin; Domestic Science Teacher Diploma, 1904, Stout Institute. Instructor, 1904.

CLARK H. BROWN, Director of Manual Training Diploma, 1908, I. S. T. C. Instructor, 1906.

HOME ECONOMICS.

MARY L. TOWNSEND, M. Di., 1899, I. S. T. C.; B. A., Wellesley College, 1896; Graduate Domestic Science Course, Drexel Institute, 1901. Professor, 1907.

ALICE MARGARET HEINZ, Teacher of Domestic Science Diploma, 1909, I. S. T. C. Instructor, 1910.

STUDENT ASSISTANTS, 1910-1911.

HELEN KATZ, B. Di., 1909, I. S. T. C. Violin, Fall Term.

BRUCE B. LYBARGER, Violin.

HENRY C. BEINKE, Violin, Winter and Spring Terms.

BRIAN C. CONDIT, Violin.

E. LAURA MUHS, Piano.

MARGUERITE BENNETT, Piano.

MYRTLE ARNOLD, Chemistry, Fall Term.

RALPH DIEHL, Chemistry Laboratory, Fall Term.

FRED VORHIES, Physics Laboratory, Winter and Spring Terms.
ALIDA CHASE, Drawing, Winter and Spring Terms.
PLEATUS BURGESS, Drawing, Winter and Spring Terms.
MAYME STRASSER, Penmanship, Winter and Spring Terms.

OTHER OFFICERS OF ADMINISTRATION.

JAMES E. ROBINSON, Superintendent of Construction and of Bildings and Grounds, 1901.

MRS. MARION McFARLAND WALKER, B. L., Ferry Hall, Lake Forest, 1880; Professor of Applied English, I. S. T. C., 1890-97; Substitute Instructor in English, 1907-08. Dean of Women, 1908. Lecturer on Social Ethics and Faculty Visitor.

LILIAN G. GOODWIN, Secretary of the College, 1909.

GEORGE S. DICK, B. Di., 1897, B. S., 1888, I. S. T. C.; B. Ph., 1897, Cornell. Registrar and Examiner, 1911.

MRS. ANNIE M. POTTER, Matron of Hospital and Hed Nurse, 1909.

LIBRARY.

*ELLEN D. BISCOE, Graduate New York State Library School, 1896. Librarian, 1907.

MARY DUNHAM, B. A., 1898, Indiana. Librarian, January, 1911.

ETHEL L. AREY, B. Di., 1893; M. Di., 1895, I. S. T. C. Loan Desk Attendant, 1896.

MATTIE FARGO, B. L. S., 1906, Illinois State Library School. Cataloger and Shelf-lister, 1906.

IVA M. HUNTLEY, M. Di., 1907, I. S. T. C. Assistant Cataloger and Accession Clerk, 1907.

**MABEL E. MASTAIN, M. Di., 1908, I. S. T. C. Assistant, 1908.

RACHEL HAIGHT, Graduate Drexel Institute, 1911. Reference Assistant, May, 1911.

BERTHA L. SHARP, Student, University of Illinois Library School. Assistant, 1911.

PRESIDENT'S OFFIS.

ANNA R. WILD, Secretary, 1896.
LILIAN G. GOODWIN, Secretary, 1898.

*Resignd, November 9, 1910.
**Resignd, October 8, 1910.

MILLICENT WARRINER, Stenograher, 1900.

L. BEATRICE WILBUR, Record Clerk, 1906.

EVELYN V. MORTON, Stenographer, 1910.

HAZEL E. BROWN, Stenographer, 1910.

EMMA DEINES, Clerk, 1910.

FACULTY COMMITTEES, 1911-1912.

I.—Examining Committees.—Opening Days of Terms.
1. *High School Graduate Examiner*—C. S. Cory.
2. *Teachers' Certificate Examiner*—H. H. Seerley, Anna R. Wild.
3. *Unclassified Student Examiner*—G. S. Dick.

II.—Executiv Committees.

1. *Reclassification of and Advisor of College Course Students*— Hed of the Department with which the major is taken.
2. *Reclassification and Advisor of all other Students*—The President and The Registrar.
3. *Literary Societies*—The English Department.
4. *Oratorical Association Representativs, Appointed by the Associations*—John Barnes, S. A. Lynch, Bertha Martin, Ira S. Condit.
5. *Debating Leag Representativs, Appointed by the Leag*—John Barnes, S. A. Lynch, Reuben McKitrick, Charles H. Meyerholz.
6. *Athletic Board*—C. H. Bailey, C. S. Cory, E. J. Cable, Charles H. Meyerholz, R. F. Seymoud, Humbert F. Pasini, and Student Representativs appointed by the men students.
7. *College Graduate Courses*—C. P. Colgrove.
8. *Lecture Course*—Charles H. Meyerholz, Frank Ivan Merchant, Louis Begeman.
9. *Musical Festival*—S. A. Lynch, George S. Dick, Reuben McKitrick, Lillian V. Lambert, Myra E. Call, C. A. Fullerton, John Ross Frampton, B. W. Merrill, Anna Gertrude Childs.
10. *Disciplin and Work of Students in Teams of all Kinds*—H. H. Seerley, R. F. Seymour, S. A. Lynch, Ira S. Condit, Sara M. Riggs, G. W. Samson, S. F. Hersey.
11. *Credits Accepted from Other Educational Institutions*—D. S. Wright, G. W. Newton, W. W. Gist, Louis Begeman, Sara F. Rice, Myra E. Call, G. W. Walters.
12. *Viseing Committee on Scheduling of Students*—G. W. Walters, G. W. Newton, Sara F. Rice.

13. *Golf House and Grounds*—J. B. Knoepfler, C. S. Cory, A. C. Page.
14. *Museum*—M. F. Arey, G. W. Newton, G. W. Walters.

III.—General Committees.

1. *Committee on Students applying for College work when they have entrance deficiences*—Ira S. Condit, W. W. Gist, Sara F. Rice, Louis Begeman, E. J. Cable.

2. *Advisory Committee to College Examiner on Students coming from non-accredited high schools*—J. B. Knoepfler, Frank Ivan Merchant, Henrietta Thornton, Sara M. Riggs, Charles S. Cory.

3. *Advisory Committee to Dean of Women*—Sara F. Rice, Lillian V. Lambert, Bertha L. Patt, George S. Dick, Ira S. Condit.

4. *Hospital Committee*—Dean of Women, Matron and Hed Nurse, Secretary of the College.

IOWA STATE TEACHERS COLLEGE
THE COURSE OF STUDY

REQUIREMENTS FOR ADMISSION.

Applicants for unconditional admission to the College Course, hereafter printed in detail, must be at least sixteen years of age and must present satisfactory records from accredited secondary schools showing a total of fifteen units of work in accordance with the standards approved by the Iowa State Board of Education, as fully set out in detail in Bulletin No. 1 of the Board on Secondary School Relations. The term unit as here used signifies a year's work where the class hours are forty-five minutes, the number of class hours per week being not less than five.

I.   CONSTANTS.

Groups of Subjects—		Units
1.	One Foren Language	2
2.	English	3
3.	Algebra	1½
4.	Plane Geometry	1
5.	History	1
6.	Electivs	6½
	Total	15

II.   ELECTIVS.

In selecting the units that are known as electivs in the above requirement, the total that may be accepted for any one group always includes those units required for constants. The maximum number of units that may be offerd on certificate from an accredited high school are as follows:

Groups of Subjects—			Units
1.	Foren Language—		4
	(1) Greek	2 to 4	
	(2) Latin	2 to 4	
	(3) French	2 to 4	
	(4) Spanish	2 to 4	
	(5) German	2 to 4	
2.	English		4

3. History, Civics and Economics   4
    (1) Ancient History   ½ to 1
    (2) Medieval and Modern
              History   ½ to 1
    (3) Civil Government   ½ to 1
    (4) Economics   ½
    (5) General History in place
              of (1) and (2)   1
    (6) U. S. History— 3rd and
              4th years   ½ to 1
    (7) English History   ½ to 1

4. Mathematics   4
    (1) Solid Geometry   ½
    (2) Plane Trigonometry   ½
    (3) Advanced Algebra   ½

5. Science   4½
    Physics   1
    Chemistry   1
    Physiography   ½ to 1
    Botany   ½ to 1
    Zoology   ½ to 1
    Physiology   ½
    Geology   ½
    Astronomy   ½
    Agriculture   ½ to 1

6. Commercial Subjects   2
    Adv. Arithmetic (after Algebra)   ½
    Bookkeeping   ½ to 1
    Commercial Geography   ½
    Commercial Law   ½
    Industrial History   ½

7. Industrial Subjects   2
    Freehand and Mechanical
              Drawing   ½ to 1
    Manual Training—i. e. Shop
              Work   ½ to 2
    Domestic Science   ½ to 1
    Stenography   ½ to 1

Credit is not given for English grammar or United States history, unless taken in the latter part of the course, nor for arithmetic unless taken after algebra.

OUTLINE OF THE COLLEGE COURSE GIVING DISTRI-
BUTION OF WORK AND DIRECTIONS CONCERNING
THE OPPORTUNITIES OFFERD.

THE COLLEGE COURSE.

Degree: Bachelor of Arts in Education.
First Grade State Certificate Standard.

FRESHMAN YEAR.

A	B	C
1. Electiv.	1. Electiv.	1. Electiv.
2. Electiv.	2. Electiv.	2. Electiv.
3. Rhetoric.	3. Education I.	3. Education II.

SOPHOMORE YEAR.

A	B	C
1. Electiv.	1. Electiv.	1. Electiv.
2. Electiv.	2. Electiv.	2. Electiv.
3. Education III.	3. Education IV.	3. Electiv.

JUNIOR YEAR.

A	B	C
1. Electiv.	1. Electiv.	1. Electiv.
2. Electiv.	2. Electiv.	2. Electiv.
3. Electiv.	3. Education V.	3. Education VI.
		or VII.

SENIOR YEAR.

A	B	C
1. Electiv.	1. Electiv.	1. Electiv.
2. Electiv.	2. Electiv.	2. Electiv.
3. Prac. Teaching.	3. Prac. Teaching.	3. Electiv.

Majors.—It is necessary for the student who takes the College
Course to select one major study with some one department at the
close of the Freshman year. A major consists of at least two full
years of work, thus covering six term credits. After the major is
decided the student is under the direction of the department in
which the major belongs, and the Hed of the Department becomes
his adviser during the rest of his course. The different majors
that are offerd are in the following lines.

1. English and Public Speaking.
2. Mathematics.

3. Mathematics and Physics.
4. History, Government, and Economics.
5. Latin.
6. German.
7. Greek.
8. Physical Science.
9. Natural Science.
10. General Science.
11. Home Economics.
12. Drawing.
13. Physical Education.
14. Manual Training.
15. Any other arrangement approved by the Faculty.

DISTRIBUTION OF CREDITS IN THE COLLEGE COURSE.

The following outline gives the distribution of studies that is
required for graduation from the college course, each credit being
12 weeks of 5 lessons a week.

I. *English Courses*   Number of Credits
    1. English   12
    2. Foren Language   3
    3. History, Government and Economics   3
    4. Science and Mathematics   3
    5. Professional   8
    6. Electiv   7
                                                       ___
        Total   36

7. Other work required.
    (a) Vocal Music—one term.
    (b) Electiv Work from Home Economics, Drawing,
Commercial Studies or Manual Training—two terms.
    (c) Physical Training—two years.
    (d) Literary Society Work—four years.

II. *Foren Language Courses*
    1. Foren Language   12
    2. English   3
    3. History, Government and Economics   3
    4. Science and Mathematics   3
    5. Professional   8
    6. Electiv   7
                                                       ___
        Total   36

7. Same as in English Courses.

III. *History, Government and Economics Courses.*
1. History, Government and Economics 12
2. English 3
3. Science and Mathematics 3
4. Foren Language 3
5. Professional 8
6. Electiv 7

Total 36
7. Same as in English Courses.

IV. *Science and Mathematics Courses.*
1. Science and Mathematics 15
2. English 3
3. Foren Language 3
4. History, Government and Economics 3
5. Professional 8
6. Electiv 4

Total 36
7. Same as in English Courses

V. *Home Economics, Drawing, Physical Education and Manual Training Courses.*
1. Home Economics, etc. 9
2. English 3
3. Foren Language 3
4. History, Government and Economics 3
5. Science and Mathematics 6
6. Professional 8
7. Electiv 7

Total 39

8. Other work required.
   (a) Vocal Music—one term.
   (b) Physical Training—two years.
   (c) Literary Society Work—four years.

OTHER PRIVILEGES ALLOWD IN ALL COURSES.

In addition to the required work necessary for graduation from the College Course as above specified, students are allowd to pursue work in vocal music, instrumental music, drawing, manual training, sewing, cooking, penmanship or other art subjects, provided not more than a total of four hours of work a day are thus scheduled.

These subjects are of such importance in public school work that this liberal plan has been adopted, it being recognized that a knowledge of these subjects greatly increases the opportunities of a teacher both as to location and as to superior salary.

DEPARTMENT SUBJECTS IN THE COLLEGE COURSE.

This tabular arrangement gives the entire program of studies with the nomenclature adopted by the Faculty for the College Course.

The numbers by which the courses in the different departments are to be designated are given below:

Professional.

    Required Work—

        I.   First Term Psychology.
        II.   Second Term Psychology.
        III.   School Management.
        IV.   History of Education.
        V.   Philosophy of Education.
        VI.   American Education, or VII. Experimental Psychology.
        XI.—XII.   Practis Teaching.

    Electiv Courses—

        VIII.   School Supervision.
        IX.   Educational Classics.
        X.   Lecture Course on Genetic, Social and Sex Psychology, 3 hours, ½ credit.
        XIII.   Practis Teaching.

English.

    (a)   Language and Literature—

        I.   Rhetoric.
        II.   English Literature.
        III.   Shakespeare.
        IV.   Epic Poetry in English.
        V.   The English Romantic Movement.
        VI.   The Development of the English Drama.
        VII.   The History of the English Language and Anglo Saxon.
        VIII.   Anglo Saxon and Middle English.
        IX.   Literary Criticism.

     X. The Development of the English Novel.
    XI. English of the Nineteenth Century.
   XII. Theme Writing and Story Telling.
  XIII. Teaching English.
  XIV. American Literature.

(b) Elocution and Public Speaking—

     XV. Elocution I.
   XVI. Elocution II.
  XVII. Applied Drama.
XVIII.—XIX.—XX. Repertoire I., II., III.
  XXI. Principles of Expression.
 XXII. Public Speaking I.
XXIII. Public Speaking II.
XXIV. Argumentation.

Latin and Greek.

  Latin—

      I. Cicero, Cato Major.
     II. Livy.
    III. Horace, Epodes and Odes.
IV.—V.—VI. Latin Composition.
VII.—VIII.—IX. Roman Literature.
X.—XI.—XII. Historical Latin Grammar.
XIII.—XIV.—XV. Senior Electiv.
XVI.—XVII.—XVIII. Elementary Latin for High
      School Graduates.

Note. Only Courses I.—XV. can be counted as part of a Latin Major.

  Greek—

    I.—II. Lessons.
  III.—IV.—V. Anabasis.
    VI. Plato.
VII.—VIII.—IX. Homer.

German and French.

  German—

    I.—II. Lessons—Grammar.
   III. Immensee and Hoeher als die Kirche.
   IV. Die Journalisten.
    V. Wilhelm Tell.
   VI. German Prose Composition.

VII.   Emilia Galotti and Lyrics and Ballads.
VIII.   Nathan der Weise.
  IX.   Iphigenie auf Tauris and Die Braut vonMessina.
   X.   German Language and Literature.
  XI.   Modern German Prose and Scientific German.
 XII.   One or more German Classics, with composition and
          conversation thruout the year.

French—

    I.   Lessons—Grammar and Pronunciation.
   II.   Lessons, with reading easy French.
  III.   L'Abbe Constantin, Le Voyage de Monsieur Perri-
          chon.
  IV.—V.—VI.   Novels, stories, dramas, with dictation ex-
ercises, composition and spoken French. The reading will be se-
lected from such texts as Hugo's Les Miserables, Feuillet's Jeune
Homme Pauvre, Souvestre's Un Philosophe sous les Toits, Sand's
La Mare au Diable, Augier's Le Gendre de M. Poirier, Loti's
Pecheur d'Islande, Moliere's comedies, and Erckmann-Chatrian's
historical novels.
Mathematics.

    I.   Solid Geometry.
   II.   College Algebra.
  III.   Plane Trigonometry.
  IV.   Spherical Trigonometry and Surveying.
   V.   History and Teaching of Mathematics.
  VI.   Analytical Geometry.
 VII.   Differential Calculus.
VIII.   Integral Calculus.

Chemistry.

    I. II.   General Inorganic.
  III. IV.   Qualitativ Analysis.
   V. VI.   Quantitativ Analysis.
 VII.   Special Methods in Quantitativ Analysis.
VIII. IX.   Household Chemistry.
   X.   Food Analysis.

Physics.

    I.   Mechanics of Solids and Fluids.
   II.   Sound and Light.
  III.   Heat, Electricity, and Magnetism.

IV. Teachers' Special Course.
V. Adv. Laboratory Work in General Physics.
VI. Adv. Laboratory Work in Electricity.

Natural Science.
I. Physiology I.
II. Botany I.
III. Hygiene and Sanitation.
IV.—V. Zoology I. and II.
VI. Physiography I.
VII.—VIII. Geology I. and II.
IX. Mineralogy.
X. Astronomy.
XI. Commercial Geography of North America.
XII. Commercial Geography of Europe.
XIII. Influences of Geography upon American History.
Major—
Zoology I.
Physiography I.
Geology I.
Physiology I.
Botany I.
Hygiene and Sanitation.

History.
I. American History.
II. English History.
III. Greek History.
IV. Roman History.
V. Medieval History.
VI. Modern History, 16th—17th Centuries.
VII. Eighteenth Century History.
VIII. Nineteenth Century History.
IX. Method History or Teachers' History.

Government.
I. American Government.
II.—III. American Constitutional History.
IV. English Government.
V. Modern European Governments.
VI. International Law.
VII. Constitutional Law.
VIII. English Constitutional History.

Economics.
    I. General Economics.
    II. Economic and Social Problems.
    III. American Industrial History.
    IV. English Industrial History.
    V. Money and Banking.
    VI. Industrial Corporations.

Drawing.

* I.—II. Cast drawing	½ credit each
III. History of Architecture	1 ”
IV. History of Painting	1 ”
* V. Perspectiv	½ ”
* VI. Still-life	½ ”
* VII—VIII. Water color	½ ” each
* IX. Design	½ ’
* Manual Training, Physical Education or Home Economics.	3 credits

Manual Training.

I—II. Manual Training Methods.	
III. Organization and Economics of Manual Training.	
* IV—V—VI—VII. Mechanical Drawing	½ credit each
* VIII—IX—X—XI. Design and Construction in Wood	½ credit each
* XII. Wood Turning	½ credit
* XIII—XIV. Design and Construction in Sheet Metal	½ ” ”
* XV. Primary Handwork	½
* XVI. Elementary Handwork	½ ”

Note. Courses I., II., III., VI., VII., IX., X., XII., and
XIII. constitute a Manual Training Major.

Home Economics.

* I—II—III. Sewing	½ credit each
* IV—V—VI—VII. Elementary Food Theory.	½ ” ”
* VIII—IX. Dietetics	½ ” ”
* X. Demonstrations	¼ ”
* XI. Principles of the Selection and Preparation of Foods	1¼ ”

* XII.   Household Management   2-5 credits
* XIII. Household Architecture   2-5   ”
* XIV.   Methods, Home Economics   1-5   ”
* Manual Training, Physical Education or
    Drawing   2   ”

Note. In Manual Training, Home Economics and Drawing Majors here outlined the fractions given specify the particular value of said courses when applied to the College Course.

Physical Education.

I—II.   Anatomy.
* III.   Hygiene.
* IV.   Theories and Systems of Physical Education.
*-V.   Physical Department Methods.
* VI.   History and Literature of Physical Training.
* VII.   Anthropometry and Physical Diagnosis.
* VIII. Physiology of Exercise.
* IX.   Medical Gymnastics and Massage.

* Not accepted as general electivs on course other than those in which majors are chosen in Home Economics, Drawing, Physical Education and Manual Training.

REQUIREMENTS IN DETAIL FOR OTHER DIPLOMAS THAT ARE GRANTED FOR SPECIAL STUDY AND TRAINING.

Master of Didactics Diploma.—For the completion of the requirements twenty-seven college credits must be acquired by candidates, distributed as follows: English, 3; Foren Language, 3; History, Government and Economics, 3; Science and Mathematics, 3; Professional, 7; Electiv, 8. Other work required is as follows: Vocal Music, one term; Electiv Work from Home Economics, Drawing, Commercial Studies or Manual Training, two terms; Physical Training, two years; Literary Society Work, three years. This diploma gives the right to hold a first grade state certificate, and, hence, the special requirements of the state certificate are here provided.

Bachelor of Didactics Diploma.—For the completion of the requirements eighteen college credits must be acquired by candidates, Government and Economics, 2; Science and Mathematics, 2; Pro-distributed as follows: English, 2; Foren Language, 2; History, Other required work will be:

fessional,6; Electiv, 4.   Other work required is as follows: Vocal
Music, one term; Electiv Work from Home Economics, Drawing,
Commercial Studies or Manual Training, two terms; Physical
Training, two years; Literary Society Work, two years.   This di-
ploma gives the right to hold the second grade state certificate as
all the special requirements are here provided.

Both of these courses are adapted to the practical needs of elementary and grade teachers as well as to those of principals of elementary, graded and village schools.   When students have completed the two terms of practis teaching here provided and after-
ward continue their study for the Bachelor of Arts in Education degree, an additional term of practis teaching becomes a special requirement in the final year.

THE PROFESSIONAL COURSE OF STUDY FOR COLLEGE GRADUATES.

The Iowa State Teachers College has developt professional
courses for college graduates that deserv special recognition for
their   practical   features   and   for   their   large   professional
helpfulness.   College graduatees of decided success in teaching   can   complete   one   of   these   courses   by   attending   three
successiv summer terms and doing special assignd work during
the interim.   Before graduation they will need to establish proofs
of their success being excellent and positiv.   Where practis teaching
is omitted with the consent of the department, other professional
credits may be substituted on arrangement with the department.
Those not having this standard of success are developt and traind
by the Practis Teaching department, which is in activ work during
the fall, winter and spring terms of each school year.   For inexperienced teachers, the regular sessions are better adapted, as the
training schools are then regularly in session.

I.   *Professional Course in Education.*

First Term.
1.   Advanced Psychology.
2.   School Management.
3.   History of Education.

Second Term.
1.   Philosophy of Education.
2.   American Education.
3.   Practis Teaching.

Third Term.

1. Experimental Psychology.
2. Educational Classics.
3. Practis Teaching.

College graduates who complete this course will be entitled to receive the degree of Bachelor of Arts in Education and a First Grade State Certificate.

II. *Professional Course with Electivs.*

1. Education		3 credits
2. Practis Teaching		2 credits
3. Scholastic Studies		4 credits
Total required		9 credits

Graduates of approved colleges can complete this course in one year, and will receive the diploma of Master of Didactics and a First Grade State Certificate, provided they meet all requirements demanded by the State Board of Educational Examiners.

OBSERVATIONS ON THESE COURSES.

1. Some branches of the above work can be personal, individual studies, laboratory and library in character, on lines outlined by the Professional department. These studies are to be carefully made and results submitted to the department for examination, criticism and instruction. The library is so strong in Pedagogy that this work is of great and lasting professional value.

2. For entrance upon this course a complete detail of all work taken at the college must be filed.

3. Substitutions will be granted for efficient pedagogical work taken at a college with a strong professional department. Great liberty will be allowd to such grade of students so as to enable them to prepare both wisely and well for the best public servis in any special line of school work, but in every case a year's attendance at this college is required. Such students are excused from orations and literary society work if they apply to the Faculty for such release.

4. Any college graduate interested in this course is requested to write for further information to the President of the Iowa State Teachers College or to C. P. Colgrove.

III.   *Professional Course as Special Teachers.*

College graduates desiring special training in such work as supervisors of music, physical education, manual training, home economics, drawing, kindergarten or primary teaching, are granted a one year course arranged to suit their scholarship and attainments. When they satisfy the Faculty of their qualifications the appropriate diploma will be granted.

JUNIOR COLLEGE COURSES.

Standards Required and Honors Conferd.

Conditions of Admission.   The standards adopted by the State Board of Education as required for entrance upon the College Course are the same for the Junior College Courses except that graduates of four year high schools may be admitted without foren language credits, provided they have equivalent credits in other kinds of high school work..

The Diploma Conferd.   The junior college courses each cover two years of strong work in scholastic, general professional and special professional lines. They are the equivalent in standard of special excellence with other college courses of similar length but they are organized to give special attention to some one line of definit training, hence are not substitutes for the requirements of the four years college course.   For the completion of these two years of study and training, a Special Teacher Diploma is awarded and a five year state certificate of some kind is granted.

For the completion of an additional year of study, a Director's or Supervisor's Diploma is awarded as an additional recommendation of qualification and training for executiv work along these specialties of teaching.   When a three-year course is printed, the third year is the supervisor's or director's course.

In some particular departments where students complete the full line of special professional work required, such as music and art, department certificates may be obtaind by such persons as do not desire to complete the scholastic and the general professional work required for a diploma.

In all junior college courses the electiv studies must be chosen from the list of branches and term's work designated as of full college grade.   These elections must be made by consulting the heds of the departments involvd in order to avoid all mistakes.

THE ELEMENTARY TEACHERS COURSE.

First Year.

A	B	C
1. Education I.	1. Education II.	1. Education III.
2. Rhetoric.	2. College Electiv.	2. College Electiv.
3. Free Electiv.	3. Free Electiv.	3. Free Electiv.
4. Vocal Music.	4. Drawing.	4. Drawing.

Physical Training, Literary Society Work.

Second Year.

A	B	C
1. Education IV.	1. Practis Teaching.	1. Practis Teaching.
2. College Electiv.	2. College Electiv.	2. College Electiv.
3. Free Electiv.	3. Free Electiv.	3. Free Electiv.
4. Review.	4. Review.	4. Review.

Physical Training, Literary Society Work.

1. The free electivs may be secondary subjects not pursued in high school, foren language or college subjects. These must be chosen in such a way that state certificate requirements are met.

2. Three reviews must be selected from the following subjects: Penmanship, Physiology, U. S. History, English Grammar, Arithmetic, and Geography, unless the student has received satisfactory credits for such work in the eleventh or twelfth grades of an accredited high school aided by the State.

THE PRIMARY TEACHERS COURSE.

First Year.

A	B	C
1. Primary Methods	1 Primary Methods	1. Primary Methods
2. Psychology.	2. Elocution.	2. Botany.
3. Pri. Handwork.	3. Psychology.	3. Obs. in Training School.
4. Rhetoric.	4. Vocal Music.	4. Vocal Music.

Physical Training, five hours a week.

Literary Society Work.

Second Year.

A	B	C
1. Sch. Management	1. Hist. of Educ'n.	1. Kg. Theory&Ob.
2. Drawing.	2. Drawing.	2. Drawing.
3. Zoology.	3. Eng. Literature.	3. Electiv.
4. Criticism and Practis.	4. Criticism and Practis.	4. Criticism and Practis.

Literary Society Work.

THE KINDERGARTEN TEACHERS COURSE.

First Year.

A	B	C
1. Kg. Theory.	1. Kg. Theory.	1. Kg. Practis.
2. Psychology.	2. Psychology.	2. El. Handwork.
3. Rhetoric.	3. Vocal Music.	3. Vocal Music.
4. Drawing.	4. Drawing.	4. Nature Study.

Physical Training.
Literary Society Work.

Second Year.

A	B	C
1. Kg. Theory.	1. Kg. Theory.	1. Kg. Theory.
2. Kg. Practis.	2. Kg. Practis.	2. Sch. Management.
3. Elocution.	3. Hist. of Educ'n.	3. Primary Theory.
4. Electiv.	4. Electiv.	4. Electiv.

Physical Training.
Literary Society Work.

Supervisor Year.

A	B	C
1. Kg. Theory.	1. Kg. Theory.	1. Psychology.
2. Phil. of Educ'n.	2. Sch. Supervision.	2. Kg. Practis.
3. Harmony.	3. Public Speaking.	3. Hist. of Painting.
4. Electiv.	4. Electiv.	4. Electiv.

Literary Society Work.

THE PUBLIC SCHOOL MUSIC TEACHERS COURSE.

First Year.

A	B	C
1. Psychology.	1. Eng. Literature.	1. Nature Study.
2. Rhetoric.	2. Psychology.	2. 6th term Music
3. 3rd term Music.	3. 4th term Music,	Methods (1)
Sightsinging (3)	Sightsinging &	Harmony (2)
Ele. Harm'y (2)	Methods (3),Hist.	Hist. of Music (2)
	of Music (2).	3. 5th term Music
		Adv. Sight-sing-
		ing (2)
		Harmony (2)
		Methods (1)

Physical Training.

Literary Society Work.

Second Year.

A	B	C
1. Sound.	1. History.	1. Hist. of Education.
2. Elocution.	2. Sch. Management	2. 9th term Music.
3. 7th term Music	3. 8th term Music	Supervision (2)
Hist. of Music (2)	Musical Appre-	Harmony (2)
Harmony (2)	ciation (2)	Theory of
Conducting (1)	Harmony (2)	Music (1)
4. Observation	Child Voice (1)	3. Practis Teaching.
(half credit)	4. Prac. Teaching.	

Physical Training.

Literary Society Work.

The figure in parenthesis indicates the number of recitation hours per week, when less than five hours a week are given.

Two years of voice are required (one lesson per week.)

One year of piano is required (one lesson per week.)

Students completing all the music work required in the above course and the practis teaching, in addition to one term of psychology, one term of school management, one term of elocution. and two electivs in English, may be granted a certificate from the department.

THE DRAWING TEACHERS COURSE.

First Year.

A	B	C
1. Cast Drawing. .	1. Cast Drawing.	1. Hist. of Painting.
2. Greek History.	2. Medieval Hist.	2. Psychology.
3. Elocution.	3 Psychology.	3. Phys. Sci. Elect.
4. Rhetoric.	4. Hist. of Arch. &	4. Electiv.
	Sculpture.	
	Physical Training.	
	Literary Society Work.	

Second Year.

A	B	C
1. Still Life.	1. Perspectiv.	1. Supervision in Art
2. Zoology.	2. El. Handwork.	2. Mathematics.
3. Pol. Sci. Electiv.	3. Eng. Literature.	3. Hist. of Educa'n.
4. Sch. Management.	4. Prac. Teaching.	4. Prac. Teaching.
	Physical Training.	
	Literary Society Work.	

Third Year.

A	B	C
1. Water Color.	1. Mech. Drawing	1. Design.
2. Profes'l Electiv	2. Geology	2. Chemistry.
3. Physiography.	3. Phil. of Education	3. Botany.
4. Literary Critic'm	4. Sheet Metal W'k.	4. Electiv.
	Literary Society Work.	

THE MANUAL TRAINING TEACHERS COURSE.

First Year.

A	B	C
1. Rhetoric.	1. College Algebra	1. Eng. Literature
2. Psychology.	2. Psychology.	2. Sch. Managem't
3. Com. Geog. of	3. Prim. Handwork	3. Bench Work.
N. Am.	4. 2nd Drawing.	4. Design.
4. 1st Drawing.	5. Mech. Drawing.	5. Mech. Drawing.
	Physical Training.	
	Literary Society Work.	

Second Year.

A	B	C
1. Trigonometry.	1. Hist. of Educa'n	1. XIX. Cent. Hist.
2. Man. Training Methods I.	2. Man. Training Methods II.	2. Physics I.
3. Bench Work.	3. Bench Work.	3. Bench Work.
4. Sheet Metal W'k.	4. Ele. Handwork.	4. Mech. Drawing
5. Special Electiv.	5. Prac. Teaching	5. Prac. Teaching.

Physical Training.

Literary Society Work.

THE HOME ECONOMICS TEACHERS COURSE.

First Year.

A	B	C
1. Principles of Selection of Foods.	1. Principles of Selection of Foods	1. Principles of Selection of Foods
2. Elementary Food Theory.	2. Elementary Food Theory.	2. Elementary Food Theory.
3. Sewing.	3. Sewing.	3. Household Manag't
4. Inorg. Chemistry.	4. Inorg. Chemistry.	4. Sewing.
5. Rhetoric.	5. Sanitation.	5. Qual. Analysis
		6. Methods—Home Economics.
		7. Psychology.

Physical Training.

Literary Society Work.

Second Year.

A	B	C
1. Elementary Food Theory.	1. Dietetics.	1. Demonstrations
2. Dietetics.	2. Household Architecture.	2. Food Analysis
3. Household Chem.	3. Household Chem.	3. History of Educ'n.
4. Adv. Physiology	4. Psychology.	4. School Manag't.
5. Practis Teaching	5 Practis Teaching	5. Practis Teaching

Physical Training.

Literary Society Work.

THE PHYSICAL EDUCATION TEACHERS COURSE.

First Year.

A	B	C
1. Electiv.	1. Chemistry I.	1. Chemistry II.
2. Electiv.	2. Elocution	2. Electiv.
3. Rhetoric.	3. Psychology.	3. Psychology.
	Physical Training.	
	Literary Society Work.	

Second Year.

A	B	C
1. Theories and Systems of Phys Ed	1. Phys. Dept. Meth's.	1. Hist. and Lit. of Phys. Training.
2. Anatomy I.	2. Anatomy II.	2. Hygiene.
3. Sch. Managem't	3. Hist. of Educ'n.	3. Electiv.
	Physical Training.	
	Literary Society Work.	

Third Year.

A	B	C
1. Anthropom'y & Phys. Diagno's	1. Prac. Teaching	1. Physiology of Exercise.
2. Adv. Physiology	2. Electiv.	2. Electiv.
3. Electiv.	3 Phil. of Educ'n.	3. Med. Gymnastics and Massage.
	Physical Training.	
	Literary Society Work.	

SPECIAL COURSE FOR COLLEGE GRADUATES.

A	B	C
1. Theories and Systems of Phys. Ed.	1. Phys. Dept. Meth's.	1. Hist.and Lit. of Ph Training.
2. Anatomy I.	2. Anatomy II.	2. Hygiene.
3. Adv. Physiology	3. Electiv.	3. Phys. of Exercise
4. Anthropom'y and Phys. Diagnosis	4 Prac. Teaching.	4. Medical Gym. & Massage.
	Physical Training.	

1. Com. Corresp.
2. Com. Arithmetic
3. Adv. Penmanship
4. Am. Ind. History

1. Eng. Composition
2. 2nd Term Book-
   keeping
3. Electiv.
4. Psychology

Physical Training.
Literary Society Work.

1. Rhetoric.
2. 3rd Term Book-
   keeping
3. Electiv.
4. Psychology.

Second Year.

A	B	C
1. Sch. Managem't.	1. Am. Government	1. Gen. Economics
2. Electiv.	2. Electiv.	2. Electiv.
3. Com. Geog. of N. America.	3. Com. Geog. of Europe	3 Commercial Law
4. Eng. Literature	4. Practis Teaching.	4. Practis Teaching.

Physical Training.
Literary Society Work.

Note.—The electiv terms work here represented are to be stenography and typewriting to the extent that will give efficiency, and such other practical training as the department may find necessary to require.

SPECIAL TEACHER COURSES.

STANDARDS OF COUNTY AND STATE CERTIFICATES PREPARATION AND TRAINING FOR ELEMENTARY SCHOOL WORK.

1.   The Uniform County Certificates Course.

Conditions of Admission. Age, sixteen years; scholarship, possessing of a third grade uniform county certificate, a country school diploma or equivalent scholarship establisht by credentials of instructors or by examination.

Variations Provided. (1) Those presenting country school diplomas or equivalent scholarship are assignd two term work in arithmetic, English grammar, U S. history, geography and elementary civics. (2) Those presenting uniform county certificates will be excused from all subjects markt 85 per cent. or above, will be required to take one term work in these subjects if markt 75 per cent. and below 85 per cent., and will be required to take two term work if below 75 per cent.

High School Work.   Those not qualified to meet the above standards of age or scholarship can be receivd and given instruction in the elementary and high schools maintaind in the Training Department of the College.

Second Grade Uniform County Certificates.   Those possessing second grade county certificates are admitted to study such subjects as are needed to prepare them for first grade certificate standard.

First Year.

A	B	C
1. Arithmetic.	1. Geography.	1. U. S. History.
2. Eng. Grammar.	2. Algebra.	2. Algebra.
3. Physiology.	3. Didactics.	3. Reading.
4. Orthography.	4. Penmanship.	4. Vocal Music.

Physical Training.

Second Year.

A	B	C
1. Eng. Composition	1 Electiv.	1. Ele. Civics.
2. Ele. Physics.	2. Ele. Physics.	2. Methods of Teach.
3. Electiv.	3. Ele. Economics	3. Electiv.
4. Electiv.	4. Electiv.	4. Electiv.

Physical Training.

The electiv terms work here outlined is physiography, English, general history, botany, vocal music, drawing and elocution. When this work is all completed a department certificate will be granted by the Department of Professional Instruction in Education.

THREE YEAR SPECIAL TEACHER COURSES.

Second Grade State Certificate Standard.

II.   The Three Year Elementary Teachers Course.

Conditions of Admission. Teachers possessing a first grade uniform county certificate are unconditionally admitted to this course and to all special-teacher three year courses here provided. Students completing the Uniform County Certificate Course given by this College will be granted unconditional admission with credit for work alredy done in Physics, Algebra, General History, and other subjects classified in the three years elementary teachers course as requirements.

Variations and Equivalents. (1) Students who have com-pleted two years of standard high school work in a creditable manner will be granted admission provided the subjects studied in the high school can be considerd equivalent tothe first grade uniform county certificate. (2) Students who have completed more than two years work of a standard high school will be given temporary ad-vanced credit upon this course in proportion to the quality and quantity of work shown by their credentials, said credit to become permanent provided the work they do in the College justifies such recognition. (3) Students coming with any other credentials can have their status determind by a committee of the Faculty

First Year.

A	B	C
1. Algebra*	1. Plane Geometry	1. Plane Geometry
2. Physics. *	2. Bookkeeping.	2. Vocal Music
3. Gen. History *	3. Elocution.	5. Prin. of Education
4. Electiv.	4. Electiv.	4. Electiv.
	Physical Training.	

Second Year.

A	B	C
1. Drawing	1. Drawing.	1. Math. Electiv.
2. Psychology.	2. Psychology	2. Sch. Managem't
3 Solid Geometry	3. Sanitation.	3 Gen. Botany
4. Electiv.	4. Electiv.	4. Electiv.
	Physical Training.	
	Literary Society Work.	

Third Year.

A	B	C
1. Rhetoric.	1. Eng. Electiv	1. Science Electiv.
2. Econ. Electiv.	2. Govt. Electiv	2. Hist. Electiv.
3 Hist. of Educ'n	3. Prac. Teaching	3. Prac. Teaching
4. Electiv.	4. Electiv.	4. Electiv.
	Literary Society Work.	

*Two terms work if elementary teachers course was not com-pleted at this College or in an equivalent school.

Note on Electivs. The word "Electiv" as used in the Elementary Teachers Course means that a reasonable range of studies, both college and secondary, can be obtain. These are to be selected under advice by the President's Offis or by the Faculty adviser appointed for such purpose. This plan permits the study of Latin, German, English classics, or other equivalent subjects during the time. If a student determins to finally take the College Course the study of four terms of either Latin or German and six terms of English is necessary because these credits are required for college admission in the state educational institutions of Iowa. Students who are admitted to this course on partial high school course credentials are required to take as electivs three terms' work from arithmetic, English grammar, U. S. history, penmanship, physiology or geography as the President's Offis may determin.

III.   Other Special Teacher Three Year Courses.
1.   Primary Teacher Course.
2.   Kindergarten Teacher Course.
3.   Public School Music Teacher Course.
4.   Manual Training Teacher Course.
5.   Home Economics Teacher Course.
6.   Drawing Teacher Course.
7.   Elementary Teacher Course.
8.   Commercial Teacher Course.

Admission. All these special teacher courses require as a minimum for entrance upon their study a first grade uniform county certificate or its equivalent.

The Courses Offerd. The first year's work is to be completed before beginning on the special work that the particular line selected will require. These selections for the year's study will depend largely upon the particular quality and quantity of scholarship alredy possest by the student. The branches from which the course shall be chosen shall consist of secondary studies such as algebra, botany, general history, economics, civil government, elocution, English classics, drawing, vocal music, Latin, German, and other acceptable subjects. The decision in each case shall be made on the basis of advice given by the President's Offis or by some member of the Faculty appointed as an adviser of these classes of students.

The Second and Third Years. The full requirements for these years are publisht in detail elsewhere in this Bulletin under the classification, "Junior College Courses." These can be enterd upon without restriction after the First Year before mentiond has been satisfactorily completed.

SPECIAL MUSIC TEACHER COURSES.

Conditions of Admission. Students are admitted to these music courses on liberal terms as to preparatory training and are encouraged to begin early enough to develop the skill and capability for professional artistic success that are so notably demanded in teachers of these kinds.

To become a candidate for graduation, the student must have attaind to the scholastic qualifications required of secondary schools for full college entrance. These scholastic conditions may be acquired in any good secondary school or may be accomplisht in the certificate courses at the College.

Conditions of Graduation. A special Teacher Diploma will be awarded to such persons as complete satisfactorily any one of the courses here outlined, but as skill and capability as musicians are also essential qualities to be attaind, the exact time necessary to complete any one of these courses can not be stated in school years. The candidate must have sufficient proficiency in the special line chosen to secure the recommendation of the professors in charge of the work to become an applicant for graduation. The courses as here mapt out, outside of the attainment in capability as a musician, can be satisfactorily completed in three years.

THE PIANO COURSE.

Piano lessons must be continued thru the entire period of study, two lessons a week. A second study—voice or orchestral instrument—must also be carried, with either one or two lessons a week, each term except the last year.

Other required work will be:

First Year.

A	B	C
Elem'ts of Music 5	Elem'ts of Music 5	German 5
German 5	German 5	Music History 2
Music History 2		Ear Training 2

Second Year.

A	B	C
Harmony 2	Harmony 2	Harmony 2
Music History 2	Eng. Literature 5	Psychology 5
Sound 5		

Third Year.

A	B	C
Harmony 2	Harmony 2	Harm. Analysis 2
Psychology 5	Medieval Hist. 5	Modern History 5

Piano—9 terms, once or twice a week (at least.)

Second Study—6 terms, once or twice a week (at least.)

The figures after the subjects indicate the number of recitation periods per week.

THE VIOLIN COURSE.

Violin lessons must be continued thru the entire period of study—two lessons per week. The piano work must be carried for two years successfully with at least one lesson a week. Attendance at two orchestra rehearsals and one class in ensemble playing is also required each week.

First Year.

A	B	C
Elem'ts of Music 5	Elem'ts of Music 5	Music History 2
German 5	German 5	German 5
Music History 2		Ear Training 2

Second Year.

A	B	C
Harmony 2	Harmony 2	Harmony 2
Music History 2	Eng. Literature 5	Psychology 5
Sound 5		

Third Year.

A	B	C
Harmony 2	Harmony 2	Harm. Analysis 2
Psychology 5	Medieval Hist. 5	Modern History 5

The figures after the subjects indicate the number of recitation periods per week.

THE VOICE COURSE.

Three years of voice lessons (two a week), and two years piano lessons (one a week), will be required.

First Year.

A	B	C
Elem'ts of Music 5	Elem'ts of Music 5	German 5
German 5	German 5	Elem'ts of Music 5
Music History 2	Theory of Phys. Training 5	Ear Training 2

Second Year.

A	B	C
Harmony 2	Harmony 2	Harmony 2
Music Hist. 2	Eng. Literature 5	Psychology 5
Scund 5		

Third Year.

A	B	C
Harmony 2	Harmony 2	Harm. Analysis 2
Psyhcology 5	French 5	French 5
French 5	Medieval Hist. 5	Modern Hist. 5

The figures after the subjects indicate the number of recitation periods per week.

PROGRAM OF RECITATIONS.

Explanatory Note.

This program of recitations is printed for the full school year, presenting the work for the Fall, Winter and Spring terms. The work is organized on the basis of the past year, and may be expanded if numbers enrol should demand it.

The nomenclature used gives in order: 1. The College Course. 2. The Junior College Courses. 3. The Teachers' Certificate Courses, for each term. The electivs in Home Economics, Drawing, Manual Training or Physical Education which may apply on a college course in case a major is taken in one of these lines, will be found listed with the subjects belonging to the Junior College Courses. All subjects of college grade required in the Junior College Courses are included under the College Course.

The program of Physical Training, excepting the Theory, will be found at the end of the program for each term.

The subject of study is given in the terminology adopted by the departments, complete explanation being given in the Catalog and Circular for 1911. The name of the teacher is given following each subject assignd for the term, and the Arabic numeral following the teacher's name gives the hour at which the recitation will occur.

The following are the hours of work in the school for the year:

First Hour ...... 8:00 to 8:55.
Second Hour ...... 8:55 to 9:50.
Assembly ...... 9:50 to 10:20.
Third Hour ...... 10:20 to 11:15.
Fourth Hour ...... 11:15 to 12:10.
Fifth Hour ...... 1:30 to 2:25.
Sixth Hour ...... 2:25 to 3:20.
Seventh Hour ...... 3:20 to 4:15.
Eighth Hour ...... 4:15 to 5:00.

Of these the first to fifth, inclusiv, are regarded as regular class hours.

Students' Offis Hours. Students having business with the President's offis will receive attention from 7:30 to 9:50 a. m. and 1:00 to 2:00 p. m. Please note this and do not come other business hours except in emergencies that are unusual.

Library Hours. School days, 7:30 a. m. to 5:00 p. m. and 6:00 to 9:30 p. m. Saturdays, 7:30 a. m. to 12:00.

Literary Societies. Fridays, 2:25 p. m. Saturdays, 7:00 p. m.

Faculty Meetings. Mondays, 2:25 p. m.

Assignment for Rehearsals of Musical Societies.

> Choral Society .... Tuesdays, 6:30 p. m.
> Cecilians .... Wednesdays, 2:25 p. m.
> Euterpeans .... Tuesdays, 2:25 p. m.
> Young Ladies' Glee Club .... Mondays, 2:25 p. m.
> Minnesingers .... Wednesdays, 2:25 p. m.
> Troubadours.... Tuesdays, 2:25 p. m.
> Orchestra .... Mondays and Thursdays, 3:30 p. m.
> Band .... Tuesdays and Fridays, 3:30 p. m.
> Ensemble Class .... Wednesdays, 3:00 p. m.
> Junior Band .... Wednesdays, 3:30 p. m.

FALL TERM.

COLLEGE COURSE.

PROFESSIONAL INSTRUCTION IN EDUCATION. I. 1st Psychology, *Mr. Samson* 1-3. II. 2nd Psychology, *Mr. Samson* 2-5. III. School Management, *Mr. Colgrove* 2-3-5. IV. History of Education, *Mr. Walters* 1-3-4. VI. American Education, *Mr. Colgrove* 1. VII. Experimental Psychology, *Mr. Mount* 5. IX. Educational Classics, *Mr. Walters* 2.

TRAINING IN TEACHING. Illustrativ Teaching, *Mr. Bender* (Tuesday, Wednesday, Thursday) 3-5-6.

ENGLISH. (*a*) *Language and Literature.* I. Rhetoric, *Mr. Lynch* 3-5; *Mr. Gist* 1-4; *Miss Carpenter* 1; *Miss Lambert* 2; *Miss Gregg* 5; *Miss Hearst* 4; *Miss Lodge* 4. II. (a).English Literature, *Mr. Lynch* 2; *Mr. Gist* 5. III. Shakespeare, *Mr. Gist* 2. VI. The Development of the English Drama, *Miss Lambert* 1. XII. Theme Writing and Story Telling, *Miss Carpenter* 2. XIV. American Literature, *Miss Lambert* 4. (*b*) *Elocution and Public Speaking.* XV. Elocution I., *Miss*

Martin 2; —————— 2. XVI. Elocution II., *Miss Martin*
3. XIX. Repertoire II., *Miss Martin* 1. XXII. Public Speaking I., *Mr. Barnes* 2. XXIII. Public Speaking II., *Mr. Barnes* 3.

LATIN AND GREEK. (1) *Latin.* I. Cicero (Cato Major), *Mr. Merchant* 1-3. IV. Latin Composition (Tuesday, Thursday), *Mr. Merchant* 2. VII. Plautus and Terence (Monday, Wednesday, Friday), *Mr. Merchant* 2. X. Historical Latin Grammar (Monday, Wednesday, Friday), *Mr Merchant* 5. XIII. Senior Electiv (Tuesday, Thursday), *Mr. Merchant* 5. XVI. (a) Elementary Latin (Introductory Work), *Miss Call* 3; (b) Elementary Latin (Ovid), Miss Call 1. (2) *Greek.* I. Lessons (Monday, Wednesday, Friday), *Miss Call* 2.

GERMAN AND FRENCH. (1) *German.* I. Grammar, *Mr. Knoepfler* 4. II. Grammar, —————— 5. IV. Die Journalisten, *Miss Lorenz* 3. V. Wilhelm Tell, *Miss Lorenz* 1. VI. Prose Composition, *Miss Lorenz* 5. VII. Emilia Galotti and Lyrics and Ballads, *Miss Lorenz* 2. X. Language and Literature, *Mr. Knoepfler* 2. (2) *French.* I. Lessons, *Mr. Knoepfler* 1. IV. Novels, Stories, etc., *Mr. Knoepfler* 3.

MATHEMATICS. I. Solid Geometry, *Mr. Wright* 5. II. College Algebra, *Mr. Condit* 3. III. Plane Trigonemetry, *Mr. Cory* 4. VI. Analytical Geometry, *Mr. Condit* 1.

CHEMISTRY. I. General Inorganic, *Mr. Bond* 4. I. General Inorganic (For Home Economics students),*Mr. Getchell* 1. II. General Inorganic, *Mr. Getchell* 2. III. IV. Qualitativ Analysis, *Mr. Bond* 3. V. VI. Quantitativ Analysis, *Mr. Bond* 5. VIII. Household Chemistry, *Mr. Getchell* 3.

PHYSICS. I. Mechanics of Solids and Fluids, *Mr. Begeman* 3. V. VI. Advanced Laboratory Work, *Mr. Begeman* 6.

NATURAL SCIENCE. I. Physiology I., *Mr. Newton* 1. IV. Zoology I., *Mr. Arey* 1. VI. Physiography I., *Mr. Cable* 3. IX. Mineralogy, *Mr. Cable* 4. XI. Commercial Geography of North America, *Miss Aitchison* 5.

HISTORY. I. American, *Miss Riggs* 1. III. Greek, *Miss Rice* 3. VI. Modern, *Miss Riggs* 4. IX. Method, *Miss Riggs* 2.

GOVERNMENT. I. American Government, *Mr. Meyerholz* 2. II. American Constitutional History I., *Mr. Meyerholz* 5. VI. International Law, *Mr. Meyerholz* 4.

ECONOMICS. I. General Economics, *Mr. McKitrick* 2. II. Economic and Social Problems, *Mr. McKitrick* 1. III. American Industrial History, *Mr. McKitrick* 3.

MANUAL TRAINING. I. Manual Training Methods I., *Mr. Bailey* 1.

PHYSICAL EDUCATION. I. Anatomy I., *Mr. Seymour* 4.

JUNIOR COLLEGE COURSES.

PROFESSIONAL INSTRUCTION IN EDUCATION. 1st Psychology, *Mr. Mount* 1-2-4; *Miss Buck* 3-5. 1st Primary Methods, *Miss Mc Govern* 2-3-4. 2nd Primary Methods, *Miss McGovern* 1.

TRAINING IN TEACHING. Primary Criticism, *Miss Hatcher* 6. Kindergarten Theory (Junior), *Miss Ward* 1. Kindergarten Theory (Senior), *Miss Ward* 5. Kindergarten Practis, *Miss Dowdell* 2-3.

MATHEMATICS. Commercial Arithmetic, *Mr. Cory* 5.

PHYSICS. Sound, *Mr. Begeman* 5.

NATURAL SCIENCE. Zoology, *Mr. Arey* 2-3-4.

DRAWING. Water Color, *Miss Thornton* 1. 1st Primary Drawing, *Miss Thornton* 2-3; *Miss Schuneman* 1. 1st Kindergarten Drawing, *Miss Schuneman* 3. Cast Drawing, *Miss Patt* 5. Still Life, *Miss Thornton* 5; *Miss Patt* 3-4; *Miss Schuneman* 5. Perspectiv, *Miss Patt* 2.

COMMERCIAL. Advanced Penmanship, *Mr. Cummins* 4. Business Correspondence, *Mr. Coffey* 2. Shorthand, *Mr. Coffey* 3. Typewriting, *Mr. Coffey* 5.

MUSIC. 3rd Music, *Mr. Fullerton* 2. 4th Music, (a) History (Tuesday, Friday), *Miss Childs;* (b) Sightsinging and Methods (Monday, Wednesday, Thursday), *Miss Stenwall* 4. 7th Music (a) Conducting (Wednesday), *Mr. Fullerton;* (b) Harmony (Tuesday, Friday), *Mr. Frampton;* (c) History (Monday, Thursday), *Miss Childs* 1.

PHYSICAL EDUCATION. Anatomy I.,*Mr. Seymour* 4. Theories and Systems of Physical Education, *Mr. Seymour* 3. Anthropometry and Physical Diagnosis, *Mr. Seymour* 5.

MANUAL TRAINING. Manual Training Methods I., *Mr. Bailey* 1. 1st Mechanical Drawing, *Mr. Bailey* 4. Advanced Mechanical Drawing, *Mr. Bailey* 5. Sheet Metal Work, *Mr. Bailey* 3. 1st Bench Work, *Mr. Brown* 2. Advanced Bench Work, *Mr. Brown* 4-5. Wood Turning, *Mr. Brown* 4-5. Individual Work in the

Shop, *Mr. Brown* 6-7. Primary Handwork, *Mrs. McMahon* 1-2-3-5.

HOME ECONOMICS. 1st Sewing, *Miss Heinz* 8:55 to 9:50 and 10:20 to 11:15. Principles of the Selection and Preparation of Foods, *Miss Townsend* (Monday, Wednesday), 1:30 to 2:25. Elementary Food Theory, *Miss Townsend* and *Miss Heinz* (Monday, Wednesday), 2:25 to 5:00. Dietetics, *Miss Townsend* (Tuesday, Thursday), 11:15 to 12:10 and 1:00 to 2:25.

COUNTY AND STATE CERTIFICATE COURSES.

PROFESSIONAL INSTRUCTION IN EDUCATION. Didactics, *Miss Buck* 2. Methods, *Miss Buck* 4. Principles of Education, *Mr. Dick* 4.

ENGLISH. (a) *Language and Literature.* Orthography, *Miss Oliver* 1-2. 1st half English Grammar, *Miss Hearst* 1;—————4. 2nd half English Grammar, *Miss Hearst* 2. Complete English Grammar, *Miss Gregg* 2-3-4. 1st half English Composition, *Miss Lodge* 1. Complete English Composition, *Miss Lodge* 5. 1st English Classics, *Miss Oliver* 4. 2nd English Classics, *Miss Hearst* 5. American Literature, *Miss Carpenter* 4. (b) *Elocution and Public Speaking.* Reading, *Miss Falkler* 1. Elocution, *Miss Falkler* 2-3-4;—————3.

LATIN AND GREEK. *Latin.* 1st Latin Lessons, *Miss Call* 4. 2nd Caesar, —————3.

GERMAN AND FRENCH. *German.* 3rd German, —————4.

MATHEMATICS. 1st half Arithmetic, *Miss Seals* 4; *Miss Lambert* 2-3. 2nd half Arithmetic, *Mr. Cory* 2. Complete Arithmetic, *Mr. Condit* 5; *Mr. Cory* 1. 1st Algebra, *Miss Seals* 3-5. 2nd Algebra, *Miss Seals* 2; *Miss Lambert* 5. Two term Algebra, *Miss Lambert* 1. 3rd Algebra, *Mr. Condit* 2. Beginning Geometry, *Mr. Wright* 2-4. Middle Geometry, *Mr. Wright* 3. Solid Geometry, *Mr. Wright* 5.

PHYSICS. 1st Physics, *Mr. Hersey* 2-3; *Mr. Kadesch* 1-4. 2nd Physics, *Mr. Hersey* 5; *Mr. Kadesch* 2.

NATURAL SCIENCE. 1st half Geography, *Miss Aitchison* 2. 2nd half Geography, *Miss Aitchison* 1. Complete Geography, *Miss Aitchison* 3. Physiology, *Mr. Newton* 2-3. Physiography, *Mr. Cable* 1-2. General Botany, *Mr. Newton* 5.

HISTORY. 1st half U. S. History, *Miss Rice* 4; *Mr. Peter-*

son 5. 2nd half U. S. History, *Miss Rice* 5. Complete U. S. History, *Miss Riggs* 5. 1st General History, *Miss Rice* 2.

GOVERNMENT. Iowa and U. S. Civics (Review), *Mr. Meyerholz* 1. Iowa History and Civics, *Mr. Peterson* 4. U. S. Civics, *Mr. Peterson* 2.

ECONOMICS. Elementary Economics, *Mr. McKitrick* 4; *Mr. Peterson* 3.

DRAWING. 1st Drawing, *Miss Thornton* 5; *Miss Patt* 3-4; *Miss Schuneman* 5. 2nd Drawing, *Miss Patt* 2.

COMMERCIAL. 1st Penmanship, *Mr. Cummins* 2-3; *Mr. Coffey* 1. 1st Bookkeeping, *Mr. Cummins* 1.

MUSIC. 1st Vocal Music, *Mr. Fullerton* 3; *Miss Stenwall* 5; —————1-2. 2nd Vocal Music, *Miss Stenwall* 2-3;———— ——————4.

HOME ECONOMICS. Sewing, *Miss Heinz* 8:00 to 8:55. Elementary Food Theory and Laboratory Cooking, *Miss Townsend* (Tuesday, Thursday), 2:30 to 4:45.

PHYSICAL TRAINING.

1st term Physical Training—
 Miss Hussey (Monday, Wednesday) 6·
  (Tuesday, Thursday) 7.
 Miss Hallingby (Tuesday, Thursday) 6.
 Miss Samson (Monday, Wednesday) 4.
  (Tuesday, Thursday) 5.

2nd term Physical Training—
 Miss Samson (Tuesday, Thursday) 6.

3rd term Physical Training—
 Miss Hallingby (Tuesday, Thursday) 7.

1st term Primary Physical Training—
 Miss Hussey (Daily) 4.
 Miss Hallingby (Daily) 5.

Swimming.
 Mr. Pasini (Tuesday, Thursday) 3-5-6.
 Miss Hussey (Tuesday, Thursday) 3.
  (Monday, Wednesday) 7.*
 Miss Hallingby (Tuesday, Thursday) 4.
  (Monday, Wednesday) 6-7.

Miss Samson (Monday, Wednesday) 3-5.
Tennis.
   Mr. Seymour (Tuesday, Thursday) 6.
          .(Monday, Wednesday, Friday) 7.*
   Mr.` Pasini (Monday, Wednesday, Friday) 3-5.
   Miss Hallingby (Monday, Wednesday) 4.
   Miss Samson (Tuesday, Thursday) 3-4-7.
Hockey.
   Miss Samson (Monday, Wednesday) 6.
Basketball.
   Miss Samson (Monday, Wednesday) 7.
Cricket.
   Miss Hussey (Tuesday, Thursday) 6.
Golf.
   Mr. Seymour (Tuesday, Thursday) 7.*
Track Athletics.
   Mr. Seymour (Monday, Wednesday, Friday) 6.
Soccer Football.
   Mr. Pasini (Monday, Wednesday, Friday) 6.
Football Squad.
   Mr. Pasini (Daily) 7-8.

*Required of Juniors and Seniors of Physical Education Department.

WINTER TERM.
COLLEGE COURSE.

PROFESSIONAL INSTRUCTION IN EDUCATION. I. 1st Psychology, *Mr. Samson* 2-5. II. 2nd Psychology, *Mr. Samson* 1-4. III. School Management, *Mr. Colgrove* 1-2-3-5. IV. History of Education, *Mr. Walters* 2-3-5. V. Philosophy of Education, *Mr. Walters* 1. VII. Experimental Psychology, *Mr. Mount* 5.

ENGLISH. (a) *Language and Literature.* I. Rhetoric, *Mr. Lynch* 5; *Mr. Gist* 4; *Miss Lodge* 2. II. (a) English Literature, *Mr. Lynch* 4; *Mr. Gist* 5; *Miss Carpenter* 2; *Miss Lambert* 3. (b) English Literature, *Miss Lambert* 5. III. Shakespeare, *Mr. Gist* 3. IV. Epic Poetry in English, *Mr. Lynch*

2. V. The English Romantic Movement, *Miss Carpenter* 4. VI. The Development of the English Drama, *Miss Lambert* 1. VIII. Anglo Saxon and Middle English, *Mr. Gist* 2. XIV. American Literature, *Miss Carpenter* 1. (*b*) *Elocution and Public Speaking.* XVI. Elocution II., *Miss Martin* 2;——————2. XVII. Applied Drama, *Miss Martin* 4. XVIII. Repertoire I., *Miss Martin* 3. XXII. Public Speaking I., *Mr. Barnes* 2. XXIV. Argumentation, *Mr. Barnes* 3.

LATIN AND GREEK. (1) *Latin.* II. Livy, *Mr. Merchant* 1-3. V. Latin Composition (Tuesday, Thursday), *Mr. Merchant* 2. VIII. Catullus (Monday, Wednesday, Friday), *Mr. Merchant* 2. XI. Historical Latin Grammar (Monday, Wednesday, Friday), *Mr. Merchant* 5. XIV. Senior Electiv (Tuesday, Thursday), *Mr. Merchant* 5. XVII. (a) Elementary Latin (Caesar), *Miss Call* 3; (b) Elementary Latin (Vergil), *Miss Call* 1. (2) *Greek.* II. Lessons (Monday, Wednesday, Friday), *Miss Call* 2.

GERMAN AND FRENCH. (1) *German.* II. Grammar, *Mr. Knoepfler* 5. III. Immensee and Hoeher als die Kirche, *Miss Lorenz* 5. V. Wilhelm Tell, *Miss Lorenz* 3. VI. Prose Composition, *Miss Lorenz* 1. VIII. Nathan der Weise, *Miss Lorenz* 2. XI. Modern German Prose and Scientific German, *Mr. Knoepfler* 2. (2) *French.* II. Lessons, *Mr. Knoepfler* 1. V. Novels, Stories, etc., *Mr. Knoepfler* 3.

MATHEMATICS. I. Solid Geometry, *Mr. Wright* 3. II. College Algebra, *Mr. Cory* 2. III. Plane Trigonometry, *Mr. Condit* 1-2. VII. Differential Calculus, *Mr. Condit* 3.

CHEMISTRY. I. General Inorganic, *Mr. Bond* 2. II. General Inorganic, *Mr. Bond* 4; II. General Inorganic (for Home Economics students), *Mr. Getchell* 1. III.—IV. Qualitativ Analysis, *Mr. Bond* 1. VI. Quantitativ Analysis, *Mr. Bond* 5-6. VII. Special Methods in Quantitativ Analysis, *Mr. Getchell* 5-6. IX. Household Chemistry, *Mr. Getchell* 3.

PHYSICS. I. Mechanics of Solids and Fluids, *Mr. Begeman* 3. II. Sound and Light, *Mr. Begeman* 1.

NATURAL SCIENCE. III. Hygiene and Sanitation, *Mr. Newton* 2-5. VII. Geology I., *Mr. Cable* 2. XII. Commercial Geography of Europe, *Miss Aitchison* 5. XIII. Influences of Geography upon American History, *Mr. Cable* 4.

HISTORY. IV. Roman, *Miss Rice* 2. V. Medieval, *Miss*

Riggs 5. VII. Eighteenth Century, *Miss Riggs* 1.

ECONOMICS. I. General Economics, *Mr. McKitrick* 5.
IV. English Industrial History, *Mr. McKitrick* 3. V. Money
and Banking, *Mr. McKitrick* 2.

GOVERNMENT. I. American Government, *Mr. Meyer-
holz* 2. III. American Constitutional History II., *Mr. Meyerholz*
4. IV. English Government, *Mr. Meyerholz* 3.

DRAWING. III. History of Architecture and Sculpture,
Miss Thornton 1.

MANUAL TRAINING. II. Manual Training Methods II., *Mr.
Bailey* 2.

PHYSICAL EDUCATION. II. Anatomy II., *Mr. Seymour* 4.

JUNIOR COLLEGE COURSES.

PROFESSIONAL INSTRUCTION IN EDUCATION. 1st Psychology, *Miss Buck* 1. 2nd Psychology, *Mr. Dick* 2; *Mr. Mount*
2-3-4. 1st Primary Methods, *Miss McGovern* 4. 2nd Primary
Methods, *Miss McGovern* 1-2-3.

TRAINING IN TEACHING. Primary Criticism, *Miss Hatcher*
6. Kindergarten Theory (Junior), *Miss Ward* 1. Kindergarten
Theory (Senior), *Miss Ward* 5. Kindergarten Practis, *Miss Dowdell* 2-3.

MATHEMATICS. Commercial Arithmetic, *Mr. Cory* 5.

NATURAL SCIENCE. Structural Botany, *Mr. Arey* 1-2. Hygiene and Sanitation, *Mr. Newton* 2-5.

DRAWING. History of Architecture and Sculpture, *Miss
Thornton* 1. 2nd Primary Drawing, *Miss Schuneman* 2-3-4. 2nd
Kindergarten Drawing, *Miss Thornton* 3. Cast Drawing, *Miss
Patt* 5. Still Life, *Miss Thornton* 2-4; *Miss Patt* 3; *Miss Schune-
man* 1. Perspectiv, *Miss Patt* 1-2.

COMMERCIAL. Advanced Penmanship, *Mr. Cummins* 4. 2nd
Bookkeeping, *Mr. Cummins* 5. Business Correspondence, *Mr.
Coffey* 1. 1st Shorthand, *Mr. Coffey* 2. 2nd Shorthand, *Mr. Cof-
fey* 5. Typewriting, *Mr. Coffey* 3.

MUSIC. 3rd Music, (a) Harmony (Tuesday, Thursday),
Mr. Fullerton; (b) Sightsinging (Monday, Wednesday, Friday),
Miss Stenwall 2. 4th Music, (a) Sightsinging and Methods (Mon-
day, Wednesday, Thursday), *Miss Stenwall;* (b) History (Tues-

day, Friday), *Miss Childs* 1. 5th Music, *Mr. Fullerton* 5. 8th Music, (a) Appreciation (Wednesday, Friday), *Mr. Fullerton;* (b) Harmony (Monday, Thursday), *Mr. Frampton;* (c) Child Voice (Tuesday), *Miss Stenwall* 1.

PHYSICAL EDUCATION. Anatomy II., *Mr. Seymour* 4. Physical Department Methods, *Mr. Seymour* 5.

MANUAL TRAINING. Manual Training Methods II., *Mr. Bailey* 2. Sheet Metal Work, *Mr. Bailey* 3. 1st Mechanical Drawing, *Mr. Bailey* 4. Advanced Mechanical Drawing, *Mr. Bailey* 5. 1st Bench Work, *Mr. Brown* 2. Advanced Bench Work, *Mr. Brown* 4-5. Wood Turning, *Mr. Brown* 4-5. Individual Work in the Shop, *Mr. Brown* 6-7. Elementary Handwork, *Mrs. McMahon* 1. Primary Handwork, *Mrs. McMahon* 2-3-5.

HOME ECONOMICS, 2nd Sewing, *Miss Heinz* 8:55 to 9:50 and 10:20 to 11:15. Principles of the Selection and Preparation of Foods, *Miss Townsend* (Monday, Wednesday), 1:30 to 2:25. Elementary Food Theory, *Miss Townsend* (Monday, Wednesday), 2:25 to 5:00. Dietetics, *Miss Townsend* (Tuesday,Thursday), 3:30. Household Architecture, *Miss Townsend* (Tuesday, Thursday), 11:15 to 12:10.

COUNTY AND STATE CERTIFICATE COURSES.

PROFESSIONAL INSTRUCTION IN EDUCATION. Didactics, *Miss Buck* 3. Methods, *Miss Buck* 2-5. Principles of Education, *Mr. Dick* 4.

ENGLISH. (a) *Language and Literature.* Orthography, *Miss Oliver* 1-2. 1st half English Grammar, *Miss Hearst* 2; ———— ————5. 2nd half English Grammar, *Miss Hearst* 3-4. Complete English Grammar, *Miss Gregg* 3-4-5. 1st half English Composition, *Miss Gregg* 2. 2nd half English Composition, *Miss Lodge* 1. Complete English Composition, *Miss Lodge* 4. 1st English Classics,*Miss Oliver* 4. 2nd English Classics, *Miss Hearst* 5. (b) *Elocution and Public Speaking.* Reading, *Miss Falkler* 1. Elocution, *Miss Falkler* 2-3-5; ———————— 4.

LATIN AND GREEK. *Latin.* 2nd Latin Lessons, *Miss Call* 4. 1st Cicero's Orations, ———————— 3.

GERMAN AND FRENCH. *German.* 1st German, ———————— ————5. 4th German (Die Journalisten), ———————— 4.

MATHEMATICS. 1st half Arithmetic, *Mr. Cory* 4; *Miss Seals*

5. 2nd half Arithmetic, *Miss Seals* 4; *Miss Lambert* 2-3. Complete Arithmetic, *Mr. Cory* 1. 1st Algebra, *Miss Seals* 2; *Miss Lambert* 5. 2nd Algebra, *Miss Seals* 1. Two term Algebra, *Mr. Condit* 5. 3rd Algebra, *Miss Lambert* 4. Beginning Geometry, *Mr. Wright* 4. Middle Geometry, *Mr. Wright* 2-5. Solid Geometry, *Mr. Wright* 3.

PHYSICS. 1st Physics, *Mr. Hersey* 1-3; *Mr. Kadesch* 4. 2nd Physics, *Mr. Kadesch* 2-5. 3rd Physics, *Mr. Hersey* 5.

NATURAL SCIENCE. 1st half Geography, *Miss Aitchison* 1. 2nd half Geography, *Miss Aitchison* 2. Complete Geography, *Miss Aitchison* 3. Physiology, *Mr. Newton* 3-4. Physiography, *Mr. Cable* 1-5. Hygiene and Sanitation, *Mr. Newton* 2-5.

HISTORY. 1st half U. S. History, *Miss Rice* 4; *Mr. Peterson* 5. 2nd half U. S. History, *Miss Rice* 5. Complete U. S. History, *Miss Riggs* 4. 1st General History, *Miss Rice* 3. 2nd General History, *Miss Riggs* 2.

GOVERNMENT. Iowa and U. S. Civics (Review), *Mr. Meyerholz* 1. Iowa History and Civics, *Mr. Peterson* 4. U. S. Civics, *Mr. Peterson* 3.

ECONOMICS. Elementary Economics, *Mr. McKitrick* 1; *Mr. Peterson* 2.

DRAWING..—1st Drawing, *Miss Thornton*, 2-4; *Miss Patt* 3; *Miss Schuneman* 1. 2nd Drawing, *Miss Patt* 1-2.

COMMERCIAL.—1st Penmanship, *Mr. Cummins* 1-3. 1st Bookkeeping, *Mr. Cummins* 2.

MUSIC. 1st Vocal Music, *Mr. Fullerton* 3; *Miss Stenwall* 5; —————————1. 2nd Vocal Music, *Miss Stenwall* 4; ————— —————2-3.

HOME ECONOMICS. Sewing, *Miss Heinz* 8:00 to 8:55. Elementary Food Theory and Laboratory Cooking, *Miss Townsend* and *Miss Heinz* (Tuesday, Thursday), 1:15 to 3.20.

PHYSICAL TRAINING.

1st term Physical Training.

Miss Hussey (Tuesday, Thursday) 6.

Miss Hallingby (Monday, Wednesday) 7.

2nd term Physical Training.

Miss Hussey (Monday, Wednesday) 5.

Miss Hallingby (Tuesday, Thursday) 6

Miss Samson (Monday, Wednesday) 4-6.

(Tuesday, Thursday) 7.

3rd term Physical Training.
> *Miss Hallingby* (Monday, Wednesday) 4.
> *Miss Samson* (Monday, Wednesday) 7.

2nd term Primary Physical Training.
> *Miss Hussey* (Daily) 4.
> *Miss Hallingby* (Daily) 5.

Swimming.
> *Mr. Pasini* (Tuesday, Thursday) 6-7.

Rythm.
> *Miss Hallingby* (Monday, Wednesday) 6.
> (Tuesday, Thursday) 7.

Games.
> *Miss Hallingby* (Tuesday, Thursday) 4.

Advanced Games.
> *MissHussey* (Monday, Wednesday) 6.
> *Miss Samson* (Monday, Wednesday) 5.
> (Tuesday, Thursday) 6.

Basketball.
> *Miss Samson* (Tuesday, Thursday) 3-4.

Gilbert Work.
> *Miss Hussey* (Tuesday, Thudsday) 7.*

Medical Gymnastics.
> *Miss Hussey* (Monday, Wednesday) 7.*

First Year Gymnastics.
> *Mr. Pasini* (Monday, Wednesday, Friday) 4-6.

Second Year Gymnastics.
> *Mr. Pasini* (Monday, Wednesday, Friday) 7.

Advanced Gymnastics.
> *Mr. Seymour* (Tuesday, Thursday) 7.*

Gymnastic Dancing.
> *Mr. Seymour* (Tuesday, Thursday) 6.*

Indoor Games.
> *Mr. Pasini* (Tuesday, Thursday) 4.

Basketball Squad.
> *Mr. Pasini* (Daily) 8.
> *Required of Juniors and Seniors of Physical Education De
partment.*

SPRING TERM.

COLLEGE COURSE.

PROFESSIONAL INSTRUCTION IN EDUCATION.—I. 1st Phychology, *Mr. Samson* 1-4. II. 2nd Psychology, *Mr. Samson* 2-5. III. School Management, *Mr. Colgrove* 1-2-3; *Miss Buck* 4. IV. History of Education, *Mr. Walters* 1-3-4. V. Philosophy of Education, *Mr. Walters* 2. VII. Experimental Psychology, *Mr. Mount* 5. VII. School Supervision, *Mr. Dick* 4. X. Lecture Course on Genetic, Social, and Sex Psychology, (½ credit), *Mr. Colgrove* 7.

ENGLISH. (*a*) *Language and Literature.* I. Rhetoric, *Mr. Gist* 1-5; *Mr. Lynch* 5. II. (a) English Literature, *Mr. Lynch* 4: *Miss Carpenter* 1-3. (b) English Literature, *Miss Lambert* 3. III. Shakespeare, *Mr. Gist* 2. VIII. Anglo Saxon and Middle English, *Mr. Gist* 4. IX. Literary Criticism, *Miss Carpenter* 4. X. The Development of the English Novel, *Miss Lodge* 5. XI. English of the Nineteenth Century, *Miss Lambert* 1. XIII. Teaching English, *Mr. Lynch* 2. XIV. American Literature, *Miss Lambert* 4. (*b*) *Elocution and Public Speaking.* XVI. Elocution II., *Miss Martin* 2; ——————— 2. XXI. Principles of Expression, *Miss Martin* 1. XXII. Public Speaking I., *Mr. Barnes* 2. XXIII. Public Speaking II., *Mr. Barnes* 3.

LATIN AND GREEK. (1) *Latin.* III. Horace, Epodes and Odes, *Mr. Merchant* 1-3. VI. Latin Composition (Tuesday, Thursday), *Mr. Merchant* 2. IX. Cicero's Letters (Monday, Wednesday, Friday), *Mr. Merchant* 2. XII. Historical Latin Grammar (Monday, Wednesday, Friday), *Mr. Merchant* 5. XV. Senior Electiv (Tuesday, Thursday), *Mr. Merchant* 5. XVIII. (a) Elementary Latin (Cicero), *Miss Call* 3; (b) Elementary Latin (Vergil), *Miss Call* 1. (2) *Greek.* III. Anabasis (Monday, Wednesday, Friday), *Miss Call* 2.

GERMAN AND FRENCH.—(1) *German.* 1. Grammar, *Miss Lorenz* 2. III. Immensee and Hoeher als die Kirche, *Miss Lorenz* 3. IV. Die Journalisten, *Miss Lorenz* 5. V. Wilhelm Tell, ——————————— 4. VI. Prose Composition, *Mr. Knoepfler* 4. IX. Iphigenie auf Tauris and Die Braut von Messina, *Miss Lorenz* 1. XII. Classics, *Mr. Knoepfler* 2. (2) *French.* III. L'Abbe Constantin, Le Voyage de Monsieur Perrichon, *Mr. Knoepfler* 1. VI. Novels, Stories, etc., *Mr. Knoepfler* 3.

MATHEMATICS. I. Solid Geometry (for High School Graduates), *Mr. Wright* 4; Solid Geometry, *Mr. Wright* 5. II. College Algebra, *Mr. Condit* 2. III. Plane Trigonometry, *Mr. Cory* 1. IV. Spherical Trigonometry and Surveying, *Mr. Condit* 5. V. History and Teaching of Mathematics, *Mr. Wright* 3. VIII. Integral Calculus, *Mr. Condit* 1.

CHEMISTRY.—I. General Inorganic, *Mr. Bond* 1. II. General Inorganic, *Mr. Bond* 4. III. IV. Qualitativ Analysis, *Mr. Bond* 3. V. VI. Quantitativ Analysis, *Mr. Getchell* 5-6. VII. Special Methods in Quantitativ Analysis, *Mr. Getchell* 1. X. Food Analysis, *Mr. Getchell* 3.

PHYSICS.—I. Mechanics of Solids and Fluids, *Mr. Begeman* 3. III. Heat, Electricity and Magnetism, *Mr. Begeman* 5.

NATURAL SCIENCE.—II. Botany I., *Mr. Newton* 1-2 (Laboratory work, Tuesday, Friday, 3-5). V. Zoology II., *Mr. Arey* 3. VIII. Geology II., *Mr. Cable* 2. X. Astronomy, *Mr. Cable* 4. XI. Commercial Geography of North America, *Miss Aitchison* 5.

HISTORY.—II. English, *Miss Rice* 1. VI. Modern, *Miss Riggs* 2. VIII. 19th Century, *Miss Riggs* 4.

GOVERNMENT. I. American Government, *Mr. Meyerholz* 5. V. Modern European Governments, *Mr. Meyerholz* 1. VII. Constitutional Law, *Mr. Meyerholz* 3.

ECONOMICS. I. General Economics, *Mr. McKitrick* 5. II. Economic and Social Problems, *Mr. McKitrick* 1. VI. Industrial Corporations, *Mr. McKitrick* 2.

DRAWING. IV. History of Painting, *Miss Thornton* 1.

MANUAL TRAINING. III. Organization and Economics of Manual Training, *Mr. Bailey* 2.

JUNIOR COLLEGE COURSES.

PROFESSIONAL INSTRUCTION IN EDUCATION. 1st Psychology, *Mr. Mount* 1-2. 2nd Psychology, *Mr. Mount* 4. 1st Primary Methods, *Miss McGovern* 4. 3rd Primary Methods, *Miss McGovern* 1-2-3.

TRAINING IN TEACHING. Observation in Training School (Primary), *Miss Hatcher* 2. Primary Theory (for Kindergarten Students), *Miss Hatcher* 5. Primary Criticism, *Miss Hatcher* 6. Kindergarten Theory and Observation (for Primary Students), *Miss Ward* 2. Kindergarten Theory (Senior), *Miss Ward* 4. Kindergarten Practis, *Miss Dowdell* 2-3.

MATHEMATICS. Commercial Arithmetic, *Mr. Condit* 3.

NATURAL SCIENCE. Structural Botany, *Mr. Arey* 1. Nature Study, *Mr. Arey* 2.

DRAWING. History of Painting, *Miss Thornton* 1. Supervision in Art, *Miss Thornton* 2. Design, *Miss Patt* 4. 3rd Primary Drawing, *Miss Schuneman* 1-4-5. Still Life, *Miss Thornton* 3; *Miss Patt* 2. Perspectiv, *Miss Thornton* 4; *Miss Patt* 3-5; *Miss Schuneman* 2.

COMMERCIAL. Advanced Penmanship, *Mr. Cummins* 4. 2nd Bookkeeping, *Mr. Cummins* 3. 3rd Bookkeeping, *Mr. Cummins* 1. Commercial Law, *Mr. Coffey* 1. 2nd Shorthand, *Mr. Coffey* 2. 3rd Shorthand, *Mr. Coffey* 3. Typewriting, *Mr. Coffey* 4.

MUSIC. 3rd Music, (a) Harmony (Tuesday, Thursday), *Mr. Fullerton;* (b) Sightsinging (Monday, Wednesday, Friday), *Miss Stenwall* 3. 4th Music, (a) Sightsinging and Methods (Monday, Wednesday, Thursday), *Miss Stenwall;* (b) History (Tuesday, Friday), *Miss Childs* 1. 5th Music, *Mr. Fullerton* 2. 6th Music, (a) Harmony (Tuesday, Friday), *Mr. Fullerton;* (b) Methods (Wednesday), *Miss Stenwall;* (c) History (Monday, Thursday), *Miss Childs* 4. 9th Music, (a) Supervision (Wednesday, Friday), *Mr. Fullerton;* (b) Harmony (Monday, Thursday), *Mr. Frampton;* (c) Theory (Tuesday), *Miss Stenwall* 1.

PHYSICAL EDUCATION. Physiology of Exercise, *Mr. Seymour* 3. Hygiene, *Mr. Pasini* 4. Medical Gymnastics and Massage, *Mr. Seymour* 4. History and Literature of Physical Training, *Mr. Seymour* 5.

MANUAL TRAINING. Organization and Economics of Manual Training, *Mr. Bailey* 2. Sheet Metal Work, *Mr. Bailey* 3. 1st Mechanical Drawing, *Mr. Bailey* 1. Advanced Mechanical Drawing, *Mr. Bailey* 5. 1st Bench Work, *Mr. Brown* 2. Advanced Bench Work, *Mr. Brown* 4-5. Wood Turning, *Mr. Brown* 4-5 Individual Work in the Shop, *Mr. Brown* 6-7. Elementary Handwork, *Mrs. McMahon* 1. Primary Handwork, *Mrs. McMahon* 2-4-5.

HOME ECONOMICS. 3rd Sewing, *Miss Heinz* 8:00 to 8:55 and 8:55 to 9:50. Principles of the Selection and Preparation of Foods, *Miss Townsend* (Monday, Wednesday), 1:30 to 2:25. Elementary Food Theory, *Miss Townsend* and *Miss Heinz* (Monday, Wednesday), 2:25 to 5:00. Demonstrations, *Miss Townsend* (Tuesday, Thursday), 3:30 to 5:30. Methods, Home Economics, *Miss Townsend* (Friday), 1:30 to 2:25. Household Management, *Miss Townsend* (Tuesday, Thursday, Friday), 11:15 to 12:10.

COUNTY AND STATE CERTIFICATE COURSES.

PROFESSIONAL INSTRUCTION IN EDUCATION. Didactics, *Miss Buck* 2. Methods, *Miss Buck* 5. Principles of Education, *Mr. Dick* 3.

ENGLISH. (*a*) *Language and Literature.* Orthography, *Miss Oliver* 1-2. 1st half English Grammar, *Miss Gregg* 3;—————— 1. 2nd half English Grammar, *Miss Hearst* 2-3. Complete English Grammar, *Miss Gregg* 4-5. 1st half English Composition, *Miss Lodge* 1. 2nd half English Composition, *Miss Gregg* 2. Complete English Composition, *Miss Lodge* 4. 1st English Classics, *Miss Oliver* 4. 2nd English Classics, *Miss Hearst* 5. American Literature, *Miss Hearst* 1. (*b*) *Elocution and Public Speaking.* Reading, *Miss Falkler* 2. Elocution, *Miss Falkler* 1-3-4; ————————————5.

LATIN AND GREEK. *Latin.* 1st Caesar, *Miss Call* 4. 2nd Cicero, ——————— 3.

GERMAN AND FRENCH. *German.* 2nd German,——————— ———————— 5.

MATHEMATICS. 1st half Arithmetic, *Miss Seals* 4; *Miss Lambert* 3. 2nd half Arithmetic, *Mr. Cory* 2-5. Complete Arithmetic, *Miss Lambert* 2. 1st Algebra, *Miss Seals* 5. 2nd Algebra, *Miss Seals* 1. Two term Algebra, *Miss Lambert* 1. 3rd Algebra, *Miss Seals* 3; *Miss Lambert* 5. Beginning Geometry, *Mr. Cory* 4. Middle Geometry, *Mr. Wright* 2. Solid Geometry, *Mr. Wright* 5.

PHYSICS. 1st Physics, *Mr. Hersey* 1-3. 2nd Physics, *Mr. Hersey* 5; *Mr. Kadesch* 2. 3rd Physics, *Mr. Kadesch* 1-4.

NATURAL SCIENCE. 1st half Geography, *Miss Aitchison* 2. 2nd half Geography, *Miss Aitchison* 1. Complete Geography, *Miss Aitchison* 3. Physiology, *Mr. Newton* 4. Physiography, *Mr. Cable* 3-5. General Botany, *Mr. Newton* 1-2.

HISTORY. 1st half U. S. History, *Miss Rice* 3; *Mr. Peterson* 1. 2nd half U. S. History, *Miss Rice* 2. Complete U. S. History, *Miss Riggs* 1. 1st General History, *Miss Rice* 4. 2nd General History, *Miss Riggs* 3.

GOVERNMENT. Iowa and U. S. Civics (Review), *Mr. Meyerholz* 2. Iowa History and Civics, *Mr. Peterson* 5. U. S. Civics, *Mr. Peterson* 3.

ECONOMICS. Elementary Economics, *Mr. McKitrick* 3; *Mr. Peterson* 4.

DRAWING. 1st Drawing, *Miss Thornton* 3; *Miss Patt* 2. 2nd Drawing, *Miss Thornton* 4; *Miss Patt* 3-5; *Miss Schuneman* 2.

COMMERCIAL. 1st Penmanship, *Mr. Cummins* 1-3; *Mr. Coffey* 5. 1st Bookkeeping, *Mr. Cummins* 2.

MUSIC. 1st Vocal Music, —————————— 1-2. 2nd Vocal Music,*Miss Stenwall* and —————————— 3; *Miss Stenwall* 5.

HOME ECONOMICS. Sewing, *Miss Heinz* 10:20 to 11:15. Elementary Food Theory and Laboratory Cooking, *Miss Townsend* (Tuesday, Thursday), 1:15 to 3:20.

PHYSICAL TRAINING.

1st term Physical Training.
   Miss Hussey (Tuesday, Thursday) 5.
2nd term Physical Training.
   MissHallingby (Tuesday, Thursday) 5-7.
3rd term Physical Training .
   Miss Hussey (Monday, Wednesday) 6.
   Miss Hallingby (Tuesday, Thursday) 6.
   Miss Samson (Monday, Wednesday) 5.
              (Tuesday, Thursday) 7.
Swimming.
   Mr. Pasini (Tuesday, Thursday) 5-6.
   Miss Hussey (Monday, Wednesday) 3-5.
              (Tuesday, Thursday) 3.
   Miss Hallingby (Tuesday, Thursday) 4.
              (Monday, Wednesday) 7.
   Miss Samson (Monday, Wednesday) 4-6.
Tennis.
   Mr. Pasini (Monday, Wednesday, Friday) 5
   Miss Hallingby (Monday, Wednesday) 3-4.
   Miss Samson (Tuesday, Thursday) 3-5-6.
              (Monday, Wednesday) 7.
Rythm.
   Miss Hallingby (Monday, Wednesday) 6.
Advanced Rythm.
   Miss Hussey (Tuesday, Thursday) 7.
Advanced Gymnastics.
   Miss Hussey (Monday, Wednesday) 7.*

Athletics.
>   *Miss Hallingby* (Monday, Wednesday) 5.
>   *Miss Samson* (Tuesday, Thursday) 4.

Medical Gymnastics.
>   *Miss Hussey* (Tuesday, Thursday) 7.*

Track Athletics.
>   *Mr. Seymour* (Monday, Wednesday, Friday) 6.

Track Squad.
>   *Mr Seymour* (Daily) 7-8.*

Baseball.
>   *Mr. Pasini* (Monday, Wednesday, Friday) 6.

Baseball Squad.
>   *Mr. Pasini* (Daily) 7-8.*

Required of Juniors and Seniors of Physical Education Department.

BULLETIN

OF THE

Iowa State Teachers College

CEDAR FALLS, IOWA

COURSES OF STUDY

AND

PROGRAM OF RECITATIONS

FOR THE SCHOOL YEAR

1912-1913

Vol. XIII. No. 2

JULY, 1912

Issued Quarterly. Publisht the State Teachers College. Enterd at the Postoffis at Cedar Falls, Iowa, as Second Class Matter

Vol. XIII   *JUNE, 1912*   *No. 2*

BULLETIN

OF THE

IOWA STATE TEACHERS COLLEGE

CEDAR FALLS, IOWA

COURSES OF STUDY

AND

PROGRAM OF RECITATIONS

FOR SCHOOL YEAR 1912-1913

Where the spelling in this Bulletin varies from the conventional form, it has been adopted for its simplicity and its preference for common usage.

Iowa State Teachers College

SCHOOL CALENDAR FOR 1912-1913

FALL TERM—TWELVE WEEKS

1912

Sept. 3.—Tuesday, Enrollment, without penalty, 8:00 a. m. to 4:00 p. m.

Sept. 4.—Wednesday, Chapel Exercises, 9:00 a. m. to 9:30 a. m.; Recitations begin 8:00 a. m., half-hour class periods; Enrollment with penalty, 1:30 p. m. to 4:00 p. m.

Sept. 5.—Thursday, Training Schools open, 9:00 a. m.

Oct. 23, 24, 25.—Wednesday, Thursday, Friday, Examination for County Uniform Certificates, beginning Wednesday, 8:00 a. m.

Nov. 26.—Tuesday, Recitations close at noon.

Nov. 25, 26, 27.—Monday, Tuesday, Wednesday, State Certificate Examination, beginning Monday, 8:00 a. m.

WINTER TERM—TWELVE WEEKS

1912

Dec. 3.—Tuesday, Enrollment, without penalty, 8:00 a. m to 4:00 p. m.

Dec. 4.—Wednesday, Chapel Exercises, 9:00 a. m. to 9:30 a. m.; Recitations begin 8:00 a. m., half-hour class periods; Enrollment, with penalty, 1:30 p. m. to 4:00 p. m.

Dec. 20.—Friday, Holiday Recess Begins at noon.

1913

Jan. 6.—Monday, Recitations Resumed, 8:00 a. m.

Iowa State Teachers College

The Course of Study

REQUIREMENTS FOR ADMISSION.

Applicants for unconditional admission to the College Course, hereafter printed in detail, must be at least sixteen years of age and must present satisfactory records from accredited secondary schools showing a total of fifteen units of work in accordance with the standards approved by the Iowa State Board of Education, as fully set out in detail in Bulletin No. 1 of the Board on Secondary School Relations. The term unit as here used signifies a year's work where the class hours are forty-five minutes, the number of class hours per week being not less than five.

I. CONSTANTS.

Groups of Subjects—	Units
1. One Foreign Language	2
2. English	3
3. Algebra	1½
4. Plane Geometry	1
5. History	1
6. Electives	6½
Total	15

II. ELECTIVES.

In selecting the units that are known as electives in the above requirement, the total that may be accepted for any one group always includes those units required for constants. The maximum number of units that may be offered on certificate from an accredited high school are as follows:

Groups of Subjects—		*Units*
1. Foreign Language—		4
(1) Greek	2 to 4	
(2) Latin	2 to 4	
(3) French	2 to 4	
(4) Spanish	2 to 4	
(5) German	2 to 4	
2. English		4
3. History, Civics and Economics		4
(1) Ancient History	½ to 1	
(2) Medieval and Modern History	½ to 1	
(3) Civil Government	½ to 1	
(4) Economics	½	
(5) General History in place of (1) and (2)	1	
(6) U. S. History—3rd and 4th years	½ to 1	
(7) English History	½ to 1	
4. Mathematics		4
(1) Solid Geometry	½	
(2) Plane Trigonometry	½	
(3) Advanced Algebra	½	
5. Science		4½
Physics	1	
Chemistry	1	
Physiography	½ to 1	
Botany	½ to 1	
Zoology	½ to 1	
Physiology	½	
Geology	½	
Astronomy	½	
Agriculture	½ to 1	
6. Commercial Subjects		2
Adv. Arithmetic (after Algebra)	½	
Bookkeeping	½ to 1	
Commercial Geography	½	
Commercial Law	½	
Industrial History	½	

7. Industrial Subjects   2
        Freehand and Mechanical
            Drawing   ½ to 1
        Manual Training—i. e. Shop
            Work   ½ to 2
        Domestic Science   ½ to 1
        Stenography   ½ to 1

Credit is not given for English grammar or United States history, unless taken in the latter part of the course, nor for arithmetic unless taken after algebra.

OUTLINE OF THE COLLEGE COURSE GIVING DISTRIBUTION OF WORK AND DIRECTIONS CONCERNING THE OPPORTUNITIES OFFERED.

THE COLLEGE COURSE.

Degree: Bachelor of Arts in Education.
First Grade State Certificate Standard.

Freshman Year.

A	B	C
1. Elective.	1. Elective.	1. Elective.
2. Elective.	2. Elective.	2. Elective.
3. Rhetoric.	3. Education I.	3. Education II.

Sophomore Year.

A	B	C
1. Elective.	1. Elective.	1. Elective.
2. Elective.	2. Elective.	2. Elective.
3. Education III.	3. Education IV.	3. Elective.

Junior Year.

A	B	C
1. Elective.	1. Elective.	1. Elective.
2. Elective.	2. Elective.	2. Elective.
3. Elective.	3. Education V.	3. Education VI.

Senior Year.

A	B	C
1. Elective.	1. Elective.	1. Elective.
2. Elective.	2. Elective.	2. Elective.
3. Practise Teach-ing.	3. Practise Teach-ing.	3. Elective.

Majors.—It is necessary for the student who takes the College Course to select one major study with some one department at the close of the Freshman year. A major consists of at least two full years of work, thus covering six term credits. After the major is decided the student is under the direction of the department in which the major belongs, and the Head of the Department becomes his advisor during the rest of his course. The different majors that are offered are in the following lines·

1. English.
2. Public Speaking.
3. Latin.
4. German.
5. French.
6. Mathematics.
7. Physics.
8. Chemistry.
9. Earth Science.
10. Biological Science.
11. History.
12. Government.
13. Economics.
14. Education.
15. Drawing.
16. Manual Training.
17. Hcme Economics.
18. Physical Education.

DISTRIBUTION OF CREDITS IN THE COLLEGE COURSE.

The following outline gives the distribution of studies that is required for graduation from the college course, each credit being 12 weeks of 5 lessons a week.

I. *Professional Courses.*   Number of Credits.

    1. Professional 14
    2. English 3
    3. Foreign Language 3
    4. History, Government and Economics ... 3
    5. Science and Mathematics 3
    6. Elective 10
        Total 36
    7. Other work required:
       (a) Physical Training—two years.
       (b) Literary Society Work—four years.

II. *English Courses.*
    1. English 12
    2. Foreign Language 3
    3. History, Government and Economics ... 3
    4. Science and Mathematics 3
    5. Professional 8
    6. Elective 7
        Total 36
    7. Same as in Professional Courses.

III. *Foreign Language Courses.*
    Foreign Language 12
    English 3
    History, Government and Economics ... 3
    Science and Mathematics 3
    Professional 8
    Elective 7
        Total 36
    7. Same as in Professional Courses.

IV. *History, Government and Economics Courses.*
    1. History, Government and Economics ... 12
    2. English 3
    3. Science and Mathematics 3
    4. Foreign Language 3
    5. Professional 8
    6. Elective 7
        Total 36
    7. Same as in Professional Courses.

V. *Science and Mathematics Courses.*

1.	Science and Mathematics	15
2.	English	3
3.	Foreign Language	3
4.	History, Government and Economics	3
5.	Professional	8
6.	Elective	4
	Total	36

7. Same as in Professional Courses.

VI. *Home Economics, Drawing, Physical Education and Manual Training Courses.*

1.	Home Economics, etc.	9
2.	English	3
3.	Foreign Language	3
4.	History, Government and Economics	3
5.	Science and Mathematics	6
6.	Professional	8
7.	Elective	7
	Total	39

8. Other Work Required:
    (a) Physical Training—two years.
    (b) Literary Society Work—four years.

OTHER PRIVILEGES ALLOWED IN ALL COURSES.

In addition to the required work necessary for graduation from the College Course as above specified, students are allowed to pursue work in vocal music, instrumental music, drawing, manual training, sewing, cooking, penmanship or other art subjects, provided not more than a total of four hours work a day is thus scheduled. These subjects are of such importance in public school work that this liberal plan has been adopted, it being recognized that a knowledge of these subjects greatly increases the opportunities of a teacher both as to location and as to superior salary.

DEPARTMENT SUBJECTS IN THE COLLEGE COURSE

This tabular arrangement gives the entire program of studies with the nomenclature adopted by the Faculty for the College Course.

The numbers by which the courses in the different departments are to be designated are given below:

Professional.

Required Work—

    I—II. Psychology, I., II.
    III. School Management.
    IV. History of Education.
    V. Philosophy of Education.
    VI. School Administration.
    VII—VIII. Practise Teaching.

Elective Courses—

    IX. Experimental Psychology.
    X. Genetic Psychology.
    XI. Educational Classics.
    XII. Lecture Course on Social and Sex Psychology, 3 hours, ½ credit.
    XIII. Rural School Problems.
    XIV. Practise Teaching.

English.

    I. College Rhetoric.
    II. Theme Writing and Story Telling.
    III. Public Speaking I.
    IV. Argumentation.
    V. The Art of Oratory—Public Speaking II.
    VI. Advanced Exposition.
    VII. English Literature.
    VIII. Anglo-Saxon.
    IX. Middle English and History of the English Language.
    X. Shakespeare.
    XI. Literary Criticism.
    XII. The English Romantic Movement.
    XIII.—XIV. History of the English Drama I., II.
    XV. English Literature of the Nineteenth Century.
    XVI. American Literature.
    XVII. The Development of the English Novel.
    XVIII—XIX. Elocution I., II.
    XX. Applied Drama.

XXI—XXII—XXIII. Repertoire I., II., III.
XXIV. Principles of Expression.
XXV. The Teaching of English.

Note. In curricula where two terms of English are required, course I and course VII are to be taken, unless otherwise specified in the curriculum. In curricula where three terms of English are required, the courses to be taken are I, VII, and *one* of the following courses: II, V, VI. Courses II, V, VI and VII are electives for other students; and all other courses are free electives, except where Elocution or Public Speaking is prescribed in certain curricula.

Latin and Greek.

Latin—
    I. Cicero, Cato Major.
    II. Livy.
    III. Horace, Epodes and Odes.
    IV—V—VI. Latin Composition.
    VII—VIII—IX. Roman Literature.
    X—XI—XII. Historical Latin Grammar.
XIII—XIV—XV. Senior Electives.
XVI—XXI. College Elementary Latin.

Note. Only courses I—XV can be counted as a part of a Latin Major.

Greek—
    I—II. Lessons.
    III. Anabasis.
    IV. Plato.
    V—VI.—Homer.

German and French.

German—
    I. Die Jungfrau von Orleans.
    II. German Prose Composition.
    III. Emilia Galotti, Lyrics and Ballads.
    IV. Nathan der Weise.
    V. Iphigenie auf Tauris.
    VI. Der dreissigjaehrige Krieg.
    VII. Modern German Prose or Scientific German.
    VIII. Selections from German Classics.

Notes. 1. The above outline of work is for students who have had a minimum of two years of German in an accredited high school, or its equivalent. Students who have met in some other foreign language the required entrance conditions, may take beginning German for college credit. Of this there are four terms; namely, German IX, X, XI, and XII.

2. Other authors of similar grade will be read at times instead of those here listed.

French—
    I. Lessons—Grammar and Pronunciation.
    II. Grammar continued; Les Prisonniers du Caucase, and other easy French.
    III. Le Voyage de Monsieur Perrichon, and L'Abbe Constantin.
    IV. La Mare au Diable, and L'Histoire d'un jeune Homme pauvre.
    V. Le Gendre de M. Poirier, and Un Philosophe sous les Toits.
    VI. Le Pecheur d'Islande, and Le Bourgeois Gentilhomme.

Mathematics.
    I. Solid Geometry.
    II. College Algebra I.
    III. Plane Trigonometry.
    IV. College Algebra II.
    V. Spherical Trigonometry and Surveying.
    VI. History and Teaching of Mathematics.
    VII. Analytical Geometry.
    VIII. Differential Calculus.
    IX. Integral Calculus.

Chemistry.
    I—II. General Inorganic.
    III. Qualitative Analysis.
    IV—V. Quantitative Analysis.
    VI. Special Methods in Quantitative Analysis.

Physics.

     I. Mechanics and Sound.
    II. Light and Heat.
   III. Electricity and Magnetism.
   IV. Teachers' Special Course.
    V. Adv. Laboratory Work in General Physics.
   VI. Adv. Laboratory Work in Electricity.

Natural Science.

     I. Physiology I.
  II—III. Botany I., II.
   IV. Hygiene and Sanitation.
  V—VI—VII. Zoology I, II, III.
VIII. Physiography I.
 IX—X. Geology I., II.
   XI. Mineralogy.
  XII. Astronomy.
 XIII. Commercial Geography of North America.
 XIV. Commercial Geography of Europe.
  XV. Influences of Geography upon American History.

History.

     I. American History.
    II. English History.
   III. Greek History.
   IV. Roman History.
    V. Medieval History.
   VI. Renaissance and Reformation.
  VII. Eighteenth Century History.
VIII. Nineteenth Century History.
   IX. Method History or Teachers' History.

Government.

     I. American Government.
  II—III. American Constitutional History I, II.
   IV. English Government.
    V. Modern European Governments.
   VI. Municipal Government.
  VII. International Law.
VIII. Constitutional Law.
   IX. English Constitutional History.

Economics.
     I.   General Economics.
    II.   Economic and Social Problems.
   III.   American Industrial History.
   IV.   English Industrial History.
    V.   Money and Banking.
   VI.   Industrial Corporations.

Drawing.

* I—II. Cast Drawing	½ credit each	
III. History of Architecture	1 "	
IV. History of Painting	1 "	
* V. Perspective	½	
* VI. Still life	½	
* VII—VIII. Water color	½ " each	
* IX. Design	½	
* Manual Training, Physical Education or Home Economics	3 credits	

Manual Training.

I—II. Manual Training Methods	1 credit each	
III. Organization and Economics of Manual Training	1	
* IV—V—VI—VII. Mechanical Drawing	½ " each	
* VIII—IX—X—XI. Design and Construction in Wood	½ " each	
* XII. Wood Turning	½	
* XIII—XIV. Design and Construction in Sheet Metal	½ " each	
* XV. Primary Handwork	½	
* XVI. Elementary Handwork	½ ..	

Note. Courses in I, II, III, VI, VII, IX, X, XII, and XIII constitute a Manual Training Major.

Home Economics.

* I—II—III. Sewing	½ credit each	
* IV—V—VI—VII. Elementary Food Theory	½ " "	
* VIII—IX. Dietetics	½ " "	
* X. Demonstrations	¼	

* XI. Principles of the Selection and
　　Preparation of Foods　　　　$1\frac{1}{4}$ credits
* XII. Household Management　　2-5 credit
* XIII. Household Architecture　　2-5 credit
* XIV. Methods, Home Economics　1-5 credit
* Manual Training, Physical Education or
　　Drawing　　　　　　　　　2 credits

Note. In Manual Training, Home Economics and Drawing Majors here outlined the fractions given specify the particular value of said courses when applied to the College Course.

Physical Education.

　I—II. Anatomy.
* III. Hygiene.
* IV. Physical Department Methods.
* V. Playground Methods.
* VI. History and Literature of Physical Training.
* VII. Anthropometry and Physical Diagnosis.
* VIII. Physiology of Exercise.
* IX. Medical Gymnastics and Massage.

Other General Electives.

Music—

Music I.　　　　　　　　　$\frac{1}{2}$ credit
Music II.　　　　　　　　　$\frac{1}{2}$ credit
Harmony I, II, III, IV.　　　2 credits
History of Music I,II.　　　　1 credit

THE JUNIOR COLLEGE COURSE.

In conformity with the custom of the State Teachers College to give a diploma for two years work in the institution after possessing the secondary scholarship of a fully accredited high school, the Junior College Course is provided. This course is distributed as to the number of term credits as follows:

* Not accepted as electives on courses other than those in which majors are chosen in Home Economics, Drawing, Physical Education or Manual Training.

Departments of Work	Number of Credits
English	2
Foreign Language	2
History, Government and Economics	2
Science and Mathematics	2
Professional and Training	6
Elective	4
Total	18

In addition, the candidate for the diploma must have two years of Physical Training and two years of Literary Society Work.

STATE CERTIFICATE REQUIREMENTS.

This diploma may or may not entitle the holder to the Second Grade State Certificate. Those who desire to secure this honorary credential as a teacher must have studied either in the high school or the Teachers College, or have passed a teachers' certificate examination of high grade, the following: 1. Arithmetic; 2. Geography; 3. English Grammar; 4. United States History; 5. Vocal Music; 6. Physiology; 7. Civics (including civil government of Iowa); 8. Algebra (including Quadratics, ratio, proportion, variation and logarithms); 9. Physics; 10. Economics (including the topics: the marginal theory of value and the laws of distribution, money—its nature and history in the United States, the quantity theory, monopolies and trusts, public ownership, or regulation); 11. Bookkeeping (single and double entry); 12. Drawing (including composition, illustrative and elementary perspective); 13. Descriptive Botany; 14. English Composition.

THE DIPLOMAS MASTER OF DIDACTICS AND BACHELOR OF DIDACTICS TO BE DISCONTINUED.

Under regulations adopted by the State Board of Education January 3, 1912, the diploma, Bachelor of Didactics, will be discontinued in 1913 and in its place the Junior College Diploma will be issued. The diploma, Master of Didactics, will be discontinued in 1914 as a recognition for completing a three year course of college grade and will only be used as a diploma to be granted to such college graduates as take the one year professional course elsewhere outlined for such class of students.

THE PROFESSIONAL COURSE OF STUDY FOR COLLEGE GRADUATES.

The Iowa State Teachers College has developed professional courses for college graduates that deserve special recognition for their practical features and for their large professional helpfulness. College graduates of decided success in teaching can complete one of these courses by attending three successive summer terms and doing special assigned work during the interim. Before graduation they will need to establish proofs of their success being excellent and positive. Where practise teaching is omitted with the consent of the department, other professional credits may be substituted on arrangement with the department. Those not having this standard of success are developed and trained by the Practise Teaching department, which is in active work during the fall, winter and spring terms of each school year. For inexperienced teachers, the regular sessions are better adapted, as the training schools are then regularly in session.

I. Professional Course in Education.

First Term.

1. Advanced Psychology.
2. School Management.
3. History of Education.

Second Term.

1. Philosophy of Education.
2. School Administration.
3. Practise Teaching.

Third Term.

1. Experimental Psychology.
2. Educational Classics.
3. Practise Teaching.

II.   PROFESSIONAL COURSE WITH ELECTIVES.

1.	Education	3 credits
2.	Practise Teaching	2 credits
3.	Scholastic Studies	4 credits
	Total required	9 credits

Graduates of approved colleges can complete either course in one year of efficient study and training, and will receive the diploma of Master of Didactics and a First Grade State Certificate, provided they meet all the requirements demanded by the State Board of Educational Examiners.

Observations on These Courses.

1.   Some branches of the above work can be personal, individual studies, laboratory and library in character, on lines outlined by the Professional department. These studies are to be carefully made and results submitted to the department for examination, criticism and instruction. The library is so strong in Pedagogy that this work is of great and lasting professional value.

2.   For entrance upon this course a complete detail of all work taken at the College must be filed.

3.   Substitutions will be granted for efficient pedagogical work taken at a college with a strong professional department. Great liberty will be allowed to such grade of students so as to enable them to prepare both wisely and well for the best public services in any special line of school work, but in every case a year's attendance at this college is required. Such students are excused from literary society work if they apply to the Faculty for such release.

III.   PROFESSIONAL COURSE AS SPECIAL TEACHERS.

College graduates desiring special training in such work as supervisors of music, physical education, manual training, home economics, drawing, kindergarten, or primary teaching, are granted a one year course arranged to suit their scholarship and attainments. When they satisfy the Faculty of their qualifications the appropriate diploma will be granted.

SPECIAL TEACHER COURSES.
Standards Required and Honors Conferred.

Conditions of Admission. The standards adopted by the State Board of Education as required for entrance upon the College Course are the same for the Special Teacher Courses except that graduates of four year high schools may be admitted without foreign language credits, provided they have equivalent credits in other kinds of high school work.

The Diploma Conferred. The Special Teacher courses each cover two years of strong work in scholastic, general professional and special professional lines. They are the equivalent in standard of special excellence with other college courses of similar length but they are organized to give special attention to some one line of definite training. For the completion of these two years of study and training, a Special Teacher Diploma is awarded and a five year state certificate of a special kind is granted by the State Board of Examiners.

For the completion of an additional year of study, a Director or Supervisor Diploma is awarded as an additional recommendation of qualification and training for executive work along these specialties of teaching. When a three-year course is printed, the third year is the supervisor or director course.

In some particular departments where students complete the full line of special professional work required, such as music and art, department certificates may be obtained by such persons as do not desire to complete the scholastic and the general professional work required for a diploma.

In all Special Teacher Courses the elective studies must be chosen from the list of branches and term's work designated as of full college grade. These elections must be made by consulting the heads of the departments involved in order to avoid all mistakes.

THE ELEMENTARY TEACHERS COURSE.
First Year.

A	B	C
1. Education I.	1. Education II.	1. Education III.
2. Rhetoric	2. College Elective	2. College Elective.
3. Free Elective	3. Free Elective	3. Free Elective
4. Vocal Music.	4. Drawing	4. Drawing
Physical Training		Literary Society Work.

Second Year.

A	B	C
1. Education IV	1. Practise Teaching.	1. Practise Teaching.
2. College Elective	2. College Elective	2. College Elective
3. Free Elective	3. Free Elective	3. Free Elective
4. Review	4. Review	4. Review
	Physical Training	
	Literary Society Work.	

1.   The free electives may be secondary subjects not pursued in high school, foreign language or college subjects. These must be chosen in such a way that state certificate requirements are met.

2.   Two terms work in Manual Arts are also accepted on the free elective credits.

3.   Three reviews must be selected from the following subjects: Penmanship, Physiology, U. S. History, English Grammar, Arithmetic and Geography, unless the student has received satisfactory credits for such work in the eleventh or twelfth grades of an accredited high school, maintaining a normal course.

THE PRIMARY TEACHERS COURSE.

First Year.

A	B	C
1. Primary Methods.	1. Primary Methods.	1. Primary Methods.
2. Education I.	2. Elocution	2. Education III.
3. Manual Arts	3. Education II.	3. Obs. in Training School.
4. Rhetoric	4. Drawing	4. Drawing

Physical Training; one term, four lessons a week, two terms, two lessons a week.

Literary Society Work.

Second Year.

A	B	C
1. Elective	1. Education IV	1. Kg. Theory and Obs.
2. Vocal Music	2. Vocal Music	2. Botany
3. Zoology	3. Eng. Literature	3. Elective
4. Criticism and Practise	4. Criticism and Practise	4. Criticism and Practise.

Physical Training, two terms, two lessons a week.

Literary Society Work.

Criticism, two hours a week, second and third terms. Practise Teaching, five periods a week.

Notes. 1. Any other science may be substituted for Zoology and Botany provided the student has had these subjects in the secondary course.

2. One term of work in Manual Arts is able to be taken as an elective credit.

THE KINDERGARTEN TEACHERS COURSE.

First Year.

A	B	C
1 { Kg. principles (The Mother Plays) Kg. Materials (The Play Gifts) Games (Game Circle)	1 { Kg. Principles (The Mother Plays) Kg Materials (The Play Gifts) Stories (Story Telling.)	1 { Kg. Handwork (The Occupations) Kg. Lesson Plans (The Program) Life of Froebel (Kg. Origin and Growth)
2. Education I.	2. Education II.	2. Education III.
3. Rhetoric	3. Vocal Music	3. Vocal Music
4. Drawing	4. Drawing	4. Nature Study

Physical Training.

Literary Society Work.

Second Year.

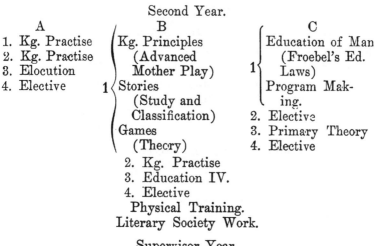

A	B	C
1. Kg. Practise	1 { Kg. Principles (Advanced Mother Play) Stories (Study and Classification) Games (Theory)	1 { Education of Man (Froebel's Ed. Laws) Program Making.
2. Kg. Practise		
3. Elocution		
4. Elective		
	2. Kg. Practise	2. Elective
	3. Education IV.	3. Primary Theory
	4. Elective	4. Elective
	Physical Training.	
	Literary Society Work.	

Supervisor Year.

A	B	C
1. Kg. Theory	1. Kg. Theory	1. Education IX.
2. Education V.	2. Education VI.	2. Kg. Practise
3. Harmony	3. Public Speaking	3. Hist. of Painting
4. Elective	4. Elective	4. Elective
	Literary Society Work.	

Note. Two terms work in Manual Arts are able to be taken as elective credits.

THE PUBLIC SCHOOL MUSIC TEACHERS COURSE.

First Year.

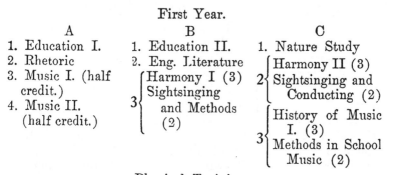

A	B	C
1. Education I.	1. Education II.	1. Nature Study
2. Rhetoric	2. Eng. Literature	2 { Harmony II (3) Sightsinging and Conducting (2)
3. Music I. (half credit.)	3 { Harmony I (3) Sightsinging and Methods (2)	
4. Music II. (half credit.)		3 { History of Music I. (3) Methods in School Music (2)

Physical Training.
Literary Society Work.

Second Year.

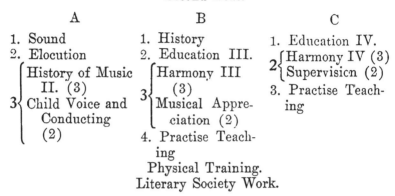

A	B	C
1. Sound	1. History	1. Education IV.
2. Elocution	2. Education III.	2 { Harmony IV (3) / Supervision (2)
3 { History of Music II. (3) / Child Voice and Conducting (2)	3 { Harmony III (3) / Musical Appreciation (2)	3. Practise Teaching
	4. Practise Teaching	
	Physical Training.	
	Literary Society Work.	

Two years of Voice are required (one lesson per week.)

One year of Piano is required (one lesson per week.)

Notes. 1. The figures in parentheses indicate the number of recitation hours per week, when less than five hours a week is given. "Music I." consists of sightsinging and chorus work. "Music II." in addition to sightsinging and chorus work includes elementary theory of music, history of music, and musical appreciation aided by the pianola and victrola.

2. Students completing all the music work required in the above course and the practise teaching, in addition to one term of psychology, one term of school management, one term of elocution, and two electives in English, may be granted a certificate from the department.

THE DRAWING TEACHERS COURSE.

First Year.

A	B	C
1. Cast Drawing	1. Cast Drawing	1. Hist. of Painting
2. Greek History	2. Medieval Hist.	2. Education III.
3. Education I.	3. Education II.	3. El. Handwork
4. Rhetoric.	4. Hist. of Arch. and Sculpture	4. Botany I.
	Physical Training.	
	Literary Society Work.	

Second Year.

A	B	C
1. Still Life	1. Perspective	1. Supv. in Art
2. Elocution	2. Elective	2. Mathematics
3. Elective	3. Eng. Literature	3. Elective
4. Education IV.	4. Prac. Teaching	4. Prac. Teaching

Physical Training.
Literary Society Work.

A Director's Course will be planned for anyone who desires to take an additional year.

THE MANUAL TRAINING TEACHERS COURSE.

First Year.

A	B	C
1. Education I.	1. Education II.	1. Education III.
2. Rhetoric	2. Eng. Lit.	2. Mathematics
3. Pri. Handwork	3. Elem. Handwork	Elective
4. Mech. Drawing	4. 1st Drawing	3. Design
		4. Mech. Drawing
		5. Bench Work

Physical Training.
Literary Society Work.

Second Year.

A	B	C
1. Education IV.	1. Prac. Teaching	1. Prac. Teaching
2. Man. Tr. Methods	2. Man. Tr. Methods	2. Physics I.
3. Bench Work	3. Coll. Elective	3. Coll. Elective
4. Sheet Metal Work	4. Bench Work	4. Bench Work
5. Mech. Drawing	5. Special Elective	5. Special Elective

Physical Training.
Literary Society Work.

THE HOME ECONOMICS TEACHERS COURSE.

First Year.

A	B	C
1. Elementary Food Theory	1. Elementary Food Theory	1. Elementary Food Theory
2. Sewing	2. Sewing	2. Sewing
3. Principles of Foods	3. Principles of Foods	3. Principles of Foods
4. Inorg. Chemistry	4. Inorg. Chemistry	4. Qual. Analysis
5. Rhetcric	5. Education I.	5. Education II.
		6. Household Mgt.
		7. Methods, Home Econ.

Physical Training.
Literary Society Work.

Second Year.

A	B	C
1. Elementary Food Theory	1. Dietetics	1. Food Analysis
2. Dietetics	2. Household Arch.	2. Demonstrations
3. Household Chem.	3. Household Chem.	3. Education IV.
4. Education III.	4. Sanitation	4. Adv. Physiology
5. Practise Teaching	5. Practise Teaching	5. Practise Teaching

Physical Training.
Literary Society Work.

Note. The course in Home Economics here printed may be taken during three of four years by selecting scholastic studies under the direction of the Faculty.

THE PHYSICAL EDUCATION TEACHERS COURSE.

First Year.

A	B	C
1. Anatomy I.	1. Anatomy II.	1. Adv. Physiology
2. Elocution I.	2. Elocution II.	2. Rhetoric
3. Education I.	3. Education II.	3. Education III.

Physical Training.
Literary Society Work.

Second Year.

A	B	C
1. Phys. Dept. Meth.	1. Playground Meth.	1. Hist. and Lit. of Phys. Training
2. Elective	2. Elective	2. Elective
3. Hygiene	3. Chemistry I.	3. Chemistry II.

Physical Training.
Literary Society Work.

Third Year.

A	B	C
1. Anthro. and Phys. Diagnosis	1. Practise Teaching	1. Physiology of Exercise
2. Practise Teaching	2. Education IV.	2. Med. Gym. and Massage
3. Elective	3. Elective	3. Education X (3 hrs.)
4. Vocal Music	4. Elective	4. Mech. Drawing

Physical Training.
Literary Society Work.

Notes. 1. The diploma given is that of *Director of Physical Education.*

2. Students contemplating becoming candidates for the Bachelor of Arts in Education Degree should make that fact known at the beginning of the course.

THE COMMERCIAL TEACHERS COURSE.

First Year.

A	B	C
1. Com'l Arithmetic	1. Accounting	1. Prac. of Banking
2. Adv. Penmanship.	2. Eng. Composition	2. Commercial Correspondence
3. Shorthand and Typewriting	3. Shorthand and Typewriting	3. Shorthand and Typewriting
4. Education I.	4. Education II.	4. Education III.

Physical Training.
Literary Society Work.

Second Year.

A	B	C
1. Am. Government	1. Coll. Economics	1. Money and Banking
2. Rhetoric	2. Eng. Literature	2. Com'l Law
3. Elective	3. Com'l Geog. N. A.	3. Com'l Geog. Europe
4. Education IV.	4. Practise Teaching	4. Practise Teaching

Physical Training.
Literary Society Work.

THE NORMAL COURSES.

I. COUNTY CERTIFICATE STANDARD.

First Year.

A	B	C
1. Arithmetic	1. Arithmetic	1. Physiology
2. Reading	2. Geography	2. Geography
3. English Grammar	3. English Grammar	3. Eng. Composition
4. Orthography	4. U. S. History	4. U. S. History
5. Vocal Music	5. Vocal Music	5. Penmanship

Second Year.

A	B	C
1. Manual Arts	1. Didactics	1. Methods
2. Algebra	2. Algebra	2. El. Civics
3. Eng. Composition	3. El. Physics	3. El. Physics
4. El. Econcmics	4. Agriculture	4. Agriculture or Manual Arts

Notes: 1. Admission to this course requires country school diploma or equivalent scholarship.

2. Abridgements will be given for all subjects on uniform county certificates showing 75 per cent. or above.

3. A certificate will be awarded, giving statement of qualifications attained, on completion of this course.

II. The Normal Course.

Second Grade State Certificate Standard.

Recognition: The Normal Diploma.

First Year.

A	B	C
1. Algebra	1. Algebra	1. Physics
2. *Sanitation	2. General History	2. General History
3. Eng. Classics	3. * Bookkeeping	3. * Elocution
4. Vocal Music	4. Drawing	4. Drawing
	Physical Training.	

Second Year.

A	B	C
1. Physics	1. * Physiography	1. General Botany
2. Plane Geometry	2. Plane Geometry	2. * Solid Geometry
3. Psychology	3. Psychology	3. Sch. Management
4. * Drawing	4. Choral Music	4. Eng. Classics
	Physical Training.	
	Literary Society Work.	

Third Year.

A	B	C
1. Rhetoric	1. English Literature	1. Am. Government
2. College Algebra I. or Trigonometry	2. Economics I.	2. Am. History
3. History of Education	3. Practise Teaching	3. Practise Teaching
4. Special Elective	4. Special Elective	4. Special Elective

Literary Society Work.

Notes. 1. The Special Electives required in the third year shall be taken from Vocal Music, Drawing, Manual Arts, Home Economics, Commercial Studies and Agriculture at the preference of the student.

2. Admission to this course requires a first grade uniform county certificate or its equivalent. Abridgement will be made by

---

*Foreign language to the extent of at least one year may be substituted.

the Examiner for work done in standard and reputable schools.

3. Two terms work in Manual Arts are able to be selected as elective credits.

III.   SPECIAL NORMAL COURSES.

Special State Certificate Standard.

Recognition: Special Normal Diplomas.

1. Primary Normal Course.
2. Kindergarten Normal Course.
3. Public School Music Normal Course.
4. Manual Training Normal Course.
5. Home Economics Normal Course.
6. Drawing Normal Course.
7. Commercial Normal Course.

Notes: 1.   Admission to all the Special Normal Courses requires First Grade Uniform County Certificate or its equivalent.

2. The First Year of these special courses will be planned by the Registrar to suit the individual condition of scholarship and the individual needs that are essential to the special course chosen.

3. These special courses are not planned on any theory that such persons would desire to take a College Course following their graduation.

4. The Second and Third Years of these special courses are the same as those adopted by the Faculty for Special Teacher Courses.

SPECIAL MUSIC TEACHER COURSES.

Conditions of Admission.   Students are admitted to these music courses on liberal terms as to preparatory training and are encouraged to begin early enough to develop the skill and capability for professional artistic success that are so notably demanded in teachers of these kinds.

To become a candidate for graduation, the student must have attained to the scholastic qualificatons required for full college entrance. These scholastic conditions may be acquired in any good secondary school or may be accomplished in the certificate courses at the College.

Conditions of Graduation. A special Teacher Diploma will be awarded to such persons as complete satisfactorily any one of the courses here outlined, but as skill and capability as musicians are also essential qualities to be attained, the exact time necessary to complete any one of these courses can not be stated in school years. The candidate must have sufficient proficiency in the special line chosen to secure the recommendation of the professors in charge of the work to become an applicant for graduation. The courses as here mapped out, outside of the attainment in capability as a musician can be satisfactorily completed in three years.

THE PIANO COURSE.

Piano lessons must be continued through the entire period of study, two lessons a week. A second study—voice or orchestral instrument—must also be carried, with either one or two lessons a week, each term except the last year.

Other work required will be:

First Year.

A	B	C
Elem'ts of Music 5	English Composi-	German 5
German 5	tion 5	Music History 2
Music History 2	German 5	

Second Year.

A	B	C
Harmony 2	Harmony 2	Harmony 2
Music History 2	Eng. Literature 5	Elocution 5
Sound 5		

Third Year.

A	B	C
Harmony 2	Harmony 2	Harmony 2
Psychology 5	Medieval Hist 5	Modern History 5

The figures after the subjects indicate the number of recitation periods per week.

THE VIOLIN COURSE.

Violin lessons must be continued through the entire period of study—two lessons per week. The piano work must be carried for two years successfully with at least one lesson a week. Attendance at two orchestra rehearsals and one class in ensemble playing is also required each week.

The general entrance requirements are the same as for Voice and Piano courses, except that before beginning the regular course the student must finish the preparatory which can be accomplished in one year of two lessons per week. Students may at their option take merely the music branches of the Violin course upon satisfactory completion of which they will receive a department certificate.

First Year.

A	B	C
Elem'ts of Music 5	Elem'ts of Music 5	Music History 2
German 5	German 5	German 5
Music History 2		Ear Training 2

Second Year.

A	B	C
Harmony 2	Harmony 2	Harmony 2
Music History 2	Eng. Literature 5	Psychology 5
Sound 5		

Third Year.

A	B	C
Harmony 2	Harmony 2	Harm. Analysis 2
Psychology 5	Medieval Hist. 5	Modern History 5

The figures after the subjects indicate the number of recitation periods per week.

THE VOICE COURSE.

Three years of voice lessons (two a week), and two years piano lessons (one a week), will be required.

First Year.

A	B	C
Elem'ts of Music 5	Elem'ts of Music 5	German 5
German 5	German 5	Elem'ts of Music 5
Music History 2	Theory of Phys. Training 5	

Second Year.

A	B	C
Harmony 2	Harmony 2	Harmony 2
Music Hist. 2	Eng. Literature 5	Psychology 5
Sound 5		

Third Year.

A	B	C
Harmony 2	Harmony 2	Harm. Analysis 2
Psychology 5	French 5	French 5
French 5	Medieval Hist. 5	Modern Hist. 5

The figures after the subjects indicate the number of recitation periods per week.

PROGRAM OF RECITATIONS

Explanatory Note

This program of recitations is printed for the full school year, presenting the work for the Fall, Winter and Spring terms. The work is organized on the basis of the past year, and may be expanded if numbers enrold should demand it.

The nomenclature used gives in order: 1. The College Course; 2. The Special Teacher Courses; 3. The Normal Courses, for each term. The electivs in Home Economics, Drawing, Manual Training or Physical Education which may apply on a college course in case a major is taken in one of these lines, will be found listed with the subjects belonging to the Special Teacher Courses.

The subject of study is given in the terminology adopted by the departments, complete explanation being given in the Catalog and Circular for 1912. Roman numerals indicate different terms of college work; Arabic numerals, different terms of all other work; C, complete subject.

The following are the hours of work in the school for the year:

First Hour	8:00 to	8:55
Second Hour	8:55 to	9:50
Assembly	9:50 to	10:20
Third Hour	10:20 to	11:15
Fourth Hour	11:15 to	12:10
Fifth Hour	1:30 to	2:25
Sixth Hour	2:25 to	3:20
Seventh Hour	3:20 to	4:15
Eighth Hour	4:15 to	5:00

Of these the first to fifth, inclusiv, are regarded as regular class hours.

Library Hours—School days, 7:30 a. m. to 9:30 p. m. Saturdays, 7:30 a. m. to 12:00.

Literary Societies—Fridays, 2:25 p. m.   Saturdays, 7:00 p. m.

Faculty Meetings—Mondays, 2:25 p. m.

Assignment for Rehearsals of Musical Societies.

Choral Society—Tuesdays, 6:30 p. m.
Cecilians—Wednesdays, 2:25 p. m.
Euterpeans—Tuesdays, 2:25 p. m.
Young Ladies' Glee Club—Mondays, 2:25 p. m.
Minnesingers—Wednesdays, 2:25 p. m.
Troubadours—Tuesdays, 2:25 p. m.
Orchestra—Mondays and Thursdays, 3:30 p. m.
Band—Tuesdays and Fridays, 3:30 p. m.
Ensemble Class—Wednesdays, 3:30 p. m.
Band Classes—Wednesdays, 3:30 p. m.

FALL TERM

First Period

College Courses

Analytical Geometry—*Mr. Condit.*
Economic and Social Problems—*Mr. McKitrick.*
Educational Classics—*Mr. Walters.*
Elocution I.—*Miss Martin.*
French IV.—*Mr. Knoepfler.*
German III (Emilia Galotti; Lyrics and Ballads)—*Miss Lorenz.*
History of English Drama I.—*Miss Lambert.*
History of Music II. (Mon., Wed., Thurs.)—*Miss Childs.*
Latin I. (Cato Major)—*Mr. Merchant.*
Latin XIX. (Ovid)—*Miss Call.*
Manual Training Methods I.—*Mr. Bailey.*
Method History—*Miss Riggs.*
Psychology I.—*Mr. Samson.*
Rhetoric—*Mr. Gist.*
Rhetoric—*Miss Carpenter.*
School Management—*Mr. Colgrove.*

Special Teacher Courses

Chemistry I. (Home Economics)—*Mr. Getchell.*
Kindergarten Theory (Junior)—*Miss Ward.*

Music (Conducting) (Fri.)—*Mr. Fullerton.*
Music (Child Voice) (Tues.)—*Miss Stenwall.*
Primary Methods 1—*Miss McGovern.*
Principles of Selection and Preparation of Foods 1 (Mon., Wed.)—*Miss Townsend.*
Psychology I.—*Mr. Mount.*
Psychology I.—*Miss Buck.*
Shorthand 3—*Mr. Coffey.*
Water Color—*Miss Schuneman.*
Zoology (Primary)—*Mr. Arey.*

Normal Courses

Agriculture 1—
Algebra 1 and 2—*Miss Lambert.*
Arithmetic C—*Mr. Cory.*
Arithmetic 1—*Miss Allen.*
Civics, Review—*Mr. Peterson.*
Civics of U. S.—*Mr. Loomis.*
Drawing 1—*Miss Patt.*
English Grammar 1—*Miss Hearst.*
Geography 2—*Miss Aitchison.*
German 1—*Miss Nolte*
Handwork—*Mrs. McMahon.*
Hygiene and Sanitation—*Mr. Newton.*
Music 1—
Orthography—*Miss Oliver.*
Penmanship 1—*Mr. Cummins.*
Physics 1—*Mr. Hersey.*
Physiography—*Mr. Cable.*
Sewing—*Miss Heinz.*

SECOND PERIOD

College Courses

American Government—*Mr. Loomis.*
American History—*Miss Riggs.*
Botany II.—
College Algebra I.—*Mr. Condit.*
Commercial Geography of North America—*Miss Aitchison.*
French I.—*Mr. Knoepfler.*
German II. (Prose Composition)—*Miss Lorenz.*

German X. (Lessons; Grammar)—*Miss Nolte.*
Greek I. (Lessons) (Mon., Wed., Fri.)—*Miss Call.*
Greek IV. (Plato) (Tues., Thurs.)—*Miss Call.*
Greek History—*Miss Rice.*
History of Education—*Mr. Walters.*
Latin IV. (Composition) (Tues., Thurs.)—*Mr. Merchant.*
Latin VII. (Roman Literature) (Mon., Wed., Fri.)—*Mr. Merchant.*
Music II.—*Mr. Fullerton.*
Psychology II.—*Mr. Samson.*
Public Speaking II.—*Mr. Barnes.*
Repertoire II.—*Miss Martin.*
Rhetoric—*Mr. Lynch.*
Rhetoric—*Miss Lambert.*
School Management—*Mr. Colgrove.*
Theme Writing and Story Telling—*Miss Carpenter.*

Special Teacher Courses

Bench Work 1—*Mr. Brown.*
Chemistry IV. (Home Economics)—*Mr. Bond.*
Drawing 1 (Primary)—*Miss Schuneman.*
Kindergarten Practis—
Primary Handwork—*Mrs. McMahon.*
Primary Methods 1—*Miss McGovern.*
Principles of Selection and Preparation of Foods 1 (Tues., Thurs.)—*Miss Townsend.*
Psychology I.—*Mr. Mount.*
Sewing 1—*Miss Heinz.*
Typewriting 1—*Mr. Coffey.*
Zoology (Primary)—*Mr. Arey.*

Normal Courses

Arithmetic C—*Mr. Cory.*
Arithmetic 1—*Miss Lambert.*
Bench Work 1—*Mr. Brown.*
Bookkeeping 1—*Mr. Cummins.*
Civics of Iowa—*Mr. Peterson.*
Elocution—*Miss Falkler.*
English Composition 1—*Miss Lodge.*
English Grammar C—*Miss Gregg.*

English Grammar 2—*Miss Hearst.*
Music 1—
Music 2—*Miss Stenwall.*
Orthography—*Miss Oliver.*
Physics 1—*Mr. Dieterich.*
Physiography—*Mr. Cable.*
Physiology—*Mr. Newton.*
Plane Geometry 1—*Mr. Wright.*

THIRD PERIOD

College Courses

American Industrial History—*Mr. McKitrick.*
Anatomy II.—*Mr. Seymour.*
Argumentation—*Mr. Barnes.*
Botany Laboratory·(Mon., Wed.)—
Chemistry I.—*Mr. Bond.*
Elocution II.—*Miss Martin.*
English Literature—*Mr. Lynch.*
German VI. (Der dreissigjaehrige Krieg)—*Mr. Knoepfler.*
German XII. (Die Journalisten)—*Miss Lorenz.*
Greek History—*Miss Rice.*
History of Education—*Mr. Walters.*
Illustrativ Teaching (Tues., Thurs.)—*Mr. Bender.*
Latin XVI. (College Elementary)—*Mr. Merchant.*
Municipal Government—*Mr. Loomis.*
Music I.—*Mr. Fullerton.*
Physics I.—*Mr. Begeman.*
Physiography I.—*Mr. Cable.*
Psychology I.—*Mr. Samson.*
Rhetoric—*Miss Hearst.*
Rhetoric—*Miss Lodge.*
School Management—*Mr. Colgrove.*
Shakespeare—*Mr. Gist.*
Zoology I.—*Mr. Arey.*

Special Teacher Courses

Advanced Hygiene—*Mr. Pasini.*
*Dietetics 1 (Tues., Thurs.)—*Miss Sheets.*
Drawing 1 (Kindergarten)—*Miss Iverson.*
Drawing 1 (Primary)—*Miss Schuneman.*

*Elementary Food Theory 4 (Mon., Wed.)—*Miss Sheets.*
Kindergarten Practis—
Physical Training 1 (Primary)—*Miss Hussey.*
Primary Handwork—*Mrs. McMahon.*
Primary Methods 1—*Miss McGovern.*
Psychology I.—*Mr. Mount.*
Sewing 1—*Miss Heinz.*
Sheet Metal Work—*Mr. Bailey.*
Shorthand 1—*Mr. Coffey.*
*Class period from 10:20 to 12:10 a. m.

Normal Courses

Algebra 3—*Mr. Condit.*
Algebra 1—*Miss Allen.*
Arithmetic 1—*Miss Lambert.*
Caesar 2—*Miss Call.*
Drawing 1—*Miss Patt.*
Didactics—*Miss Buck.*
Elementary Economics—*Mr. Peterson.*
Elocution—*Miss Falkler.*
English Classics 1—*Miss Oliver.*
English Grammar C—*Miss Gregg.*
Geography 1—*Miss Aitchison.*
German 3—*Miss Nolte.*
Music 2—*Miss Stenwall.*
Penmanship 1—*Mr. Cummins.*
Physics 1—*Mr. Hersey.*
Physiology—*Mr. Newton.*
Plane Geometry 2—*Mr. Wright.*
Swimming (Mon., Wed.)—*Miss Hallingby.*
Tennis (Tues., Thurs.)—*Miss Hallingby.*

Fourth Period

College Courses

American Literature—*Miss Lambert.*
Botany I.—
Chemistry II., III.—*Mr. Getchell.*
Elocution I.—*Miss Martin.*
English Literature—*Miss Carpenter.*
German IX. (Lessons; Grammar)—*Mr. Knoepfler.*

History of Education—*Mr. Walters.*
Mineralogy—*Mr. Cable.*
Plane Trigonometry—*Mr. Cory.*
Rhetoric—*Mr. Lynch.*
Rhetoric—*Mr. Gist.*

Special Teacher Courses

Bench Work 1—*Mr. Brown.*
*Dietetics 1 (Tues., Thurs.)—*Miss Sheets.*
Drawing 1 (Primary)—*Miss Schuneman.*
*Elementary Food Theory 4 (Mon., Wed.)—*Miss Sheets.*
Mechanical Drawing—*Mr. Bailey.*
Penmanship (Advanced)—*Mr. Cummins.*
Physical Department Methods—*Mr. Seymour.*
Physical Department Methods—*Miss Hussey.*
Physical Training 1 (Primary)—*Miss Hallingby.*
Psychology I.—*Miss Buck.*
Sewing 1—*Miss Heinz.*
Typewriting 3—*Mr. Coffey.*
*Class period from 10:20 to 12:10 a. m.

Normal Courses

Algebra 1—*Miss Allen.*
Bench Work 1—*Mr. Brown.*
Drawing 2—*Miss Patt.*
Elementary Economics—*Mr. McKitrick.*
Elocution—*Miss Falkler.*
English Grammar C—*Miss Gregg.*
General History 1—*Miss Rice.*
German 4—*Miss Nolte.*
Latin Lessons 1—*Miss Call.*
Music 1—*Miss Stenwall.*
Music 2—
Physics 1—*Mr. Dieterich.*
Plane Geometry 1—*Mr. Wright.*
Swimming (Mon., Wed.)—
Tennis (Tues., Thurs.)—
U. S. History C—*Miss Riggs.*
U. S. History 1—*Mr. Peterson.*

Fifth Period

College Courses

American Constitutional History I.—*Mr. Loomis.*
Botany I., Laboratory (Tues., Thurs.)—
Experimental Psychology—*Mr. Mount.*
General Economics—*Mr. McKitrick.*
German I. (Die Jungfrau von Orleans)—*Miss Lorenz.*
History, Renaissance and Reformation—*Miss Riggs.*
Illustrativ Teaching (Tues., Thurs.)—*Mr. Bender.*
Latin X. (Historical Grammar) (Mon., Wed., Fri.)—*Mr. Merchant.*
Latin XIII. (Senior Electiv) (Tues., Thurs.)—*Mr. Merchant.*
Psychology II.—*Mr. Samson.*
Solid Geometry—*Mr. Wright.*
Zoology, Laboratory (2 days)—*Mr. Arey.*

Special Teacher Courses

Anthropometry and Physical Diagnosis—*Mr. Seymour.*
Bench Work (Advanced)—*Mr. Brown.*
Cast Drawing—*Miss Patt.*
Commercial Arithmetic—*Mr. Cory.*
*Elementary Food Theory 1 (Mon., Wed.)—*Miss Townsend.*
*Elementary Food Theory 1 (Tues., Thurs.)—*Miss Townsend.*
*Elementary Food Theory 1 (Mon., Wed.)—*Miss Sheets.*
Mechanical Drawing—*Mr. Bailey.*
Primary Handwork—*Mrs. McMahon.*
Primary Methods 2—*Miss McGovern.*
Psychology II.—*Mr. Colgrove.*
Sound—*Mr. Begeman.*
Wood Turning—*Mr. Brown.*
Zoology, Laboratory (2 days)—*Mr. Arey.*
*Class period from 1:30 to 4:00 p. m.

Normal Courses

Algebra 2—*Miss Lambert.*
Algebra 3—*Mr. Condit.*
Arithmetic 2—*Miss Allen.*
Drawing 1—*Miss Iverson.*
English Classics 2—*Miss Hearst.*
English Composition 2—*Miss Lodge.*

*Elementary Food Theory (Tues., Thurs.)—*Miss Sheets.*
English Grammar 1—*Miss Gregg.*
General Botany—*Mr. Newton.*
Geography C—*Miss Aitchison.*
Gymnastics (Tues., Thurs.)—*Mr. Pasini.*
Physical Training 1 (Tues., Thurs.)—*Miss Hallingby.*
Physics 2—*Mr. Hersey.*
Psychology 1 (Elementary)—*Miss Buck.*
Reading—*Miss Falkler.*
Swimming (Mon., Wed.)—
Tennis (Tues., Thurs.)—
Tennis (Mon., Wed.)—*Mr. Pasini.*
U. S. History 1—*Miss Rice.*
*Class period from 1:30 to 3:20 p. m.

SIXTH PERIOD

College Courses

Botany I., Laboratory (Tues., Thurs.)—
Chemistry IV., V., VI.—*Mr. Bond.*
Illustrativ Teaching (Tues., Thurs.)—*Mr. Bender.*
Physics, Advanced Laboratory Course—*Mr. Begeman.*

Special Teacher Courses

*Elementary Food Theory 1 (Mon., Wed.)—*Miss Townsend.*
*Elementary Food Theory 1 (Tues., Thurs.)—*Miss Townsend.*
*Elementary Food Theory 1 (Mon., Wed.)—*Miss Sheets.*
Primary Criticism—*Miss Hatcher.*
*Class period from 1:30 to 4:00 p. m.

Normal Courses

Basketball (Tues., Thurs.)—*Miss Hallingby.*
Cricket (Mon., Wed.)—*Miss Hussey.*
*Elementary Food Theory (Tues., Thurs.)—*Miss Sheets.*
Hockey (Tues., Thurs.)—
Physical Training 1 (Tues., Thurs.)—*Miss Hussey.*
Soccer Foot Ball (Mon., Wed.)—*Mr. Pasini.*
Swimming (Mon., Wed.)—*Miss Hallingby.*
Swimming (Tues., Thurs.)—*Mr. Pasini.*
Tennis (Mon., Wed.)—
Track Athletics (Mon., Wed.)—*Mr. Seymour.*
*Class period from 1:30 to 3:20 p. m.

Seventh Period

Special Teacher Courses

*Elementary Food Theory 1 (Mon., Wed.)—*Miss Townsend.*
*Elementary Food Theory 1 (Tues., Thurs.)—*Miss Townsend.*
*Elementary Food Theory 1 (Mon., Wed.)—*Miss Sheets.*
Football—*Mr. Pasini.*
*Class period from 1:30 to 4:00 p. m.

Normal Courses

Football—*Mr. Pasini.*
Golf (Tues., Thurs.)—*Mr. Seymour.*
Physical Training 1 (Mon., Wed.)—*Miss Hussey.*
Physical Training 1 (Mon., Wed.)—
Physical Training 2 (Tues., Thurs.)—
Physical Training 3 (Mon., Wed.)—*Miss Hallingby.*
Swimming (Tues., Thurs.)—*Miss Hussey.*
Tennis (Mon., Wed.)—*Mr. Seymour.*
Tennis (Tues., Thurs.)—*Miss Hallingby.*

WINTER TERM

First Period

College Courses

American History—*Miss Riggs.*
Anglo-Saxon—*Mr. Gist.*
Differential Calculus—*Mr. Condit.*
English Literature—*Miss Carpenter.*
French V.—*Mr. Knoepfler.*
German IV. (Nathan der Weise)—*Miss Lorenz.*
Harmony III. (Mon., Wed., Fri.)—
History of Architecture and Sculpture—*Miss Patt.*
History of English Drama II.—*Miss Lambert.*
Latin II (Livy)—*Mr. Merchant.*
Latin XX. (Vergil)—*Miss Call.*
Philosophy of Education—*Mr. Walters.*
Psychology II.—*Mr. Samson.*
Public Speaking I.—*Mr. Barnes.*
School Management—*Mr. Colgrove.*
Zoology II.—*Mr. Arey.*

Special Teacher Courses

Drawing 1 (Primary)—*Miss Iverson.*
Chemistry II. (Home Economics)—*Mr. Getchell.*
Elementary Handwork—*Mrs. McMahon.*
Kindergarten Theory (Junior)—*Miss Ward.*
Music Appreciation (Tues., Thurs.)—*Mr. Fullerton.*
Primary Methods 2—*Miss McGovern.*
Principles of Selection and Preparation of Foods 2 (Tues.. Thurs.)—*Miss Townsend.*
Psychology I.—*Miss Buck.*
Psychology II.—*Mr. Mount.*
Shorthand 2—*Mr. Coffey.*

Normal Courses

Agriculture 2—
Algebra 2—*Miss Allen.*
Algebra 3—*Miss Lambert.*
Arithmetic C—*Mr. Cory.*
Elementary Economics—*Mr. McKitrick.*
Geography 1—*Miss Aitchison.*
Music 1—
Orthography—*Miss Oliver.*
Penmanship 1—*Mr. Cummins.*
Physics 1—*Mr. Dieterich.*
Physiography—*Mr. Cable.*
Sewing—*Miss Heinz.*

SECOND PERIOD

College Courses

Advanced Exposition—*Mr. Lynch.*
American Literature—*Miss Carpenter.*
Botany II.—
College Algebra I.—*Mr. Cory.*
Elocution II.—*Miss Martin.*
English Literature—*Miss Lambert.*
French II.—*Mr. Knoepfler.*
Geology II.—*Mr. Cable.*
German XI. (Immensee; Im Vaterland)—*Miss Nolte.*
German II. (Prose Composition)—*Miss Lorenz.*
Greek II. (Lessons) (Mon., Wed., Fri.)—*Miss Call.*

Greek V. (Homer) (Tues., Thurs.)—*Miss Call.*
History of Education—*Mr. Walters.*
Hygiene and Sanitation—*Mr. Newton.*
Latin V. (Composition) (Tues., Thurs.)—*Mr. Merchant.*
Latin VIII. (Roman Literature) (Mon., Wed., Fri.)--*Mr. Merchant.*
Manual Training Methods II.—*Mr. Bailey.*
Medieval History—*Miss Riggs.*
Money and Banking—*Mr. McKitrick.*
Music II.—*Mr. Fullerton.*
Plane Trigonometry—*Mr. Condit.*
Psychology I.—*Mr. Samson.*
Rhetoric—*Miss Lodge.*
Roman History—*Miss Rice.*
Rural School Problems—*Mr. Colgrove.*
Zoology II., Laboratory (2 days)—*Mr. Arey.*

Special Teacher Courses

Business Correspondence—*Mr. Coffey.*
Chemistry V. (Home Economics)—*Mr. Bond.*
Drawing 2. (Primary)—*Miss Schuneman.*
Kindergarten Practis—
Primary Handwork—*Mrs. McMahon.*
Primary Methods 2—*Miss McGovern.*
Psychology II.—*Mr. Mount.*
Sewing 2—*Miss Heinz.*

Normal Courses

Algebra 2—*Miss Allen.*
Arithmetic C—*Miss Lambert.*
Bench Work 1—*Mr. Brown.*
Bookkeeping 1—*Mr. Cummins.*
Civics of Iowa—*Mr. Peterson.*
Civics of U. S.—*Mr. Loomis.*
Didactics—*Miss Buck.*
English Composition 1—*Miss Gregg.*
English Grammar 1—*Miss Hearst.*
Geography 2—*Miss Aitchison.*
Music 1—*Miss Stenwall.*
Music 2—
Orthography—*Miss Oliver.*

Plane Geometry 2—*Mr. Wright.*
Reading—*Miss Falkler.*
Physics 2—*Mr. Dieterich.*

THIRD PERIOD

College Courses

American Government—*Mr. Loomis.*
Anatomy II.—*Mr. Seymour.*
Chemistry II.—*Mr. Bond.*
Elocution I.—*Miss Falkler.*
English Industrial History—*Mr. McKitrick.*
English Literature—*Mr. Lynch.*
German I. (Die Jungfrau von Orleans)—*Miss Lorenz.*
German VII. (Modern German Prose)—*Mr. Knoepfler.*
History of Education—*Mr. Walters.*
Latin XVII. (College Elementary)—*Mr. Merchant.*
Music I.—*Mr. Fullerton.*
Physics I.—*Mr. Begeman.*
Repertoire I.—*Miss Martin.*
Roman History—*Miss Rice.*
Shakespeare—*Mr. Gist.*
Solid Geometry—*Mr. Wright.*

Special Teacher Courses

Drawing 2 (Kindergarten)—*Miss Iverson.*
Drawing 2 (Primary)—*Miss Schuneman.*
Kindergarten Practis—
Penmanship (Advanced)—*Mr. Cummins.*
Primary Handwork—*Mrs. McMahon.*
Primary Methods 2—*Miss McGovern.*
Psychology II.—*Mr. Colgrove.*
Sewing 2—*Miss Heinz.*
Sheet Metal Work—*Mr. Bailey.*
Shorthand 1—*Mr. Coffey.*

Normal Courses

Algebra 1—*Miss Allen.*
Algebra 1 and 2—*Mr. Condit.*
Arithmetic 2—*Miss Lambert.*
Cicero 1—*Miss Call.*

Civics of Iowa—*Mr. Peterson.*
Drawing 1—*Miss Patt.*
English Composition 1—*Miss Lodge.*
English Grammar C—*Miss Gregg.*
English Grammar 1—*Miss Hearst.*
Geography C—*Miss Aitchison.*
German 4—*Miss Nolte.*
Methods—*Miss Buck.*
Music 2—*Miss Stenwall.*
Penmanship 1—*Mr. Cummins.*
Physics 1—*Mr. Hersey.*
Physiology—*Mr. Newton.*

FOURTH PERIOD

College Courses

Applied Drama—*Miss Martin.*
Botany II., Laboratory (Mon., Wed.)—
Chemistry I.—*Mr. Getchell.*
Eighteenth Century History—*Miss Riggs.*
Elocution I.—*Mr. Barnes.*
English Government—*Mr. Loomis.*
English Literature—*Miss Lambert.*
English Romantic Movement—*Miss Carpenter.*
German X. (Lessons; Grammar)—*Mr. Knoepfler.*
Harmony I. (Mon., Wed., Thurs.)—
History of Education—*Mr. Walters.*
Influences of Geography Upon American History—*Mr. Cable.*
Psychology II.—*Mr. Samson.*
Rhetoric—*Mr. Gist.*
School Administration—*Mr. Dick.*

Special Teacher Courses

Benchwork (Advanced)—*Mr. Brown.*
Bookkeeping 2—*Mr. Cummins.*
Drawing 1 (Primary)—*Miss Iverson.*
Drawing 2 (Primary)—*Miss Schuneman.*
Household Architecture (Tues., Thurs.)—*Miss Townsend.*
Mechanical Drawing—*Mr. Bailey.*
Music, Sight-singing and Methods (Tues., Fri.)—*Miss Stenwall.*

Physical Training 2 (Primary) (Mon., Wed.)—*Miss Hussey.*
Principles of Selection and Preparation of Foods 2 (Mon., Wed.)—*Miss Townsend.*
Psychology II.—*Mr. Mount.*
Sewing 2—*Miss Heinz.*
Typewriting 2—*Mr. Coffey.*
Woodturning—*Mr. Brown.*

Normal Courses

Algebra 1—*Miss Allen.*
Arithmetic 1—*Mr. Cory.*
Arithmetic 2—*Miss Lambert.*
Basketball (Mon., Wed.)—
Drawing 2—*Miss Patt.*
Elocution—*Miss Falkler.*
English Classics 1—*Miss Oliver.*
English Composition 2—*Miss Lodge.*
English Grammar C—*Miss Gregg.*
English Grammar 2—*Miss Hearst.*
General History 1—*Miss Rice.*
German 1—*Miss Nolte.*
Gymnastics, first year (Mon., Wed.)—*Mr. Pasini.*
Latin Lessons 2—*Miss Call.*
Music 2—
Physics 1—*Mr. Dieterich.*
Physiology—*Mr. Newton.*
Plane Geometry 1—*Mr. Wright.*
Psychology 2 (Elementary)—*Miss Buck.*
Rythm 1 (Mon., Wed.)—*Miss Hallingby.*
U. S. History 1—*Mr. Peterson.*

Fifth Period

College Courses

American Constitutional History II.—*Mr. Loomis.*
Botany II., Laboratory (Tues., Thurs.)—
Commercial Geography of Europe—*Miss Aitchison.*
Experimental Psychology—*Mr. Mount.*
General Economics—*Mr. McKitrick.*
German XII. (Die Journalisten)—*Miss Lorenz.*
Hygiene and Sanitation—*Mr. Newton.*

Latin XI. (Historical Grammar) (Mon., Wed., Fri.)—*Mr. Merchant.*
Latin XIV. (Senior Electiv) (Tues., Thurs.)—*Mr. Merchant.*
Physics II.—*Mr. Begeman.*
Plane Trigonometry—*Mr. Condit.*
Psychology I.—*Mr. Samson.*
Rhetoric—*Mr. Lynch.*
School Management—*Mr. Colgrove.*

Special Teacher Courses

Bench Work (Advanced)—*Mr. Brown.*
Cast Drawing—*Miss Patt.*
Drawing 1 (Primary)—*Miss Iverson.*
Kindergarten Theory (Senior)—*Miss Ward.*
Mechanical Drawing—*Mr. Bailey.*
Physical Training 2 (Primary) (Tues., Thurs.)—*Miss Hallingby.*
Playground Methods—*Mr. Pasini.*
Primary Handwork—*Mrs. McMahon.*
Primary Methods 1—*Miss McGovern.*
Typewriting—*Mr. Coffey.*
Woodturning—*Mr. Brown.*

Normal Courses

Arithmetic 1—*Mr. Cory.*
Baseball, Indoor (Tues., Thurs.)—
Basketball (Mon., Wed.)—*Miss Hallingby.*
Drawing 1—*Miss Schuneman.*
Elementary Economics—*Mr. Peterson.*
*Elementary Food Theory (Tues., Thurs.)—*Miss Sheets.*
Elocution—*Miss Falkler.*
English Classics 2—*Miss Hearst.*
English Grammar 2—*Miss Gregg.*
Games (Mon., Wed.)—
German 2—*Miss Nolte.*
Music 1—*Miss Stenwall.*
Penmanship 1—*Mr. Cummins.*
Physical Training 2 (Mon., Wed.)—*Miss Hussey.*
Physics 2—*Mr. Hersey.*
Physiography—*Mr. Cable.*
Plane Geometry 2—*Mr. Wright.*

U. S. History C—*Miss Riggs.*
U. S. History 2—*Miss Rice.*
*Class period from 1:30 to 3:20 p. m.

Sixth Period

College Courses

Chemistry IV., V., VI., Laboratory Courses—*Mr. Getchell.*
Physics, Advanced Laboratory Course—*Mr. Begeman.*

Special Teacher Courses

*Elementary Food Theory 2 (Mon., Wed.)—*Miss Townsend.*
*Elementary Food Theory 2 (Tues., Thurs.)—*Miss Townsend.*
*Elementary Food Theory 2 (Mon., Wed.)—*Miss Sheets.*
Primary Criticism (Tues., Thurs.)—*Miss Hatcher.*
*Class period from 2:25 to 5:00 p. m.

Normal Courses

Basketball (Tues., Thurs.)—
*Elementary Food Theory (Tues., Thurs.)—*Miss Sheets.*
Games (Mon., Wed.)—*Miss Hussey.*
Gymnastics, first year (Mon., Wed.)—*Mr. Pasini.*
Gymnastics, second year (Tues., Thurs.)—*Mr. Seymour.*
Physical Training 1 (Tues., Thurs.)—*Miss Hussey.*
Physical Training 2 (Mon., Wed.)—*Miss Hallingby.*
Physical Training 2 (Mon., Wed.)—
Rythm 1 (Tues., Thurs.)—*Miss Hallingby.*
Swimming (Tues., Thurs.)—*Mr. Pasini.*
*Class period from 1:30 to 3:20 p. m.

Seventh Period

Special Teacher Courses

Dietetics 2 (Mon., Wed.)—*Miss Townsend,* (to 7:00 p. m.)
Dietetics 2 (Tues., Thurs.)—*Miss Sheets,* (to 7:00 p. m.)
*Elementary Food Theory 2 (Mon., Wed.)—*Miss Townsend.*
*Elementary Food Theory 2 (Tues., Thurs.)—*Miss Townsend.*
*Elementary Food Theory 2 (Mon., Wed.)—*Miss Sheets.*
Medical Gymnastics and Massage (Mon., Wed.)—*Miss Hussey.*
*Class period from 2:25 to 5:00 p. m.

Normal Courses

Gilbert (Tues., Thurs.)—*Miss Hussey.*

Gymnastics, first year (Mon., Wed.)—*Mr. Pasini.*
Gymnastics, third year (Mon., Wed.)—*Mr. Seymour.*
Physical Training 1 (Mon., Wed.)—
Physical Training 2 (Tues., Thurs.)—
Physical Training 3 (Tues., Thurs.)—*Miss Hallingby.*
Rythm 1 (Mon., Wed.)—*Miss Hallingby.*
Swimming (Tues., Thurs.)—*Mr. Pasini.*

EIGHTH PERIOD

Special Teacher Courses

Basketball Team—*Mr. Pasini.*
Gymnastic Team—*Mr. Seymour.*

SPRING TERM

FIRST PERIOD

College Courses

Botany II.—
Chemistry III.—*Mr. Getchell.*
Development of the English Novel—*Miss Lodge.*
Economic and Social Problems—*Mr. McKitrick.*
English History—*Miss Rice.*
English Literature—*Miss Carpenter.*
English Literature of Nineteenth Century—*Miss Lambert.*
French VI.—*Mr. Knoepfler.*
German V. (Iphigenie auf Tauris; Die Braut von Messina)—
　　Miss Lorenz.
Harmony IV. (Mon., Wed., Thurs.)—
History of Education—*Mr. Walters.*
History of Painting—*Miss Patt.*
Integral Calculus—*Mr. Condit.*
Latin III. (Horace)—*Mr. Merchant.*
Latin XXI. (Vergil)—*Miss Call.*
Nineteenth Century History—*Miss Riggs.*
Physics III.—*Mr. Begeman.*
Psychology I.—*Mr. Samson.*
Repertoire I.—*Miss Martin.*
Rhetoric—*Mr. Gist.*
School Management—*Mr. Colgrove.*
Zoology III.—*Mr. Arey.*

Special Teacher Courses

Drawing 3 (Primary)—*Miss Schuneman.*
Mechanical Drawing—*Mr. Bailey.*
Music Supervision (Fri.)—*Mr. Fullerton.*
Music Supervision (Tues.)—*Miss Stenwall.*
Primary Methods 3—*Miss McGovern.*
Psychology I.—*Miss Buck.*
Psychology II.—*Mr. Mount.*
Sewing 3—*Miss Heinz.*
Shorthand 2—*Mr. Coffey.*

Normal Courses

Algebra 3—*Miss Allen.*
Arithmetic C—*Miss Lambert.*
Arithmetic 2—*Mr. Cory.*
Drawing 1—*Miss Iverson.*
Elementary Handwork—*Mrs. McMahon.*
English Grammar 1—*Miss Hearst.*
General Botany—*Mr. Newton.*
Geography 2—*Miss Aitchison.*
German 3—*Miss Nolte.*
Music 1—
Orthography—*Miss Oliver.*
Penmanship 1—*Mr. Cummins.*
Physics 1—*Mr. Hersey.*
Physiography—*Mr. Cable.*
U. S. History 1—*Mr. Peterson.*

SECOND PERIOD

College Courses

College Algebra II.—*Mr. Cory.*
Elocution II.—*Miss Martin.*
English History—*Miss Rice.*
English Literature—*Miss Lambert.*
French III.—*Mr. Knoepfler.*
Genetic Psychology—*Mr. Mount.*
Geology II.—*Mr. Cable.*
German I. (Die Jungfrau von Orleans)—*Miss Lorenz.*
Greek III. (Anabasis) (Mon., Wed., Fri.)—*Miss Call.*
Greek VI. (Homer) (Tues., Thurs.)—*Miss Call.*

Harmony II (Mon., Wed., Thurs.)—
History of Education—*Mr. Walters.*
Industrial Corporations—*Mr. McKitrick.*
Latin VI. (Composition) (Tues., Thurs.)—*Mr. Merchant.*
Latin IX. (Roman Literature) (Mon., Wed., Fri.)—*Mr. Merchant.*
Music II.—*Mr. Fullerton.*
Organization and Economics of Manual Training—*Mr. Bailey.*
Psychology II.—*Mr. Samson.*
Public Speaking I.—*Mr. Barnes.*
School Management—*Mr. Colgrove.*
Teaching of English—*Mr. Lynch.*
Zoology, Laboratory (2 days)—*Mr. Arey.*

Special Teacher Courses

Chemistry VI. (Home Economics)—*Mr. Bond.*
Commercial Law—*Mr. Coffey.*
Drawing 2 (Primary)—*Miss Iverson.*
Kindergarten Theory and Observation (Primary)—*Miss Ward.*
Kindergarten Practis—
Music (Sightsinging and Conducting) (Tues., Fri.)—*Miss Stenwall.*
Observation in Training School (Primary)—*Miss Hatcher.*
Primary Handwork—*Mrs. McMahon.*
Primary Methods 3—*Miss McGovern.*
Principles of Selection and Preparation of Foods 3 (Tues., Thurs.)—*Miss Townsend.*
Sewing 3—*Miss Heinz.*
Supervision in Art—*Miss Patt.*

Normal Courses

Agriculture 1—
Algebra 1—*Miss Lambert.*
Arithmetic C—*Mr. Condit.*
Bench Work 1—*Mr. Brown.*
Bookkeeping 1—*Mr. Cummins.*
Civics of U. S.—*Mr. Loomis.*
Didactics—*Miss Buck.*
Drawing 1—*Miss Schuneman.*
English Composition 1—*Miss Lodge.*
English Composition 2—*Miss Gregg.*

English Grammar 1—*Miss Hearst.*
General History 2—*Miss Riggs.*
Geography 1—*Miss Aitchison.*
German 1—*Miss Nolte.*
Orthography—*Miss Oliver.*
Physics 2—*Mr. Hersey.*
Physiology—*Mr. Newton.*
Plane Geometry 2—*Mr. Wright.*
Reading—*Miss Falkler.*

THIRD PERIOD

College Courses

Chemistry I.—*Mr. Bond.*
Constitutional Law—*Mr. Loomis.*
Elocution I.—*Miss Falkler.*
English Literature—*Mr. Lynch.*
Experimental Psychology—*Mr. Mount.*
German VIII. (German Classics)—*Mr. Knoepfler.*
German XI. (Immensee; Der Zerbrochene Krug)—*Miss Lorenz.*
History of Education—*Mr. Walters.*
History, Renaissance and Reformation—*Miss Riggs.*
Latin XVIII. (College Elementary)—*Mr. Merchant.*
Literary Criticism—*Miss Carpenter.*
Music I.—*Mr. Fullerton.*
Physics I.—*Mr. Begeman.*
Physiology I.—*Mr. Newton.*
Plane Trigonometry—*Mr. Condit.*
Public Speaking II.—*Mr. Barnes.*
School Management—*Mr. Colgrove.*
Shakespeare—*Mr. Gist.*

Special Teacher Courses

Bookkeeping 2—*Mr. Cummins.*
Drawing 2 (Primary)—*Miss Iverson.*
Household Management (Tues., Thurs., Fri.)—*Miss Townsend.*
Household Management (Thurs., Fri.)—*Miss Sheets.*
Kindergarten Theory (Junior)—*Miss Ward.*
Kindergarten Practis—
Physiology of Exercise—*Mr. Seymour.*

Primary Methods 3—*Miss McGovern.*
Principles of Selection and Preparation of Foods 3 (Mon., Wed.)—*Miss Townsend.*
Sheet Metal Work—*Mr. Bailey.*
Shorthand 3—*Mr. Coffey.*

Normal Courses

Algebra 1 and 2—*Miss Lambert.*
Arithmetic 1—*Miss Allen.*
Cicero 2—*Miss Call.*
Civics of Iowa—*Mr. Peterson.*
Elementary Economics—*Mr. McKitrick.*
English Grammar C—*Miss Gregg.*
English Grammar 2—*Miss Hearst.*
Geography C—*Miss Aitchison.*
German 4—*Miss Nolte.*
Methods—*Miss Buck.*
Music 1—*Miss Stenwall.*
Music 2—
Penmanship 1—*Mr. Cummins.*
Physical Training 3 (Tues., Thurs.)—
Physics 1—*Mr. Dieterich.*
Plane Geometry 1—*Mr. Wright.*
Sewing—*Miss Heinz.*
Swimming (Mon., Wed.)—*Miss Hallingby.*
Tennis (Mon., Wed.)—*Miss Hussey.*
Tennis (Tues., Thurs.)—*Miss Hallingby.*
U. S. History C —*Miss Rice.*
Zoology (Elementary)—*Mr. Arey.*

Fourth Period

College Courses

American Government—*Mr. Loomis.*
American Literature—*Miss Lambert.*
Argumentation—*Mr. Barnes.*
Astronomy—*Mr. Cable.*
Botany II., Laboratory (Mon., Wed.)—
Chemistry II.—*Mr. Getchell.*
English Literature—*Miss Carpenter.*
German II. (Prose Composition)—*Mr. Knoepfler.*

History of Music I. (Mon., Wed., Thurs.)—*Miss Childs.*
Middle English—*Mr. Gist.*
Physiology I.—*Mr. Newton.*
Psychology I.—*Mr. Samson.*
School Administration—*Mr. Dick.*

Special Teacher Courses

Bench Work (Advanced)—*Mr. Brown.*
Commercial Arithmetic—*Mr. Cory.*
Drawing 2 (Primary)—*Miss Iverson.*
Drawing 3 (Primary)—*Miss Schuneman.*
Kindergarten Theory (Senior)—*Miss Ward.*
Music Methods (Tues., Fri.)—*Miss Stenwall.*
Primary Handwork—*Mrs. McMahon.*
Primary Methods 1—*Miss McGovern.*
Sewing 3—*Miss Heinz.*
Typewriting 3—*Mr. Coffey.*
Woodturning—*Mr. Brown.*

Normal Courses

Algebra 3—*Miss Allen.*
Arithmetic 1—*Miss Lambert.*
Baseball (Mon., Wed.)—*Mr. Pasini.*
Caesar 1—*Miss Call.*
Drawing 2—*Miss Patt.*
Elementary Economics—*Mr. Peterson.*
Elocution—*Miss Falkler.*
English Classics 1—*Miss Oliver.*
English Grammar C—*Miss Gregg.*
German 2—*Miss Nolte.*
Music 1—
Physical Training 3 (Mon., Wed.)—*Miss Hallingby.*
Physics 2—*Mr. Hersey.*
Solid Geometry—*Mr. Wright.*
Swimming (Mon., Wed.)—*Miss Hussey.*
Swimming (Tues., Thurs.)—
Tennis (Mon., Wed.)—
Tennis (Tues., Thurs.)—*Miss Hussey.*
U. S. History C—*Miss Riggs.*
U. S. History 2—*Miss Rice.*

FIFTH PERIOD

College Courses

Commercial Geography of North America—*Miss Aitchison.*
European Governments—*Mr. Lōomis.*
Experimental Psychology—*Mr. Mount.*
General Economics—*Mr. McKitrick.*
German XII. (Die Journalisten)—*Miss Lorenz.*
History and Teaching of Mathematics—*Mr. Condit.*
Latin XII. (Historical Grammar) (Mon., Wed., Fri.)—*Mr. Merchant.*
Latin XV. (Senior Electiv) (Tues., Thurs.)—*Mr. Merchant.*
Philosophy of Education—*Mr. Walters.*
Psychology II—*Mr. Samson.*
Rhetoric—*Mr. Lynch.*
Solid Geometry—*Mr. Wright.*

Special Teacher Courses

Bench Work (Advanced)—*Mr. Brown.*
Bookkeeping 3—*Mr. Cummins.*
Chemistry III. (Home Economics)—*Mr. Getchell.*
Design—*Miss Patt.*
·Drawing 3 (Primary)—*Miss Schuneman.*
*Elementary Food Theory 3 (Mon., Wed.)—*Miss Townsend.*
*Elementary Food Theory 3 (Tues., Thurs.)—*Miss Townsend.*
*Elementary Food Theory 3 (Mon., Wed.)—*Miss Sheets.*
History and Literature of Physical Training—*Mr. Seymour.*
Mechanical Drawing—*Mr. Bailey.*
Methods, Home Economics (Fri.)—*Miss Townsend.*
Nature Study—
Primary Theory (Kindergarten)—*Miss Hatcher.*
Typewriting 2—*Mr. Coffey.*
Woodturning—*Mr. Brown.*
*Class period from 1:00 to 3:20 p. m.

Normal Courses

Algebra 2—*Miss Allen.*
Arithmetic 2—*Mr. Cory.*
Civics, Review—*Mr. Peterson.*
Drawing 2—*Miss Patt.*
*Elementary Food Theory (Tues., Thurs.)—*Miss Sheets.*

Elementary Handwork—*Mrs. McMahon.*
Elocution—*Miss Falkler.*
English Classics 2—*Miss Hearst.* ·
English Composition 2—*Miss Lodge.*
English Grammar C—*Miss Gregg.*
Gymnastics (Tues., Thurs.)—*Mr. Pasini.*
Music 2—*Miss Stenwall.*
Penmanship 1—*Mr. Cummins.*
Physical Training 2 (Mon., Wed.)—
Physical Training 3 (Mon., Wed.)—*Miss Hussey.*
Physical Training 3 (Tues., Thurs.)—*Miss Hallingby.*
Physics 2—*Mr. Dieterich.*
Physiography—*Mr. Cable.*
School Management (Elementary)—*Mr. Colgrove.*
Swimming (Mon., Wed.)—*Miss Hallingby.*
Tennis (Mon., Wed.)—*Mr. Pasini.*
Tennis (Tues., Thurs.)—
*Class period from 1:30 to 3:45 p. m.

SIXTH PERIOD ·

College Courses

Botany II., Laboratory (Tues., Thurs.)—
Chemistry IV., V., VI., Laboratory Courses—*Mr. Bond.*
Physics IV.—*Mr. Begeman.*

Special Teacher Courses

*Elementary Food Theory 3 (Mon., Wed.)—*Miss Townsend.*
*Elementary Food Theory 3 (Tues., Thurs.)—*Miss Townsend.*
*Elementary Food Theory 3 (Mon., Wed.)—*Miss Sheets.*
Primary Criticism (Tues., Thurs.)—*Miss Hatcher.*
*Class period from 1:00 to 3:20 p. m.

Normal Courses

Baseball (Mon., Wed.)—*Mr. Pasini.*
*Elementary Food Theory (Tues., Thurs.)—*Miss Sheets.*
Physical Training 1 (Tues., Thurs.)—
Physical Training 2 (Mon., Wed.)—*Miss Hallingby.*
Rythm 1 (Tues., Thurs.)—*Miss Hallingby.*
Swimming (Tues., Thurs.)—*Mr. Pasini.*
Swimming (Mon., Wed.)—

Tennis (Tues., Thurs.)—*Miss Hussey.*
Track (Mon., Wed.)—*Mr. Seymour.*
*Class period from 1:30 to 3:45 p. m.

Seventh Period

Special Teacher Courses

Baseball—*Mr. Pasini.*
Demonstrations in Cooking (Mon., Wed.)—*Miss Townsend,*
    (to 5:30 p. m.)
Demonstrations in Cooking (Mon., Wed.)—*Miss Sheets,* (to
    5:30 p. m.)
Medical Gymnastics and Massage (Mon., Wed.)—*Miss Hussey.*
Track Team—*Mr. Seymour.*

Normal Courses

Gilbert (Tues., Thurs.)—*Miss Hussey.*
Physical Training 3 (Tues., Thurs.)—
Rythm 2 (Mon., Wed.)—*Miss Hallingby.*
Swimming (Mon., Wed.)—
Tennis (Tues., Thurs.)—*Miss Hallingby.*

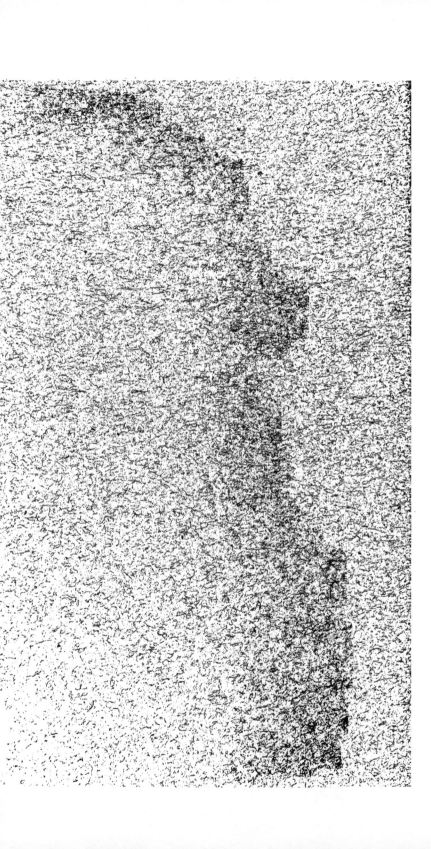

BULLETIN

OF THE

Iowa State Teachers College

CEDAR FALLS, IOWA

Courses of Study

and

Program of Recitations

FOR THE SCHOOL YEAR

1913-1914

VOL. XIV.   No. 1

JULY 1913

Issued Quarterly. Publisht by the Iowa State Teachers College.
Entered as second-class mail matter August 31, 1912,
at the post office at Cedar Falls, Iowa, under
the Act of Congress, August 24, 1912

Vol. XIV.   *JULY 1913*   *No. 1*

BULLETIN

OF THE

IOWA STATE TEACHERS COLLEGE

CEDAR FALLS, IOWA

COURSES OF STUDY

AND

PROGRAM OF RECITATIONS

FOR SCHOOL YEAR 1913-1914

Where the spelling in this Bulletin varies from the conventional form, it has been adopted for its simplicity and its preference for common usage. These forms are accepted by the later editions of Webster's and Standard Dictionaries and should be adopted by public school teachers and taught in the schools.

Iowa State Teachers College

SCHOOL CALENDAR FOR 1913-1914·

FALL TERM—TWELVE WEEKS

1913

Sept. 2. Tuesday, Enrollment without penalty, 8:00 a. m. to 4:00 p. m.

Sept. 3. Wednesday, Chapel Exercises, 9:00 a. m. to 9:30 a.m.; Recitations begin 8:00 a. m., half-hour class periods; Enrollment with penalty, 1:30 p. m. t) 4:00 p. m.

Sept. 4. Thursday, Training Schools open, 9:00 a. m.

Oct. 29, 30, 31. Wednesday, Thursday, Friday, Examination for Uniform County Certificates, beginning Wednesday, 8:00 a. m.

Nov. 25. Tuesday, Recitations close at noon.

Nov. 24, 25, 26.. Monday, Tuesday, Wednesday, State Certificate examination, beginning Monday, 8:00 a. m. Complete arrangements must be made ten days in advance.

WINTER TERM—TWELVE WEEKS

1913

Dec. 2. Tuesday. Enrollment, without penalty, 8:00 a. m. to 4:00 p. m.

Dec. 3. Wednesday, Chapel Exercises, 9:00 a. m. to 9:30 a. m. Recitations begin 8:00 a.m., half hour class periods; Enrollment, with penalty, 1:30 p. m. to 4:00 p. m.

Dec. 23. Tuesday, Holiday Recess, beginning at noon.

1914.

Jan. 6. Tuesday, Recitations resumed, 8:00 a. m.

Jan. 28, 29, 30. Wednesday, Thursday, Friday, Examination for Uniform County Certificates, beginning Wednesday, 8:00 **a. m.**

March 10. Tuesday, Recitations close at noon.

March 9, 10, 11. Monday, Tuesday, Wednesday, Examination for State Certificates, beginning Monday, 8:00 a. m. Complete arrangement must be made ten days in advance.

SPRING TERM—TWELVE WEEKS

1914
March 17. Tuesday, Enrollment, without penalty, 8:00 a.m. to 4:00 p. m.

March 18. Wednesday, Chapel Exercises, 9:00 a. m. to 9:30 a. m. Recitations begin 8:00 a. m.; half hour class periods; Enrollment, with penalty, 1:30 p. m. to 4:00 p. m.

June 5. Friday, Recitations close at noon.

June 2, 3, 4. Tuesday, Wednesday, Thursday, Examination for State Certificates, beginning Tuesday, 8:00 a. m. Complete arrangements must be made ten days in advance.

COMMENCEMENT EXERCISES—JUNE 5 to 9.

1914
June 5. Friday, Annual parade of the Women's Literary Societies, 2:00 p. m.

June 5. Friday, Commencement Concert, 7:00 p. m.

June 5. Friday, Reception to Graduating Class, Alumni and Visitors, by the Faculty, 8:30 p. m.

June 6. Saturday, Class Reunions and Special Programs.

June 6. Saturday, Anniversaries of Men's Literary Societies, 8:00 p. m.

June 7. Sunday, Baccalaureate Address by the President, 4:00 p. m.

June 7. Sunday, Alumnal, Senior and Student Prayer Service, 7:00 p. m.

June 8. Monday, Literary, Social and Business Meeting of the Alumnal Association, 10:00 a. m.

June 8. Monday, Luncheon of the Alumnal Association, 12:30 p. m.

June 8. Monday, Commencement Play, 8:00 p. m.

June 9. Tuesday, Commencement Exercises, 10:00 a. m.

SUMMER TERM—SIX WEEKS

1914

June 13. Saturday, Enrollment, 1:30 p. m. to 4:00 p. m.

June 15. Monday, Enrollment, 8:00 a. m. to 12 m.; Recitations begin 1:30 p. m.; half hour periods.

June 24, 25, 26. Wednesday, Thursday, Friday. Examination for Uniform County Certificates, beginning Wednesday, 8:00 a. m.

July 22, 23, 24. Wednesday, Thursday, Friday, Examination for State Certificates, beginning Wednesday, 8:00 a. m.

July 24. Friday, Commencement Exercises, 9:50 a. m.

July 24. Friday, Recitations close 2:25 p. m.

Iowa State Teachers College

The Course of Study

REQUIREMENTS FOR ADMISSION.

Applicants for unconditional admission to the College Course, hereafter printed in detail, must be at least sixteen years of age and must present satisfactory records from accredited secondary schools showing a total of fifteen units of work in accordance with the standards approved by the Iowa State Board of Education, as fully set out in detail in Bulletin No. 1 of the Board on Secondary School Relations. The term unit as here used signifies a year's work where the class hours are forty-five minutes, the number of class hours per week being not less than five.

I. CONSTANTS

Groups of Subjects—	*Units*
1. One Foreign Language	2
2. English	3
3. Algebra	1½
4. Plane Geometry	1
5. History	1
6. Electives	6½
Total	15

II. ELECTIVES.

In selecting the units that are known as electives in the above requirement, the total that may be accepted for any one group always includes those units required for constants. The maximum number of units that may be offered on certificate from an accredited high school are as follows:

Groups of Subjects—	*Units*
1. Foreign Language—	
(1) Greek	2 to 4
(2) Latin	2 to 4

(3) French	2 to 4	
(4) Spanish	2 to 4	
(5) German	2 to 4	
2. English		4
3. History, Civics and Economics		4
(1) Ancient History	½ to 1	
(2) Medieval and Modern History	½ to 1	
(3) Civil Government	½ to 1	
(4) Economics	½	
(5) General History in place of (1) and (2)	1	
(6) U. S. History—3rd and 4th years	½ to 1	
(7) English History	½ to 1	
4. Mathematics		4
(1) Solid Geometry	½	
(2) Plane Trigonometry	½	
(3) Advanced Algebra	½	
5. Science		4½
Physics	1	
Chemistry	1	
Physiography	½ to 1	
Botany	½ to 1	
Zoology	½ to 1	
Physiology	½	
Geology	½	
Astronomy	½	
Agriculture	½ to 1	
6. Commercial Subjects		2
Adv. Arithmetic (after Algebra)	½	
Bookkeeping	½ to 1	
Commercial Geography	½	
Commercial Law	½	
Industrial History	½	
7. Industrial Subjects		2
Freehand and Mechanical Drawing	½ to 1	
Manual Training—i. e. Shop Work	½ to 2	

Domestic Science   ½ to 1
Stenography   ½ to 1
     Credit is not given for English grammar or United States his-
tory, unless taken in the latter part of the course, nor for arithmetic
unless taken after algebra.

OUTLINE OF THE COLLEGE COURSE GIVING DISTRIBUTION OF WORK AND DIRECTIONS CONCERNING THE OPPORTUNITIES OFFERD

THE COLLEGE COURSE.

Degree: Bachelor of Arts in Education
First Grade State Certificate Standard.

Freshman Year.

A	B	C
1. Elective.	1. Elective.	1. Elective.
2. Elective.	2. Elective.	2. Elective.
3. Rhetoric.	3. Education I.	3. Education II.

Sophomore Year.

A	B	C
1. Elective.	1. Elective.	1. Elective.
2. Elective.	2. Elective.	2. Elective.
3. Education III.	3. Education IV.	3. Elective.

Junior Year.

A	B	C
1. Elective.	1. Elective.	1. Elective.
2. Elective.	2. Elective.	2. Elective.
3. Elective.	3. Education V.	3. Education VI.

Senior Year.

A	B	C
1. Elective.	1. Elective.	1. Elective.
2. Elective.	2. Elective.	2. Elective.
3. Practise Teaching.	3. Practise Teaching.	3. Elective.

Majors.—It is necessary for the student who takes the College
Course to select one major study with some one department at the

close of the Freshman year. A major consists of at least two full
years of work, thus covering six term credits. After the major is
decided the student is under the direction of the department in
which the major belongs, and the Head of the Department becomes
his advisor during the rest of his course. The different majors that
are offerd are in the following lines:

1. English.
2. Public Speaking.
3. Latin.
4. German.
5. French
6. Mathematics.
7. Physics.
8. Chemistry.
9. Earth Science.
10. Biological Science.
11. History.
12. Government.
13. Economics.
14. Education.
15. Drawing.
16. Manual Training.
17. Home Economics.
18. Physical Education.
19. Rural Education.

DISTRIBUTION OF CREDITS IN THE COLLEGE COURSE.

PRIVILEGES ALLOWD IN ALL COURSES.

In addition to the required work necessary for graduation
from the College Course as above specified, students are allowd to
pursue work in vocal music, instrumental music, drawing, manual
training, sewing, cooking, penmanship or other art subjects, provided not more than a total of four hours work a day is thus scheduled. These subjects are of such importance in public school work
that this liberal plan has been adopted, it being recognized that a
knowledge of these subjects greatly increases the opportunities of a
teacher both as to location and as to superior salary.

REQUIRED POINTS OF COLLEGE GRADE.

The following outline gives the distribution of studies that
is required for graduation from the college course, each credit being 12 weeks of 5 lessons a week.

1. *Professional Courses.*   *Number of Credits*

    (a) *General Education.*

	1. Professional	14
	2. English	3
	3. Foreign Language	3
	4. History, Government and Economics	3
	5. Science and Mathematics	3
	6. Elective	10
	Total	36

      7. Other work required:
      (a) Physical Training—two years.
      (b) Literary Society work—four years

  (b) *Special Education*—Course for teachers of Rural School Training in High Schools.

	1. Professional	12
	2. English	3
	3. Foreign Language	3
	4. History, Government and Economics	3
	5. Science and Mathematics	3
	6. Vocational Instruction	6
	7. Elective	6
	Total	36

      8. Other work required:
      (a) Special Electives in vocational instruction—See head of Department of Professional Instruction for assignment according to individual qualifications.
      (b) Physical Training—two years.
      (c) Literary Society Work—four years.

II. *English Courses.*

	1. English	12
	2. Foreign Language	3
	3. History, Government and Economics	3
	4. Science and Mathematics	3
	5. Professional	8
	6. Elective	7
	Total	36

      7. Other work required:

(a)   Physical Training—two years.
(b)   Literary Society Work—four years.

III.   *Foreign Language Courses.*

1.	Foreign Language	12
2.	English	3
3.	History, Government and Economics	3
4.	Science and Mathematics	3
5.	Professional	8
6.	Elective	7
	Total	36

7.   Same as in English Courses.

IV.   *History, Government and Economics Courses.*

1.	History, Government and Economics	12
2.	English	3
3.	Science and Mathematics	3
4.	Foreign Language	3
5.	Professional	8
6.	Elective	7
	Total	36

7.   Same as in English Courses.

V.   *Science and Mathematics Courses.*

1.	Science and Mathematics	15
2.	English	3
3.	Foreign Language	3
4.	History, Government and Economics	3
5.	Professional	8
6.	Elective	4
	Total	36

7.   Same as in English Courses.

VI.   *Home Economics, Drawing, Physical Education and Manual Training Courses.*

1.	Home Economics, or Drawing, etc.	9
2.	English	3
3.	Foreign Language	3
4.	History, Government and Economics	3
5.	Science and Mathematics	6

6.	Professional	8
7.	Elective	7
	Total	39

8. Other work required:
   (a) Physical Training—two years.
   (b) Literary Society Work—four years.

DEPARTMENT SUBJECTS IN THE COLLEGE COURSE

This tabular arrangement gives the entire program of studies with the nomenclature adopted by the Faculty for the College Course.

The numbers by which the courses in the different departments are to be designated are given below:

Professional.

Required Work—

   I—II. Psychology I, II.
   III. School Management.
   IV. History of Education.
   V. Philosophy of Education.
   VI. School Administration.
   VII—VIII. Practise Teaching.

Elective Courses—

   IX. Experimental Psychology.
   X. Genetic Psychology.
   XI. Educational Classics.
   XII. Lecture Course on Social and Sex Psychology, 3 hours, ½ credit.
   XIII. Rural School Problems.
   XIV. Practise Teaching.

English.

   I. College Rhetoric.
   II. Theme Writing and Story Telling.
   III. Advanced Exposition.
   IV. English Literature.
   V. Anglo-Saxon and History of English Language.
   VI. Anglo-Saxon and Middle English.
   VII. Shakespeare.
   VIII. Literary Criticism.
   IX. The English Romantic Movement.

X—XI.   History of the English Drama I, II.
XII.   English Literature of the Nineteenth Century.
XIII.   American Literature.
XIV.   Development of the English Novel.
XV.   Elocution I, or Public Speaking I.
XVI.   Elocution II, or Public Speaking II.
XVII.   Argumentation.
XVIII.   Applied Drama.
XIX—XX.   Repertoire I, II.
XXI.   Principles of Expression.
XXII.   The Teaching of English.

Note. In curricula where two terms of English are required, course I and course IV are to be taken, unless otherwise specified in the curriculum. In curricula where three terms of English are required, the courses to be taken are I, IV, and *one* of the following courses: II, III, XVI. Courses II, III, IV and XVI are electives for other students; and all other courses are free electives, except where Elocution or Public Speaking is prescribed in certain curricula.

Latin and Greek.

I—II—III.   Livy and Horace (Epodes and Odes.)
IV—V—VI.   Latin Composition.
VII—VIII—IX.   Roman Literature.
X—XI—XII.   Historical Latin Grammar.
XIII—XIV—XV.   Elementary Greek.
XVI—XVII——XVIII.   Senior Electives   (Latin   or Greek.)
XIX—XXIII.   College Elementary Latin.

German and French.

German—

I.   Die Jungfrau von Orleans.
II.   German Prose Composition.
III.   Emilia Galotti, Lyrics and Ballads.
IV.   Nathan der Weise.
V.   Iphigenie auf Tauris.
VI.   Der dreissigjaehrige Krieg.
VII.   Modern German Prose or Scientific German.
VIII.   Selections from German Classics.

Notes. 1. The above outline of work is for students who have had a minimum of two years of German in an accredited high

school, or its equivalent. Students who have met in some other for-
eign language the required entrance condition, may take beginning
German for college credit. Of this there are four terms; namely,
German IX, X, XI, and XII.

2.   Other authors of similar grade will be read at times instead of those here listed.

French—

I.   Lessons—Grammar and Pronunciation.
II.   Grammar continued; Les Prisonniers du Caucase,
and other easy French.
III.   Le Voyage de Monsieur Perrichon, and L'Abbe Con-
stantin.
IV.   La Mare au Diable, and L'Histoire d'un jeune Hom-
me pauvre.
V.   Le Gendre de M. Poirier, and Un Philosophe sous les
Toits.
VI.   Le Pecheur d'Islande,   and   Le   Bourgeois   Gentil-
homme.

Mathematics.

I.   Solid Geometry.
II.   College Algebra I.
III.   Plane Trigonometry.
IV.   College Algebra II.
V.   Spherical Trigonometry and Surveying.
VI.   History and Teaching of Mathematics.
VII.   Analytical Geometry.
VIII.   Differential Calculus.
IX.   Integral Calculus.

Chemistry.

I—II.   General Inorganic.
III.   Qualitative Analysis.
IV—V.   Quantitative Analysis.
VI.   Special Methods in Quantitative Analysis.

Physics.

I.   Mechanics and Sound.
II.   Light and Heat.
III.   Electricity and Magnetism.
IV.   Teachers' Special Course.

V. Adv. Laboratory Work in General Physics.
VI. Adv. Laboratory Work in Electricity

Natural Science.

I. Physiology I.
II—III. Botany I, II.
IV. Hygiene and Sanitation.
V—VI—VII. Zoology I, II, III.
VIII. Physiography I.
IX—X. Geology I, II.
XI. Mineralogy.
XII. Astronomy.
XIII. Commercial Geography of North America.
XIV. Commercial Geography of Europe.
XV. Influences of Geography upon American History.
XVI. Agriculture for Public School Teachers.

History.

I. American History.
II. English History.
III. Greek History.
IV. Roman History.
V. Medieval History.
VI. Renaissance and Reformation.
VII. Eighteenth Century History.
VIII. Nineteenth Century History.
IX. Method History or Teachers' History.

Government.

I. American Government.
II—III. American Constitutional History I, II.
IV. English Government.
V. Modern European Governments.
VI. Municipal Government.
VII. International Law.
VIII. Constitutional Law.
IX. English Constitutional History.

Economics.

I. General Economics.
II. Social and Economic Problems.
III. American Industrial History.
IV. English Industrial History.

V.   Money and Banking.
VI.   Public Finance.

Drawing—Not elective on other courses except as specified.

I—II.   Cast Drawing .... ½ credit each
* III.   History of Architecture 1   "
* IV.   History of Painting 1   "
V.   Perspective .... ½   "
VI.   Still life .... ½   :
VII—VIII.   Water color .... ½   "   each
IX.   Design .... ½   "
Manual Training, Physical Education or
    Home Economics .... 3½ credits
* Elective on College Courses.

Manual Training—Not elective on other courses except as specified.

* I—II.   Manual Training Methods I,II ..... 1 credit each
* III.   Organization and Economics of
    Manual Training
IV—V—VI—VII.   Mechanical Draw-
    ing .... ½   "   each
VIII—IX—X—XI.   Design and Con-
    struction in Wood .... ½   "   each
XII.   Wood Turning .... ½   :
XIII—XIV.   Design and Construction
    in Sheet Metal .... ½   "   each
XV.   Primary Handwork .... ½   :
XVI.   Elementary Handwork .... ½
* Elective on College Courses.
Note.   Courses   in I, II, III, VI, VII, IX, X,
XII, and XIII constitute a Manual Training Major.

Home Economics—Not elective on other courses.

I—II—III.   Sewing .... ½ credit each
IV—V—VI—VII.   Elementary Food
    Theory .... ½   "   "
VIII—IX.   Dietetics .... ½   "   "
X.   Demonstrations .... ¼
XI.   Principles of the Selection and
    Preparation of Foods .... 1¼ credits
XII.   Household Management .... 2-5 credit
XIII.   Household Architecture ...... 2-5 credit
XIV.   Methods, Home Economics ..... 1-5 credit

Manual Training, Physical Education or
Drawing   2 credits

Note. In Manual Training, Home Economics and Drawing
Majors here outlined the fractions given specify the particular value
of said courses when applied to the College Course.

Physical Education—Not elective on other courses except as
specified.

    * I—II. Anatomy I, II.
    III. Hygiene.
    IV. Physical Department Methods.
    V. Playground Methods.
    VI. History and Literature of Physical Training.
    VII. Anthropometry and Physical Diagnosis.
    VIII. Physiology of Exercise.
    IX. Medical Gymnastics and Massage.
    * Elective on College Courses.

Other Possible Electives.

Music—

Music I.	½ credit
Music II.	½ credit
Harmony I, II, III, IV.	2 credits
History of Music I, II.	1 credit

THE JUNIOR COLLEGE COURSE.

In conformity with the custom of the State Teachers College
to give a diploma for two years work in the institution after possessing the secondary scholarship of a fully accredited high school
the Junior College Course is provided. This course is distributed
as to the number of term credits as follows:

Departments of Work	Number of Credits
English	2
Foreign Language	2
History, Government and Economics	2
Science and Mathematics	2
Professional and Training	6
Elective	4
Total	18

In addition, the candidate for the diploma must have two years of Physical Training and two years of Literary Society Work.

A Junior College Diploma will be granted to any student who completes the schedule here outlined.

This diploma may or may not entitle the holder to the Second Grade State Certificate. Those who desire to secure this honorary credential as a teacher must have studied either in the high school or the Teachers College, or have past a teachers' certificate examination of high grade, the following: 1. Arithmetic; 2. Geography; 3. English Grammar; 4. United States History; 5. Vocal Music; 6. Physiology; 7. Civics (including civil government of Iowa); 8. Algebra, (including Quadratics, ratio, proportion, variation and logarithms); 9. Physics; 10. Economics (including the topics: the marginal theory of value and the laws of distribution, money—its nature and history in the United States, the quantity theory, monopolies and trusts, public ownership or regulation); 11. Bookkeeping (single and double entry); 12. Drawing (including composition, illustrative and elementary perspective); 13. Descriptive Botany; 14. English Composition.

THE DIPLOMA MASTER OF DIDACTICS TO BE DISCONTINUED.

Under regulations adopted by the State Board of Education January 3, 1912, the diploma, Master of Didactics, will be discontinued in 1914 as a recognition for completing a three year course of college grade.

THE PROFESSIONAL COURSE OF STUDY FOR COLLEGE GRADUATES.

The Iowa State Teachers College has developt professional courses for college graduates that deserve special recognition for their practical features and for their large professional helpfulness. College graduates of decided success in teaching can complete one of these courses by attending three successive summer terms and doing special assigned work during the interim. Before graduation they will need to establish proofs of their success being excellent and positive. Where practise teaching is omitted with the consent of the department, other professional credits may be substituted on arrangement with the department. Those not having this stand-

ard of success are developt and traind by the Practise Teaching Department. For inexperienced and less qualified teachers, the regular sessions are better adapted, as all the training schools are then
in session.

I. PROFESSIONAL COURSE IN EDUCATION

First Term.

1. Advanced Psychology.
2. School Management.
3. History of Education.

Second Term.

1. Philosophy of Education.
2. School Administration.
3. Practise Teaching.

Third Term.

1. Experimental Psychology.
2. Educational Classics.
3. Practise Teaching.

II. PROFESSIONAL COURSE IN EDUCATION WITH ELECTIVES.

The following schedule is suitable when college graduates have
had partial instruction in professional education:

1. Education   3 credits
2. Practise Teaching   2 credits
3. Other studies approved by the Professional
   Department   4 credits

Total required   9 credits

III. PROFESSIONAL COURSE IN EDUCATION AS SPECIAL TEACHERS.

College graduates desiring special training in such work as
high school rural teacher training, supervisors of public school
music, physical education, manual training, home economics, drawing, kindergarten, or primary teaching, are granted a one year
course arranged to suit their scholarship and attainments. When
they satisfy the Faculty of their qualifications the appropriate diploma will be granted.

Observations on These Courses.

1.   Some branches of the above work can be personal, individual studies, laboratory and library in character. on lines outlined by the Professional department.   These studies are to be carefully made and results submitted to the   department   for   examination,. criticism and instruction.   The library is so strong in Pedagogy that this work is of great and lasting professional value.

2.   For entrance upon this course a complete detail of all work taken at the College must be filed.

3.   Substitutions will be granted   for   efficient   pedagogical work taken at a college with a   strong   professional   department. Great liberty will be allowd to such grade of   students   so as to enable them to prepare both wisely and well for the best public service in any special line of school work, but in   every   case a year's attendance at this college is required.   Such students are excused from literary society work if they apply to the Faculty for such release.

4.   Students desiring to train to be special teachers in rural school education so as to be qualified to instruct in normal courses in high schools will be provided such a plan of training and can complete the work in one year if they are college graduates.   This work is now one of the more important fields of teacher education.

SPECIAL TEACHER COURSES.

Standards Required and Honors Conferred.

Conditions of Admission.   The standards adopted by the State Board of Education as required for entrance   upon   the   College Course are the same for the Special Teacher Courses except that graduates of four year high schools may be   admitted   without foreign language credits, provided they have   equivalent   credits   in other kinds of high school work.

The Diploma Conferred.   The Special Teacher courses each cover two years of strong work in scholastic, general professional and special professional lines.   They are the equivalent in standard of special excellence with other   college   courses   of   similar length but they are organized to give special attention to some one line of definite training.   For the completion of these two years of study and training, a Special Teacher Diploma is awarded and a five year state certificate of a special kind is granted by the State Board of Examiners.

For the completion of an additional year of study, a Director or Supervisor Diploma is awarded as an additional recommendation of qualification and training for executive work along these specialties of teaching. When a three-year course is printed, the third year is the supervisor or director course.

In some particular departments where students complete the full line of special professional work required, such as music and art, department certificates may be obtained by such persons as do not desire to complete the scholastic and the general professional work required for a diploma.

In all Special Teacher Courses the elective studies must be chosen from the list of branches and term's work designated as of full college grade. These elections must be made by consulting the heads of the departments involvd in order to avoid all mistakes.

THE ELEMENTARY TEACHERS COURSE.

First Year.

A	B	C
1. Education I.	1. Education II.	1. Education III.
2. Rhetoric	2. College Elective	2. College Elective
3. Free Elective	3. Free Elective	3. Free Elective
4. Vocal Music	4. Drawing	4. Drawing

Physical Training.   Literary Society Work.

Second Year.

A	B	C
1. Education IV.	1. Practise Teaching	1. Practise Teaching
2. College Elective	2. College Elective	2. College Elective
3. Free Elective.	3. Free Elective	3. Free Elective
4. Review	4. Review	4. Review

Physical Training.
Literary Society Work.

1.   The free electives may be secondary subjects not pursued in high school, foreign language or college subjects. These must be chosen in such a way that state certificate requirements are met.

2.   Two terms work in Manual Arts are also accepted on the free elective credits.

3· Three reviews must be selected from the following subjects: Penmanship, Physiology, U. S. History, English Grammar, Arithmetic and Geography, unless the student has received satisfactory credits for such work in the eleventh or twelfth grades of an accredited high school, maintaining a normal course.

THE PRIMARY TEACHERS COURSE.

First Year.

A	B	C
1. Primary Methods.	1. Primary Methods	1. Primary Methods
2. Education I.	2. Elocution I, or	2. Education III.
3. Manual Arts	Public Speaking I.	3. Obs. in Training
4. Rhetoric	3. Education II.	School
	4. Drawing	4. Drawing

Physical Training; one term, four lessons a week, two terms, two lessons a week.

Literary Society Work.

Second Year.

A	B	C
1. Elective	1. Education IV.	1. Kg. Theory and
2. Vocal Music	2. Vocal Music	Obs.
3. Zoology	3. Eng. Literature	2. Botany
4. Criticism and	4. Criticism and	3. Elective
Practise	Practise	4. Criticism and
		Practise

Physical Training, two terms, two lessons a week.

Literary Society Work.

Criticism, two hours a week, second and third terms. Practise Teaching, five periods a week.

Notes. 1. Any other science may be substituted for Zoology and Botany provided the student has had these subjects in the secondary course.

2. One term of work in Manual Arts is able to be taken as an elective credit.

THE KINDERGARTEN TEACHERS COURSE.

First Year.

A	B	C
Kg. Principles (The Mother Plays)	Kg. Principles (The Mother Plays)	Kg. Handwork (The Occupations)
Kg. Materials (The Play Gifts)	Kg. Materials (The Play Gifts)	Kg. Lesson Plans (The Program)
Games (Game Circle)	Stories (Story Telling.)	Life of Froebel (Kg. Origin and Growth)
Education I.	2. Education II.	2. Education III.
Rhetoric	3. Vocal Music.	3. Vocal Music
Drawing	4. Drawing	4. Nature Study

Physical Training
Literary Society Work

Second Year

A	B	C
Kg. Practise	Kg. Principles (Advanced Mother Play)	Education of Man (Froebel's Ed. Laws)
Kg. Practise		
Elocution I, or	Stories (Study and Classification)	Program Making
Public Speaking I.		
Elective	Games (Theory)	2. Elective
	2. Kg. Practise	3. Primary Theory
	3. Education IV.	4. Elective
	4. Elective	

Physical Training
Literary Society Work

Supervisor Year

A	B	C
Kg. Theory	1. Kg. Theory	1. Education IX.
Education V.	2. Education VI.	2. Kg. Practise
Harmony	3. Elocution II, or Public Speaking II.	3. Hist. of Painting
Elective		4. Elective
	4. Elective	

Literary Society Work.

Note. Two terms work in Manual Arts are able to be taken as elective credits.

THE PUBLIC SCHOOL MUSIC TEACHERS COURSE.

First Year.

A	B	C
1. Education I.	1. Education II.	1. Nature Study
2. Rhetoric	2. Eng. Literature	2 { Harmony II. (3) / Sightsinging and / Conducting (2)
3. Music I.	3 { Harmony I. (3) / Sightsinging / and Methods / (2)	
4. Music II.		3 { History of Music / I. (3) / Methods in School / Music (2)

Physical Training.
Literary Society Work.

Second Year.

A	B	C
1. Sound	1. History	1. Education IV.
2. Elocution I, or Public Speaking I.	2. Education III.	2 { Harmony IV. (3) / Supervision (2)
3 { History of Music II. (3) / Child Voice and / Conducting (2)	3 { Harmony III. (3) / Musical Appreciation (2)	3. Practise Teaching
	4. Practise Teaching	

Physical Training.
Literary Society Work.

Two years of Voice are required (one lesson per week.)

One year of Piano is required (one lesson per week.)

Notes. 1. The figures in parentheses indicate the number of recitation hours per week, when less than five hours a week is given. "Music I" consists of sightsinging and chorus work. "Music II" in addition to sightsinging and chorus work includes elementary theory of music, history of music, and musical appreciation aided by the pianola and victrola.

2. Students completing all the music work required in the above course and the practise teaching, in addition to one term of psychology, one term of school management, one term of elocution,

or public speaking, and two electives in English, may be granted a
certificate from the department.

THE DRAWING TEACHERS COURSE.

First Year.

A	B	C
1. Cast Drawing	1. Cast Drawing	1. Hist. of Painting
2. Greek History	2. Medieval Hist.	2. Education III.
3. Education I.	3. Education II.	3. El. Handwork
4. Rhetoric	4. Hist. of Arch. and Sculpture	4. Botany I.

Physical Training.
Literary Society Work.

Second Year.

A	B	C
1. Still Life	1. Perspective	1. Supv. in Art
2. Elocution I, or Public Speaking I.	2. Elective	2. Mathematics
3. Elective	3. Eng. Literature	3. Elective
4. Education IV.	4. Prac. Teaching	4. Prac. Teaching

Physical Training.
Literary Society Work.

THE MANUAL TRAINING TEACHERS COURSE.

First Year.

A	B	C
1. Education I.	1. Education II.	1. Education III.
2. Rhetoric	2. Eng. Literature	2. Mathematics Elective
3. Pri. Handwork	3. Elem. Handwork	3. Design
4. Mech. Drawing	4. 1st Drawing	4. Mech. Drawing
		5. Wood Work

Physical Training.
Literary Society Work.

Second Year.

A	B	C
1. Education IV.	1. Prac. Teaching	1. Prac. Teaching
2. Man. Tr. Methods	3. Man. Tr. Methods	2. Physics I.
		3. Coll. Elective

C
e Study
ony II. (3)
singing
nducting
y of M

ds in School
ic (2)

C
tion IV.
ony IV (3)
vision (2)
se Teaching

week.)

rs a week i
horus work
ork include
cal apprecia

uired
one t
of elo

3. Wood Work
4. Sheet Metal Work
5. Mech. Drawing

3. Coll. Elective
4. Wood Work
5. Special Elective

4. Wood Work
5. Special Elective

Physical Training.

Literary Society Work.

Note. Modifications in the vocational requirements here outlined will be made by the Department of Manual Training, the better to adapt the course to the special needs of individual students.

THE HOME ECONOMICS TEACHERS COURSE.

First Year.

A	B	C
1. Elementary Food Theory	1. Elementary Food Theory	1. Elementary Food Theory
2. Sewing	2. Sewing	2. Sewing
3. Principles of Foods	3. Principles of Foods	3. Principles of Foods
4. Inorg. Chemistry	4. Inorg. Chemistry	4. *Qual. Analysis
5. Rhetoric	5. Education I.	5. Education II.
		6. Household Mgt.
		7. Methods, Home Economics

Physical Training.
Literary Society Work.

Second Year.

A	B	C
1. Elementary Food Theory	1. Dietetics	1. Food Analysis
2. Dietetics	2. Household Arch.	2. Demonstrations
3. Household Chem.	3. *Household Chem.	3. Education IV.
4. Education III.	4. Sanitation	4. Adv. Physiology
5. Practise Teaching	5. Practise Teaching	5. Practise Teaching

Physical Training.
Literary Society Work.

Note. The course in Home Economics here printed may be taken during three or four years by selecting scholastic studies under the direction of the Faculty.

* Omitted in this course by election provided work in some one other department is substituted.

THE PHYSICAL EDUCATION TEACHERS COURSE

First Year.

A	B	C
1. Anatomy I.	1. Anatomy II.	1. Adv. Physiology
2. Elocution I or	2. Elocution II or	2. Rhetoric
Public Speaking I.	Public Speaking II.	3. Education III.
3. Education I.	3. Education II.	

Physical Training.
Literary Society Work.

Second Year.

A	B	C
1.Phys. Dept. Methods	1.Playground Methods	1. Hist. and Lit. of Phys. Training
2. Elective	2. Elective	2. Elective
3. Hygiene	3. Chemistry I.	3. Chemistry II.

Physical Training.
Literary Society Work.

Third Year.

A	B	C
1. Anthro. and Phys. Diagnosis	1. Practise Teaching	1. Physiology of Exercise
2. Practise Teaching	2. Education IV.	2. Med. Gym. and Massage
3. Elective	3. Elective	3. Education X.
4. Vocal Music	4. Elective	4. Mech. Drawing

Physical Training.
Literary Society Work.

Notes. 1. The diploma given is that of *Director of Physical Education.*

2. Students contemplating becoming candidates for the

Bachelor of Arts in Education Degree should make that fact known at the beginning of the course.

THE COMMERCIAL TEACHERS COURSE.

First Year.

A	B	C
1. Com'l Arithmetic	1. Accounting	1. Prac. of Banking
2. Adv. Penmanship	2. Eng. Composition	2. Commercial Correspondence
3 Shorthand and Typewriting	3. Shorthand and Typewriting	3. Shorthand and Typewriting
4. Education I.	4. Education II.	4. Education III.

Physical Training.
Literary Society Work.

Second Year.

A	B	C
1. Gen. Economics	1. Money and Banking	1. Am. Government
2. Rhetoric	2. Eng. Literature	2. Com'l Law
3. Com'l Geog. N. A.	3. Com'l Geog. Europe	3. Elective
4. Education IV.	4. Practise Teaching	4. Practise Teaching

Physical Training.
Literary Society Work.

THE NORMAL COURSES.

I. County Certificate Course.

1. *Admission on the basis of country school diploma.*

2. *Recognition for completion:* Normal Course Certificate *stating qualifications.*

First Year.

A	B	C
1. Sewing	1. Cooking	1. Cooking
2. Reading	2. English Grammar	2. English Grammar
3. Geography	3. Geography	3. U. S. History
4. Arithmetic	4. Arithmetic	4. Physiology
5. Orthography	5. Penmanship	5. Vocal Music

Second Year.

A	B	C
1. Agriculture	1. El. Economics	1. Agriculture
2. U. S. History	2. Algebra	2. El. Civics
3. Algebra	3. El. Physics	3. El. Physics
4. The Country School	4. Eng. Composition	4. Education
5. Vocal Music	5. Manual Training	5. Manual Training

Notes. Abridgements will be given for all subjects on uniform county certificates showing 75 per cent or above. This course gives all the new industrial subjects required by law for 1915.

II. THE GENERAL NORMAL COURSE FOR GRADE TEACHERS.

Admission on the basis of a first grade county certificate.

Recognition: The Normal Diploma and Second Grade State Certificate.

First Year.

A	B	C
1. Algebra	1. Algebra	1. Physics
2. *Sanitation	2. General History	2. General History
3. Eng. Classics	3. *Bookkeeping	3. *Elocution
4. Vocal Music	4. Drawing	4. Drawing
	Physical Training.	

Second Year.

A	B	C
1. Physics	1. *Physiography	1. General Botany
2. Plane Geometry	2. Plane Geometry	2. *Solid Geometry
3. Psychology	3. Psychology	3. Sch. Management
4. *Drawing	4. Elective	4. Eng. Classics

Physical Training.
Literary Society Work.

* Latin or German Elective may be substituted.

Third Year.

A	B	C
1. Rhetoric	1. English Literature	1. Am. Government
2. College Algebra 1.	2. Economics I.	2. Am. History

or Trigonometry	3. Practis Teaching	3. Practis Teaching
3. History of Educa-tion	4. Special Elective	4. Special Elective
4. Special Elective		

Literary Society Work.

Notes. 1. Students who have completed the vocational work, the algebra or the physics required in Normal Certificate Course will be granted credit in proportion to the work accomplisht, thus abridging the above requirements.

2. The special electives of the third year as designated are intended for Vocal Music and Drawing beyond the tabulated subjects in the same line, or in Manual Training, Home Economics, Commercial studies or Agriculture, as the student may elect.

III. THE VOCATIONAL NORMAL COURSE.

For rural and consolidated school teachers.

Admission: First Grade Uniform County Certificate.

Recognition: The Normal Diploma and Second Grade State Certificate.

First Year.

A	B	C
1. Sewing	1. Sewing	1. Cooking
2. Algebra	2. Algebra	2. General History
3. Penmanship & Bookkeeping	3. Drawing	3. Drawing
4. Sanitation	4. English Classics	4. English Classics
5. Vocal Music	5. Vocal Music	5. English Composition

Physical Training.

Second Year.

A	B	C
1. Cooking	1. Elocution	1. Agriculture
2. General History	2. Physiography	2. Farm Botany
3. Plane Geometry	3. Plane Geometry	3. Rural School Management
4. Psychology	4. Psychology	4. Am. History

Physical Training.
Literary Society Work.

Teaching
Elective

tional work,
icate Course
nplisht, thus

signated are
bulated sub-
Economics,
elect

Grade State

C

g
l History
ng
h Classics

C

lture
Botany
School

listory

Third Year.

A	B	C
1. Agriculture	1. Manual Training	1. Manual Training
2. Rhetoric	2. English Literature	2. Am. Government
3 Economics	3. Physics	3. Physics
4. History of Educa-	4. Practise Teaching	4. Practise Teaching
tion		

Literary Society Work.

Note. This course is arranged for the giving of special qualifications of a superior kind in modern standards. None of these courses are to be the equivalent of College Courses as they will be taught so as to give the teacher in training more practical efficiency in educating the boys and girls of the farms of the state The Practise in Teaching will be broad in its scope and notably efficient in its extent.

IV. SPECIAL NORMAL COURSES.

Special State Certificate Standard.

Recognition: Special Normal Diplomas.
1. Primary Normal Course.
2. Kindergarten Normal Course.
3. Public School Music Normal Course.
4. Manual Training Normal Course.
5. Home Economics Normal Course.
6. Drawing Normal Course.
7. Commercial Normal Course.

Notes. 1. Admission to all the Special Normal Courses requires First Grade Uniform County Certificate or its equivalent.

2. The First Year of these special courses will be planned by the Registrar to suit the individual condition of scholarship and the individual needs that are essential to the special course chosen.

3. These special courses are not planned on any theory that such persons would desire to take a College Course following their graduation.

4. The Second and Third Years of these special courses are the same as those adopted by the Faculty for Special Teacher Courses.

SPECIAL MUSIC TEACHER COURSES.

Conditions of Admission. Students are admitted to these music courses on liberal terms as to preparatory training and are encouraged to begin early enough to develop the skill and capability for professional artistic success that are so notably demanded in teachers of these kinds.

To become a candidate for graduation, the student must have attaind to the scholastic qualifications required for full college entrance. These scholastic conditions may be acquired in any good secondary school or may be accomplisht in the certificate courses at the College.

Conditions of Graduation. A special Teacher Diploma will be awarded to such persons as complete satisfactorily any one of the courses here outlined, but as skill and capability as musicians are also essential qualities to be attaind, the exact time necessary to complete any one of these courses can not be stated in school years. The candidate must have sufficient proficiency in the special line chosen to secure the recommendation of the professors in charge of the work to become an applicant for graduation. The courses as here mapped out, outside of the attainment in capability as a musician, can be satisfactorily completed in three years.

THE PIANO COURSE.

Piano lessons must be continued thru the entire period of study, two lessons a week. A second study—voice or orchestral instrument—must also be carried, with either one or two lessons a week, each term except the last year.

Other work required will be:

First Year.

A	B	C
Music II. 5	English Composi-	German 5
German 5	tion 5	Eng. Literature 5
	German 5	

Second Year.

A	B	C
History of Music I. 3	Harmony I. 3	Harmony II. 3
Sound 5	History of Music II. 3	Elocution or Public Speaking 5

Third Year.

A	B	C
Psychology 5	Harmony III. 3	Harmony IV. 3
	Medieval Hist. 5	Modern History 5

The figures after the subjects indicate the number of recitation periods per week.

THE VIOLIN COURSE.

Violin lessons must be continued thru the entire period of study—two lessons per week. The piano work must be carried for two years successfully with at least one lesson a week. Attendance at two orchestra rehearsals and one class in ensemble playing is also required each week.

The general entrance requirements are the same as for Voice and Piano courses, except that before beginning the regular course the student must finish the preparatory course which can be accomplisht in one year of two lessons per week. Students may at their option take merely the music branches of the Violin course, upon satisfactory completion of which they will receive a department certificate.

First Year.

A	B	C
German 5	Eng. Composition 5	Eng. Literature 5
	German 5	German 5

Second Year.

A	B	C
History of Music I. 3	Harmony I. 3	Harmony II. 3
Sound 5	History of Music II. 3	

Third Year.

A	B	C
Psychology 5	Harmony III. 3	Harmony IV. 3
	Medieval Hist. 5	Modern History 5

The figures after the subjects indicate the number of recitation periods per week.

THE VOICE COURSE.

Three years of voice lessons (two a week), and two years piano lessons (one a week), will be required.

First Year.

A	B	C
Music I. 5	Music II. 5	German 5
German 5	German 5	Elem'ts of Music 5
	Theory of Phys.	
	Training 5	

Second Year.

A	B	C
History of Music I. 3	Harmony I. 3	Harmony II. 3
Sound 5	Eng. Literature 5	Psychology 5
	History of Music II. 3	

Third Year.

A	B	C
Psychology 5	Harmony III. 3	Harmony IV. 3
French 5	French 5	French 5
	Medieval Hist. 5	Modern Hist. 5

The figures after the subjects indicate the number of recitation periods per week.

Program of Recitations

Explanatory Note.

This program of recitations is printed for the full school year, presenting the work for the Fall, Winter and Spring terms. The work is organized on the basis of the past year, and may be expanded if numbers enrolled should demand it.

The nomenclature used gives in order: 1. The College Course; 2. The Special Teacher Courses; 3. The Normal Courses, for each term. The electives in Home Economics, Drawing, Manual Training or Physical Education which may apply on a college course in case a major is taken in one of these lines, will be found listed with the subjects belonging to the Special Teacher Courses.

The program of Physical Training, excepting the Theory, will be found at the end of the program for each term.

The name of the teacher is given following each subject assignd for the term, and the Arabic numeral following the teacher's name gives the hour at which the recitation will occur.

The following are the hours of work in the school for the year:

First Hour ....8:00 to 8:55.
Second Hour ....8:55 to 9:50.
Assembly ....9:50 to 10:20
Third Hour.............................10:20 to 11:15
Fourth Hour ....11:15 to 12:10.
Fifth Hour ....1:30 to 2:25.
Sixth Hour ....2:25 to 3:20.
Seventh Hour ....3:20 to 4:15
Eighth Hour ....4:15 to 5:00.

Of these the first to fifth, inclusiv, are regarded as regular class hours.

Library Hours—School days, 7:30 a. m. to 9:30 p. m. Saturdays, 7:30 a. m. to 12:00.

Literary Societies—Fridays, 2:25 p. m. Saturdays, 7:00 p. m.
Faculty Meetings—Mondays, 2:25 p. m.

Assignment for Rehearsals of Musical Societies.

Choral Society—Tuesdays, 6:15 p. m.
Cecilians—Wednesdays, 2:25 p. m.
Euterpeans—Tuesdays, 2:25 p. m.
Young Ladies' Glee Club—Mondays, 2:25 p. m.
Minnesingers—Wednesdays, 2:25 p. m.
Troubadours—Thursdays—2:25 p. m.
Orchestra—Mondays and Thursdays, 3:30 p. m.
Band—Tuesdays, 3:30 p. m.
Ensemble Class—Wednesdays, 3:30 p. m.
Band Classes—Wednesdays, 3:30 p. m.

FALL TERM

COLLEGE COURSES.

Professional Instruction in Education.

> Psychology I., Mr. Samson 1-3.
> Psychology II., Mr. Samson 2-5.
> School Management, Mr. Colegrove 2-3-5.
> History of Education, Mr. Walters 2-3-4.
> Experimental Psychology, Mr. Mount 5.
> Educational Classics, Mr. Walters 1.
> School Administration, Mr. Colegrove 1.

Training in Teaching.

> Illustrative Teaching, (Tues.,Thurs.) Mr. Dick 3-5-6.

English.

> Rhetoric, Mr. Lynch 2-5; Mr. Gist 1-4; Miss Carpenter 1; Miss
>   Lambert 2-4; Mr. Barnes 1-3; Miss Hearst 3; —————3.
> Theme Writing and Story Telling, Miss Carpenter 2.
> Elocution I., Miss Martin 4; ————— 1-5.
> Elocution II., Miss Martin 2; —————3.
> English Literature, Mr. Lynch 3; Miss Carpenter 4.
> Shakespeare, Mr. Gist 3.
> History of the English Drama I., Miss Lambert 1.
> Repertoire II., Miss Martin 3.

Latin and Greek.

> Livy, Mr. Merchant 1.
> Composition, Mr. Merchant (Tues., Thurs.) 2.
> Roman Literature, Mr. Merchant (Mon., Wed., Fri.) 2.
> Historical Latin Grammar, Mr. Merchant (Tues., Thurs.) 5.
> Elementary Greek, 1st term, Mr. Merchant (Mon., Wed., Fri.) 5.
> Cicero's Orations, 1st term, Mr. Merchant 3.
> Vergil, 1st term, Miss Call 1.

German and French.

> German I. (Die Jungfrau von Orleans), Miss Lorenz 5.
> German II. (Prose Composition), Miss Lorenz 2.
> German III., (Emilia Galotti; Lyrics and Ballads), Miss Lor-
>   enz 1.
> German VI. (Der dreissigjaehrige Krieg), Mr. Knoepfler 3.
> German IX. (Lessons; Grammar), Mr. Knoepfler 4.

Fall Term.

German XII. (Die Journalisten), Miss Lorenz 3.
French I., Mr. Knoepfler 2.
French IV., Mr. Knoepfler 1.

Mathematics.

Solid Geometry, Mr. Wright 5.
College Algebra I., Mr. Condit 2-3.
Plane Trigonometry, Mr. Cory 4.
Analytical Geometry, Mr. Condit 1.

Chemistry.

Chemistry I., ——————————3.
Chemistry II., III., Mr. Reed 4.
Chemistry IV., V., Mr. Bond 5-6.

Physics.

Physics I., Mr. Begeman 2.
Physics IV., Mr. Begeman 5.
Physics, Advanced Laboratory Course, Mr. Begeman 6.

Natural Science.

Botany I., Mr. Davis 2.
Botany I., Laboratory, Mr. Davis (Mon., Tues., or Wed., Thurs.)
   3.
Zoology I., Mr. Arey 3.
Zoology I., Laboratory, Mr. Arey (Mon., Tues.) 5.
Physiography I., Mr. Cable 3
Mineralogy, Mr Cable 4.
Commercial Geography of North America, Miss Aitchison 2.
Agriculture I., Mr. Davis 5, (two laboratory periods to be ar-
   ranged by instructor.)

History

American History, Miss Riggs 2.
Greek History, Miss Rice 2-3.
Renaissance and Reformation, Miss Riggs 1.

Government.

American Government, Mr. Meyerholz 2.
American Constitutional History I., Mr. Meyerholz 5.
Municipal Government, Mr. Meyerholz 4.

Economics.

General Economics, Mr. McKitrick 5; Mr. Morgan 4.
Social and Economic Problems, Mr. McKitrick 1.
American Industrial History, Mr. McKitrick 3.

Manual Training.

Manual Training Methods I., Mr. Bailey 2.

Fall Term.   (

Physical Education.

Anatomy I., Mr. Seymour 3.

Music.

Music I., Mr. Fullerton 3.
Music II., Mr. Fullerton 2.
History of Music I., Miss Childs (Tues., Wed., Fri.) 4.
History of Music II., Miss Childs (Mon., Wed., Thurs.) 1.

SPECIAL TEACHER COURSES.

Professional Instruction in Education.

Psychology I., Miss Buck 1-3-5; Mr. Mount 2-4.
Psychology II., Mr. Mount 1.   (
Primary Methods, 1st term, Miss McGovern 1-2-3.
Primary Methods, 2nd term, Miss McGovern 5.

Training in Teaching.

Primary Criticism, Miss Hatcher 6.
Kindergarten Theory, 1st term, Miss Ward 1.
Kindergarten Practise, Miss Ward 2-3.
Montessori Conference (2 days), Miss Ward 5.

Mathematics.

Commercial Arithmetic, Mr. Cory 5.

Chemistry.

Chemistry I. (Home Econ.), Mr. Reed 1-2.
Chemistry IV. (Home Econ.), Mr. Bond 2.

Physics.

Sound, Mr. Begeman 4.

Natural Science.

Zoology I. (Primary), Mr. Arey 1-2.
Zoology, Laboratory, Mr. Arey (Wed., Thurs.) 5.

Drawing.

Drawing (Primary), 1st term, Miss Iverson 2.
Drawing (Kindergarten), 1st term, Miss Iverson 3.
Cast Drawing, Miss Iverson 5.
Water Color, Miss Thornton 1.

Manual Training.

Mechanical Drawing, Mr. Bailey 4-5.
Woodwork, 1st term, Mr. Brown 2-4.
Woodwork, Advanced, Mr. Brown 5.
Wood Turning, Mr. Brown 5-6.

Fall Term.

Sheet Metal Work, Mr. Bailey 3.
Primary Handwork, Mrs. McMahon 2-3-5.
Elementary Handwork, Mrs. McMahon 4.

Physical Education.

Hygiene, Mr. Seymour 5.
Physical Department Methods, Mr. Seymour and Miss Hussey 4.
Physical Training (Primary), 1st term, Miss Hussey 3; Miss
Wild 4.

Music.

Child Voice, Miss Stenwall (Tues.) 1.
Conducting, Mr. Fullerton (Fri.) 1.

Commercial.

Penmanship, Advanced, Mr. Cummins 4.
Shorthand, 1st term, Mr. Coffey 3.
Shorthand, 4th term, Mr. Coffey 1.
Typewriting, 1st term, Mr. Coffey 2.
Typewriting, 3rd term, Mr. Coffey 4.

Home Economics.

Sewing, 1st term—

Miss Heinz (Daily) 8:55 to 9:50.
Miss Heinz (Daily) 10:20 to 11:15.
Miss Heinz (Daily) 11:15 to 12:10.
Miss Heinz (Fri.) 1:30 to 2:25; (Mon., Wed.) 1:30 to 3:20.
Miss Freer (Daily) 8:55 to 9:50.
Miss Freer (Daily) 10:20 to 11:15.

Elementary Food Theory, 1st term—

Miss Townsend (Mon., Wed.) 1:30 to 4:30.
Miss Townsend (Tues., Thurs.) 1:00 to 3:15.
Miss Townsend (Tues., Thurs.) 3:15 to 5:30.
Miss Sheets (Tues., Thurs.) 1:00 to 3:15.
Miss Sheets (Tues., Thurs.) 3:15 to 5:30.

Elementary Food Theory, 4th term—

Miss Sheets (Mon., Tues.) 10:00 to 12:10.
——————— (Mon., Tues.,) 10:00 to 12:10.

Dietetics, 1st term—

Miss Sheets (Wed., Thurs.) 10:00 to 12:10.
——————— (Wed., Thurs.) 10:00 to 12:10.

Fall Term.

Principles of Selection and Preparation of Foods, 1st term—

Miss Townsend (Mon., Wed.) 8:00 to 8:55.
Miss Townsend (Tues., Thurs.) 8:00 to 8:55.
Miss Townsend (Tues., Thurs.) 8:55 to 9:50.

NORMAL COURSES.

Professional Instruction in Education.

Methods, Miss Buck 2.
Elementary Psychology, 1st term, Mr. Campbell 1.
The Country School, Mr. Campbell 2.
Rural Education (Didactics), Mr. Campbell 3.

English.

Orthography, Miss Oliver 1-2.
English Grammar, 1st half, Miss Hearst 1-5.
English Grammar, 2nd half, Miss Gregg 5.
English Grammar, Complete, Miss Gregg 3-4.
Reading, Miss Falkler 5.
Elocution, Miss Falkler 2-3-4.
English Classics, 1st term, Miss Oliver 3.
English Classics, 2nd term, Miss Hearst 4.
English Composition, 1st term, Miss Gregg 2; ——————— 1.
English Composition, 2nd term, ——————— 5.

Latin.

Latin Lessons, 1st term, Miss Call 2.
Caesar, 1st term, Miss Call 4.
Caesar, 2nd term, Miss Call 3.

German.

German, 1st term, Miss Nolte 1.
German, 2nd term, Miss Nolte 4.
German, 3rd term, Miss Nolte 3.
German, 4th term, Miss Nolte 2.

Mathematics.

Arithmetic, 1st half, Mr. Cory 1; Miss Lambert 3-5.
Arithmetic, 2nd half, Miss Allen 2.
Arithmetic, Complete, Mr. Cory 2.
Algebra, 1st term, Miss Allen 3-4.
Algebra, 2nd term, Miss Allen 5.
Algebra, 1st and 2nd terms, Mr. Condit 5.
Algebra, 3rd term, Miss Lambert 1-2.
Plane Geometry, 1st term, Mr. Wright 2-4.
Plane Geometry, 2nd term, Mr. Wright 3.

Physics.

Physics, 1st term, Mr. Hersey 1-3-4; Mr. Kadesch 2.
Physics, 2nd term, Mr. Kadesch 3-5.

Fall Term.

Natural Science.

Geography, 1st half, Miss Aitchison 3.
Geography, 2nd half, Miss Aitchison 1.
Geography, Complete, Miss Aitchison 4.
Physiology, Mr. Newton 2-3.
Physiography, Mr. Cable 1-2.
Agriculture, 1st term, Mr. Davis 1.
Agriculture, Short Course, Mr. Davis 4.
General Botany, Mr. Newton 5.
Hygiene and Sanitation, Mr. Newton 1.

History.

U. S. History, 1st half, Miss Rice 4-5.
U. S. History, 2nd half, —————4.
U. S. History, Complete, Miss Riggs 4-5

Government.

Civics of Iowa, Mr. Morgan 2.
Civics of United States, Mr. Morgan 1.
Civics, Review, Mr. Meyerholz 1.

Economics.

Elementary Economics, Mr. McKitrick 4; Mr. Morgan 3.

Drawing.

Drawing, 1st term, Miss Thornton, 2-3; Miss Iverson 1.
Drawing, 2nd term, Miss Thornton 4.

Music.

Vocal Music, 1st term, Miss Stenwall 4; Miss Giberson 1-2-4,
Vocal Music, 2nd term, Miss Stenwall 2-3.

Manual Training.

Rural School Manual Training, Mr. Bailey and Mrs. McMahon 1.
Woodwork, 1st term, Mr. Brown 2-4.

Commercial.

Penmanship, 1st term, Mr. Cummins 1-3.
Bookkeeping, 1st term, Mr. Cummins 2.

Home Economics.

Cooking and Household Management, 1st term—
————— (Mon., Wed.) 1:30 to 4:00.
————— (Tues., Thurs.) 1:30 to 4:00.
Sewing, 1st term —
Miss Freer, (Daily) 11:15 to 12:10.
Miss Freer (Tues., Thurs., Fri.) 1:30 to 2:25; (Tues.,
Thurs.) 2:25 to 3:20.

Fall Term.

PHYSICAL TRAINING.

1st term Physical Training (Primary).

> Miss Hussey (Daily) 3.
> Miss Wild (Daily) 4.

1st term Physical Training.

> Miss Hussey (Tues., Thurs.) 6; (Mon., Wed.) 7.
> Miss Wild (Tues., Thurs.) 5.
> Miss Nisbet (Tues., Thurs.) 7.

2nd term Physical Training.

> Miss Nisbet (Mon., Wed.) 7.

3rd term Physical Training.

> Miss Wild (Tues., Thurs.) 7.

Gymnastics.

> Mr. Seymour (Tues., Thurs.) 8.

Tennis.

> Miss Hussey (Mon., Wed.) 5.
> Miss Wild (Mon., Wed.) 3; (Tues., Thurs.) 6.
> Mr. Berkstresser (Mon., Wed.) 4; (Tues., Thurs.) 5; (Tues., Fri.) 6.
> Miss Nisbet (Tues., Thurs.) 4.
> Mr. Seymour (Mon., Wed.) 7.

Swimming.

> Miss Hussey (Tues., Thurs.) 5-7.
> Miss Wild (Tues., Thurs.) 3; (Mon., Wed.) 6.
> Mr. Berkstresser (Tues., Fri.) 4.
> Miss Nisbet (Mon., Wed.) 4-5; (Tues., Thurs.) 6.

Basket Ball.

> Miss Wild (Mon., Wed.) 7.
> Miss Nisbet (Tues., Thurs.) 5.

Baseball.

> Miss Wild (Mon., Wed.) 5.

Cricket and Baseball.

> Miss Nisbet (Mon., Wed.) 6.

Rhythm.

> Miss Hussey (Mon., Wed.) 6.

Fall Term.

Golf.

    Mr. Seymour (Tues., Thurs.) 7.

Soccer Football.

    Mr. Berkstresser (Mon., Thurs.) 6.

Track.

    Mr. Seymour (Tues., Fri.) 6.

Football Team.

    Mr. Berkstresser (Daily) 7.

WINTER TERM

Professional Instruction in Education.

Psychology I., Mr. Samson 2-4-5.
Psychology II., Mr. Samson 1.
School Management, Mr. Colegrove 1-2-3-5.
History of Education, Mr. Walters 1-2-4.
Philosophy of Education, Mr. Walters 3.
Experimental Psychology, Mr. Mount 5.

English.

Rhetoric, Mr. Lynch 5; Mr. Gist 4; Mr. Barnes 4; —————2'.
Elocution I., Miss Falkler 3; ————— 2-4.
Public Speaking I., Mr. Barnes 3.
Elocution II., Miss Martin 2; —————1.
Advanced Exposition, Mr. Lynch 2.
English Literature, Mr. Lynch 3; Miss Carpenter 1; Miss Lambert 2-4.
Anglo Saxon and History of English Language, Mr. Gist 5.
Shakespeare, Mr. Gist 3.
The English Romantic Movement, Miss Carpenter 4.
History of the English Drama II., Miss Lambert 1.
American Literature, Miss Carpenter 2.
Applied Drama, Miss Martin 4.
Repertoire I., Miss Martin 3.

Latin and Greek.

Livy and Horace (Epodes and Odes) Mr. Merchant 1.
Composition, Mr. Merchant (Tues., Thurs.) 2.
Roman Literature, Mr. Merchant (Mon., Wed., Fri.) 2.
Historical Latin Grammar, Mr. Merchant (Tues., Thurs.) 5.
Elementary Greek, 2nd term, Mr. Merchant (Mon., Wed., Fri) 5.
Cicero's Orations, 1st term, Miss Call 3.
Vergil, 2nd term, Miss Call 1.

German and French.

German I. (Die Jungfrau von Orleans), Miss Lorenz 3.
German II. (Prose Compositon), Miss Lorenz 2.
German IV. (Nathan der Weise), Miss Lorenz 1.
German VII. (Modern German Prose), Mr. Knoepfler 3.
German X. (Lessons; Grammar), Mr. Knoepfler 4.

Winter Term.

German XII. (Die Journalisten), Miss Lorenz 5.
French II., Mr. Knoepfler 2.
French V., Mr. Knoepfler 1.

Mathematics.

Solid Geometry, Mr. Wright 3.
College Algebra I., Mr. Cory 2.
Plane Trigonometry, Mr. Condit 2-3.
Differential Calculus, Mr. Condit 1.

Chemistry.

Chemistry I., Mr. Bond 4.
Chemistry II., Mr. Reed 3.
Chemistry III., IV., V., Mr. Bond 5-6.

Physics.

Physics I, Mr. Begeman 2.
Physics II., Mr. Begeman 4.
Physics IV., V., Mr. Begeman 5.
Physics, Advanced Laboratory Course, Mr. Begeman 6.

Natural Science.

Physiology I., Mr. Newton 2.
Botany II., Mr. Davis 2.
Botany II., Laboratory, Mr. Davis (Mon., Wed.) 4.
Hygiene and Sanitation, Mr. Newton 5.
Zoology II., Mr. Arey 1.
Zoology II., Laboratory, Mr. Arey (2 days) 5.
Geology I., Mr. Cable 2.
Commercial Geography of Europe, Miss Aitchison 5.
Influences of Geography upon American History, Mr. Cable 4.

History.

American History, Miss Riggs 1.
Roman History, Miss Rice 2-3.
Medieval History, Miss Riggs 2.
Eighteenth Century History, Miss Riggs 4.

Government.

American Government, Mr. Meyerholz 3.
American Constitutional History II., Mr. Meyerholz 5.
English Government, Mr. Meyerholz 4.

Economics.

General Economics, Mr. McKitrick 5; Mr. Morgan 1.
English Industrial History, Mr. McKitrick 1.
Money and Banking, Mr. McKitrick 2.

Winter Term.

Drawing.

History of Architecture and Sculpture, Miss Thornton 1.

Manual Training.

Manual Training Methods II., Mr. Bailey 2.

Physical Education.

Anatomy II., Mr. Seymour 3.

Music.

Music II., Mr. Fullerton 2.
Harmony I., Mr. Fullerton (Mon., Wed., Fri.) 4.
Harmony III., Mr. Frampton (Mon., Wed., Thurs.) 1.
History of Music II., Miss Childs (Mon., Wed., Thurs.) 3.

SPECIAL TEACHER COURSES.

Professional Instruction in Education.

Psychology I., Miss Buck 1-2.
Psychology II., Miss Buck 3-5; Mr. Mount 1-2-4.
Primary Methods, 1st term, Miss McGovern 5.
Primary Methods, 2nd term, Miss McGovern 1-2-3.

Training in Teaching.

Primary Criticism, Miss Hatcher (Tues., Thurs.) 6.
Kindergarten Theory, 2nd term, Miss Ward 1.
Kindergarten Theory, 4th term, Miss Ward 5.
Kindergarten Practise, Miss Ward 2-3.
Montessori Methods of Child Training, Miss Ward 4.

Chemistry.

Chemistry I., (Home Econ.) Mr. Bond 1.
Chemistry II. (Home Econ.) Mr. Reed 1-2.

Drawing.

Drawing (Primary), 1st term, Miss Thornton 3-4; Miss Iver-
    son 1.
Drawing (Primary), 2nd term, Miss Iverson 2.
Drawing (Kindergarten), 2nd term, Miss Iverson 3.
Cast Drawing, Miss Patt 5.
Water Color, Miss Thornton 2.

Manual Training.

Mechanical Drawing, Mr. Bailey 4-5.
Woodwork, 1st term, Mr. Brown 2.
Woodwork, 2nd term, Mr. Brown 4.
Woodwork, Advanced, Mr. Brown 5.
Wood Turning, Mr. Brown 5-6.
Sheet Metal Work, Mr. Bailey 3.

Winter Term.

Primary Handwork, Mrs. McMahon 2-3.
Elementary Handwork, Mrs. McMahon 1.

Physical Education.

Playground Methods, Mr. Seymour 5.
History and Literature of Physical Training, Mr. Seymour 4.

Music.

Appreciation, Mr. Fullerton (Tues., Fri.) 1.
Sightsinging and Methods, Miss Stenwall (Tues., Thurs.) 4.

Commercial.

Penmanship, Advanced, Mr. Cummins 3.
Bookkeeping, 2nd term, Mr. Cummins 4.
Shorthand, 1st term, Mr. Coffey 3.
Shorthand, 2nd term, Mr. Coffey 1.
Typewriting, Mr. Coffey 5.
Typewriting, 2nd term, Mr. Coffey 4.
Commercial Correspondence, Mr. Coffey 2.

Home Economics.

Sewing, 2nd term—

Miss Heinz (Daily) 8:55 to 9:50.
Miss Heinz (Fri.) 10:20 to 11:15; (Tues., Thurs.) 10:20 to 12:10.
Miss Heinz (Mon., Wed., Fri.) 11:15 to 12:10; (Mon., Wed.) 10:20 to 11:15.
Miss Heinz (Mon., Wed., Fri.) 1:30 to 2:25; (Mon., Wed.) 2:25 to 3:20.
Miss Freer (Mon., Wed., Fri.) 8:55 to 9:50: (Mon., Wed.) 8:00 to 8:55.
Miss Freer (Tues., Thurs., Fri.) 1:30 to 2:25; (Tues., Thurs.) 2:25 to 3:20.

Elementary Food Theory, 2nd term—

Miss Townsend (Mon., Wed.) 1:30 to 4:00.
Miss Sheets (Mon., Wed.) 10:00 to 12:10.
Miss Sheets (Tues., Thurs.) 10:00 to 12:10.
Miss Sheets (Tues., Thurs.) 1:30 to 4:00.
Miss Sheets (Mon., Wed.) 1:30 to 4:00.

Dietetics, 2nd term—

Miss Townsend, Miss Sheets, and ———(Tues., Wed., Thurs.) 4:00 to 7:30.

Principles of Selection and Preparation of Foods, 2nd term—

Miss Townsend (Mon., Wed.) 8:00 to 8:55.
Miss Townsend (Tues., Thurs.) 8:00 to 8:55.
Miss Townsend (Tues., Thurs.) 8:55 to 9:50.

Winter Term.

Household Architecture—
    Miss Townsend (Mon., Wed.) 3.
    Miss Townsend (Tues., Thurs.) 3.

NORMAL COURSES.

Professional Instruction in Education.

Rural Education (Didactics), Mr. Campbell 2.
Rural School Problems, Mr. Campbell 1.
Elementary Psychology, 2nd term, Mr. Campbell 3.
The Country School, Mr. Campbell 5.

Training in Teaching.

Observation (Rural School), Mr. Dick 4.

English.

Orthography, Miss Oliver 1-2.
English Grammar, 1st half, Miss Hearst 2-3-4.
English Grammar, 2nd half, Miss Gregg 5.
English Grammar, Complete, Miss Gregg 3-4.
Reading, Miss Falkler 2.
Elocution, Miss Falkler 4-5.
English Classics, 1st term, Miss Oliver 4.
English Classics, 2nd term, Miss Hearst 5.
English Composition, 1st term, Miss Gregg 2; ————3.
English Composition, 2nd term, ————4.

Latin.

Latin Lessons, 1st term, Mr. Merchant 3.
Latin Lessons, 2nd term, Miss Call 2.
Caesar, 2nd term, Miss Call 4.

German.

German, 1st term, Miss Nolte 2.
German, 2nd term, Miss Nolte 1.
German, 3rd term, Miss Nolte 4.
German, 4th term, Miss Nolte 3.

Mathematics.

Arithmetic, 1st half, Mr. Cory 4-5.
Arithmetic, 2nd half, Miss Lambert 3-4.
Arithmetic, Complete, Mr. Cory 1; Miss Lambert 2.
Algebra, 1st term, Miss Lambert 5.
Algebra, 2nd term, Miss Allen 1-2.
Algebra, 1st and 2nd terms, Mr. Condit 5.
Algebra, 3rd term, Miss Allen 3-4.
Plane Geometry, 1st term, Mr. Wright 4.
Plane Geometry, 2nd term, Mr. Wright 2-5.

Winter Term.

Physics.

Physics, 1st term, Mr. Hersey 3; Mr. Kadesch 1-4.
Physics, 2nd term, Mr. Hersey 2-5; Mr. Kadesch 3.

Natural Science.

Geography, 1st half, Miss Aitchison 1.
Geography, 2nd half, Miss Aitchison 2.
Geography, Complete, Miss Aitchison 3.
Physiology, Mr. Newton 3-4.
Physiography, Mr. Cable 1-5.
Agriculture, 2nd term, Mr. Davis 1-3.
Agriculture, Short Course, Mr. Davis 5.

History.

U. S. History, 1st half, —————2-4.
U. S. History, 2nd half, Miss Rice 1.
U. S. History, Complete, Miss Riggs 5; ————— 1
General History, 1st term, Miss Rice 4.

Government.

Civics of United States, Mr. Morgan 2.
Civics, Review, Mr. Meyerholz 1.
Iowa Civics, Mr. Morgan 3.

Economics.

Elementary Economics, Mr. McKitrick 4; Mr. Morgan 5.

Drawing.

Drawing, 1st term, Miss Patt 1-3; Miss Iverson 5.
Drawing, 2nd term, Miss Patt 4.

Music.

Vocal Music, 1st term, Miss Stenwall 2-5; Miss Giberson 1.
Vocal Music, 2nd term, Miss Stenwall 3; Miss Giberson 2-4.

Manual Training.

Handwork, Mrs. McMahon 5.
Woodwork, 1st term, Mr. Brown 2.
Woodwork, 2nd term, Mr. Brown 4.

Commercial.

Penmanship, 1st term, Mr. Cummins 1-3-5.
Bookkeeping, 1st term, Mr. Cummins 2.

Home Economics.

Cooking and Household Management, 1st term—
—————(Mon., Wed.) 1:30 to 4:00.
Cooking and Household Management, 2nd term—

Winter Term.

—————————(Tues., Thurs.) 1:30 to 4:00.

Sewing, 1st term—

Miss Freer (Daily) 10:20 to 11:15.

Sewing, 2nd term—

Miss Freer (Mon., Wed., Fri.) 1:30 to 2:25; (Mon., Wed.)
2:25 to 3:20.

PHYSICAL TRAINING

1st term Physical Training.

Miss Hussey (Tues., Thurs.) 5.

2nd term Physical Training.

Miss Hussey (Mon., Wed.) 5.
Miss Wild (Tues., Thurs.) 5; (Mon., Wed.) 6.
Miss Nisbet (Tues., Thurs.) 3-6-7.

3rd term Physical Training.

Miss Wild (Tues., Thurs.) 7.
Miss Nisbet (Mon., Wed.) 6.

Adv. Physical Training (for special students in this department)

Miss Hussey (Tues., Thurs.) 7.

2nd term Physical Training (Primary).

Miss Wild (Mon., Wed.) 4.

Gymnastics, First Year.

Mr. Berkstresser (Mon., Wed.) 4; (Mon. Thurs.) 6.

Gymnastics, Second Year.

Mr. Berkstresser (Tues., Thurs.) 7.

Gymnastics, Third Year.

Mr. Seymour (Mon., Wed.) 7.

Basket Ball.

Miss Hussey (Mon. Wed.) 4-6.
Miss Wild (Mon., Wed.) 5.
Miss Nisbet (Mon., Wed.) 3-7.
Mr. Berkstresser (Tues., Fri.) 6.

Baseball

Miss Nisbet (Tues., Thurs.) 5.

Corrective Work.

Miss Nisbet (Mon., Tues., Wed., Thurs.) 8.

Winter Term.

Rhythm, 1st term.

    Miss Wild (Tues., Thurs.) 6; (Mon., Wed.) 7.

Rhythm, 2nd term.

    Miss Hussey (Tues., Thurs.) 6.

Esthetic Dancing.

    Miss Hussey (Tues., Thurs.) 7.

Swimming.

    Mr. Berkstresser (Tues., Thurs.) 4; (Mon., Wed.) 7.

Basket Ball Team.

    Mr. Berkstresser (Daily) 8.

Gymnastic Team.

    Mr. Seymour (Daily) 8.

SPRING TERM

Professional Instruction in Education.

Psychology I., Mr. Samson 1.
Psychology II., Mr. Samson 2-4-5.
School Management, Mr. Colegrove 1-2-3-4.
History of Education, Mr. Walters 1-2-3.
Philosophy of Education, Mr. Walters 4.
Experimental Psychology, Mr. Mount 5.
Genetic Psychology, Mr. Mount 4.
Social and Sex Psychology, Mr. Colegrove 6.

English.

Rhetoric, Mr. Lynch 4; Mr. Gist 1; ————3.
Elocution I., Miss Falkler 3; ———— 1.
Public Speaking I., Mr. Barnes 1.
Argumentation, Mr. Barnes 5.
Elocution II., ————2-4.
Public Speaking II., Mr. Barnes 3.
English Literature, Mr. Lynch 1; Miss Carpenter 2-4; Miss Lambert 3.
Anglo Saxon and Middle English, Mr. Gist 4.
Shakespeare, Mr. Gist 3.
Literary Criticism, Miss Carpenter 3.
English Literature of the Nineteenth Centry, Miss Lambert 1.
American Literature, Miss Lambert 4.
Repertoire I., Miss Martin 2.
Principles of Expression, Miss Martin 1.
The Teaching of English, Mr. Lynch 2.

Latin and Greek.

Horace (Odes), Mr. Merchant 1.
Composition, Mr. Merchant (Tues., Thurs.) 2.
Roman Literature, Mr. Merchant (Mon., Wed., Fri.) 2.
Historical Latin Grammar, Mr. Merchant (Tues., Thurs.) 3.
Elementary Greek, 3rd term, Mr. Merchant (Mon., Wed., Fri.) 5.
Cicero's Orations, 1st term, Miss Call 4.
Cicero's Orations, 2nd term, Miss Call 3.
Ovid, Miss Call 1.

Spring Term.

German and French.

German I., (Die Jungfrau von Orleans), Miss Lorenz 3.
German II., (Prose Composition), Miss Lorenz 2.
German V., (Iphigenie auf Tauris; Die Braut von Messina),
Miss Lorenz 1.
German VIII. (German Classics), Mr. Knoepfler 3.
German XI. (Immensee), Mr. Knoepfler 4.
German XII. (Die Journalisten), Miss Lorenz 5.
French III., Mr. Knoepfler 2.
French VI., Mr. Knoepfler 1.

Mathematics.

Solid Geometry, Mr. Wright 5.
College Algebra I., Mr. Cory 4.
Plane Trigonometry, Mr. Cory 5.
College Algebra II., Mr. Condit 2.
Spherical Trigonometry and Surveying, Mr. Condit 5.
History and Teaching of Mathematics, Mr. Condit 3.
Integral Calculus, Mr. Condit 1.

Chemistry.

Chemistry I., Mr. Reed 3.
Chemistry II., Mr. Reed 4.
Chemistry III., IV., V., Mr. Bond 5.
Chemistry IV., V., Mr. Bond 6.

Physics

Physics I., Mr. Begeman 2.
Physics III., Mr. Begeman 4.
Physics V., VI., Mr. Begeman 5-6.

Natural Science.

Physiology I., Mr. Newton 3-4.
Botany II., Mr. Davis 1.
Botany II., Laboratory, Mr. Davis (Tues., Thurs.) 6.
Zoology III., Mr. Arey 1.
Zoology, Laboratory, Mr. Arey (by arrangement) 2.
Geology II., Mr. Cable 2.
Astronomy, Mr. Cable 4.
Commercial Geography of North America, Miss Aitchison 5.
Agriculture I., Mr. Davis 5.

History.

English History, Miss Rice 1-2.
Nineteenth Century History, Miss Riggs 1.
Method History, Miss Riggs 3.

Spring Term.

Government.

>   American Government, Mr. Meyerholz 4.
>   Modern European Governments, Mr. Meyerholz 5.
>   Constitutional Law, Mr. Meyerholz 3.

Economics.

>   General Economics, Mr. McKitrick 3; Mr. Morgan 5.
>   Social and Economic Problems, Mr. McKitrick 1.
>   Public Finance, Mr. McKitrick 2.

Drawing.

>   History of Painting, Miss Thornton 1.

Manual Training.

>   Organization and Economics of Manual Training, Mr. Bailey 2.

Music.

>   Music I., Mr. Fullerton 3.
>   Music II., Mr. Fullerton 2.
>   Harmony II., Mr. Fullerton (Mon., Wed., Thurs.) 2.
>   Harmony IV., Mr. Frampton (Mon., Wed., Thurs.) 1
>   History of Music I., Miss Childs (Mon., Wed., Thurs.) 4.

SPECIAL TEACHER COURSES.

Professional Instruction in Education.

>   Psychology I., Miss Buck 1-2.
>   Psychology II., Miss Buck 5; Mr. Mount 1-2.
>   Primary Methods, 3rd term. Miss McGovern 1-3-4.

Training in Teaching.

>   Observation in Training School (Primary), Miss Hatcher 2.
>   Primary Criticism, Miss Hatcher (Tues., Thurs.) 6.
>   Primary Theory (Kindergarten), Miss Hatcher 5.
>   Kindergarten Theory and Observation (Primary), Miss Ward 2
>   Kindergarten Theory, 3rd term, Miss Ward 3.
>   Kindergarten Theory, 5th term, Miss Ward 4.
>   Kindergarten Practise, Miss Ward 2-3.

Chemistry.

>   Chemistry I., (Home Econ.) ——————— 2.
>   Chemistry II., (Home Econ.) Mr. Reed 1.
>   Chemistry VI., (Home Econ.) Mr. Bond 2.

Natural Science.

>   Nature Study, Mr. Arey 5.

Spring Term.

Drawing.

>Drawing (Primary), 2nd term, Miss Thornton 3; Miss Iverson 1-4.
>Water Color, Miss Thornton 4.
>Design, Miss Patt 5.
>Design for Household Art, Miss Patt 1.
>Supervision in Art, Miss Thornton 2.

Manual Training.

>Mechanical Drawing, Mr. Bailey 5.
>Woodwork, 1st term, Mr. Brown 2.
>Woodwork, 2nd term, Mr. Brown 4.
>Woodwork, 3rd and 4th terms, Mr. Brown 5.
>Wood Turning, Mr. Brown 5-6.
>Sheet Metal Work, Mr. Bailey 3.
>Primary Handwork, Mrs. McMahon 2-5.
>Elementary Handwork, Mrs. McMahon 3.

Physical Education.

>Physiology of Exercise, Mr. Seymour 3.
>Medical Gymnastics and Massage, Mr. Seymour 4.

Music.

>Supervision, Mr. Fullerton (Fri.) 1; Miss Stenwall (Tues.) 1.
>Sightsinging and Conducting, Miss Stenwall (Tues., Fri.) 1.
>Methods, Miss Stenwall (Tues., Fri.) 4.

Commercial.

>Penmanship, Advanced, Mr. Cummins 4.
>Bookkeeping, 3rd term, Mr. Cummins 1.
>Shorthand, 2nd term, Mr. Coffey 1.
>Shorthand, 3rd term, Mr. Coffey 3.
>Typewriting, 2nd term, Mr. Coffey 5.
>Typewriting, 2nd and 3rd terms, Mr. Coffey 4.
>Commercial Law, Mr. Coffey 2.

Home Economics.

>Sewing, 3rd term—

>>Miss Heinz (Daily) 8:00 to 8:55.
>>Miss Heinz (Tues., Thurs., Fri.) 1:30 to 2:25; (Tues., Thurs.) 2:25 to 3:20.
>>Miss Heinz (Mon., Wed., Fri.) 10:20 to 11:15; (Mon., Wed.) 11:15 to 12:10.
>>Miss Heinz (Tues., Thurs., Fri.) 11:15 to 12:10; (Tues., Thurs.) 10:20 to 11:15.
>>Miss Freer (Tues., Thurs., Fri.) 1:30 to 2:25; (Tues., Thurs.) 2:25 to 3:20.
>>Miss Freer (Mon., Wed., Fri.) 10:20 to 11:15; (Mon., Wed.) 11:15 to 12:10.

Spring Term.

Elementary Food Theory, 3rd term—

Miss Townsend (Tues., Thurs.) 1:00 to 3:15.
Miss Sheets (Mon., Wed.) 1:00 to 3:15
Miss Sheets (Tues., Thurs.) 10:00 to 12:10.
——————(Mon., Wed.) 1:00 to 3:15.
——————(Tues., Thurs.) 10:00 to 12:10.

Demonstrations—

Miss Townsend, Miss Sheets and ——————
    (Tues., Thurs.) 1:00 to 3:15.   .
    (Tues., Thurs.) 3:30 to 5:30.
    (Mon., Wed.) 3:30 to 5:30.

Principles of Selection and Preparation of Foods, 3rd term—

Miss Townsend (Tues., Thurs.) 8:00 to 8:55.
Miss Townsend (Tues., Thurs.) 11:15 to 12:10.
Miss Townsend (Tues., Thurs.) 2:25 to 3:20.

Methods, Home Economics.

Miss Townsend (Mon.) 8:55 to 9:50.

Household Management—

Miss Townsend (Wed.) 8:55 to 9:50.

NORMAL COURSES.

Professional Instruction in Education.

Rural School Management, Mr. Campbell 5.
Rural Education (Didactics), Mr. Campbell 3.
Methods, Miss Buck 3.
Primary Methods (Rural School), Miss McGovern 2.
Rural School Problems, Mr. Campbell 1.
The Country School, Mr. Campbell 4.

Training in Teaching.

Observation (Rural School), Mr. Dick 4.

English.

Orthography, Miss Oliver 1-2.
English Grammar, 1st half, Miss Hearst 5.
English Grammar, 2nd half, Miss Hearst 3-4.
English Grammar, Complete, Miss Gregg 3-4-5.
Reading, Miss Falkler 2.
Elocution, Miss Falkler 4-5.
English Classics, 1st term, Miss Oliver 4.
English Classics, 2nd term, Miss Hearst 1.
English Composition, 1st term, —————— 2.
English Composition, 2nd term, Miss Gregg 2; ——————5.

Latin.

Latin Lessons, 2nd term, Mr. Merchant 3.
Caesar, 1st term, Miss Call 2,

Spring Term.

German.

German, 1st term, Miss Nolte 3.
German, 2nd term, Miss Nolte 2.
German, 3rd term, Miss Nolte 1.
German, 4th term, Miss Nolte 4.

Mathematics.

Arithmetic, 1st half, Miss Lambert 2.
Arithmetic, 2nd half, Mr. Cory 1-2.
Arithmetic, Complete, Miss Lambert 4; Miss Allen 1.
Algebra, 1st term, Miss Allen 5.
Algebra, 2nd term, Miss Lambert 1.
Algebra, 1st and 2nd terms, Miss Lambert 3.
Algebra, 3rd term, Miss Allen 3-4.
Plane Geometry, 1st term, Mr. Wright 3.
Plane Geometry, 2nd term, Mr. Wright 2.
Solid Geometry, Mr. Wright 4.

Physics.

Physics, 1st term, Mr. Hersey 1; Mr. Kadesch 2-3.
Physics, 2nd term, Mr. Hersey 3-4; Mr. Kadesch 5.

Natural Science.

Geography, 1st half, Miss Aitchison 4.
Geography, 2nd half, Miss Aitchison 1.
Geography, Complete, Miss Aitchison 3.
Physiology, Mr. Newton 2.
Physiography, Mr. Cable 1-5.
Agriculture, 1st term, Mr. Davis 2.
Agriculture, 3rd term, Mr. Davis 3.
Agriculture, Short Course, Mr. Davis 4.
General Botany, Mr. Newton 1.
Elementary Zoology, Mr. Arey 3.

History.

U. S. History, 1st half, Miss Rice 3.
U. S. History, 2nd half, Miss Rice 4.
U. S. History, Complete, Miss Riggs 4.
General History, 2nd term, Miss Riggs 2.

Government.

Civics of Iowa, Mr. Morgan 1.
Civics of United States, Mr. Morgan 2. ·
Civics, Review, Mr. Meyerholz 2.

Economics.

Elementary Economics, Mr. McKitrick 4; Mr. Morgan 3.

Spring Term.

Drawing.

> Drawing, 1st term, Miss Patt 3; Miss Iverson 2-5.
> Drawing, 2nd term, Miss Patt 4.

Music.

> Vocal Music, 1st term, Miss Stenwall 3-5; Miss Giberson 1.
> Vocal Music, 2nd term, Miss Giberson 3-4.

Manual Training.

> Rural School Manual Training, Mr. Bailey and Mrs. McMahon 1.
> Woodwork, 1st term, Mr. Brown 2.
> Woodwork, 2nd term, Mr. Brown 4.

Commercial.

> Penmanship, 1st term, Mr. Cummins 1-3-5.
> Bookkeeping, 1st term, Mr. Cummins 2.

Home Economics.

> Cooking and Household Management, 1st term—
>
> ———————(Mon., Wed.) 1:00 to 3:15.
>
> Cooking and Household Management, 2nd term—
>
> ———————(Tues., Thurs.) 1:00 to 3:15.
>
> Sewing, 1st term—
> Miss Freer (Daily) 8:55 to 9:50.
>
> Sewing, 2nd term —
> Miss Freer (Daily) 8:00 to 8:55.

PHYSICAL TRAINING.

1st term Physical Training.

> Miss Nisbet (Tues., Thurs.) 6.

2nd term Physical Training.

> Miss Wild (Tues., Thurs.) 6.

3rd term Physical Training.

> Miss Hussey (Mon., Wed.) 5; (Tues., Thurs.) 6.
> Miss Wild (Tues., Thurs.) 5; (Mon., Wed.) 4.
> Miss Nisbet (Tues., Thurs.) 3; (Mon., Wed.) 7.

Gymnastics.

> Mr. Seymour (Tues., Thurs.) 5.

Tennis.

> Miss Hussey (Mon., Wed.) 3; (Tues., Thrus.) 4.
> Miss Wild (Mon., Wed.) 7.

Spring Term.

>Miss Nisbet (Mon., Wed.) 4; (Tues., Thurs.) 5-7.
>Mr. Seymour (Tues., Fri.) 6.
>Mr. Berkstresser (Mon., Wed.) 5.

Swimming.

berson 1.

>Miss Hussey (Mon., Wed.) 4.
>Miss Wild (Mon., Wed.) 3-5.
>Miss Nisbet (Tues., Thurs.) 4; (Mon., Wed.) 6.
>Mr. Berkstresser .(Tues., Thurs.) 5.

. McMahon 1.

Rhythm, 1st term.

>Miss Wild (Mon., Wed.) 6.

Rhythm, 2nd term.

>Miss Wild (Tues., Thurs.) 7.

Basketball and Baseball.

>Miss Hussey (Mon., Wed.) 6.

Esthetic Dancing.

>Miss Hussey (Tues., Thurs.) 7.

Advanced Physical Training (for special students in this depart-ment.)

>Miss Hussey (Mon., Wed.) 7.

Baseball.

>Mr. Berkstresser (Tues., Fri.) 6; (Mon., Thurs.) 6; (Mon. Wed.) 4.

Track.

>Mr. Seymour (Mon., Thurs.) 6.

Golf.

>Mr. Seymour (Mon., Wed.) 5.

Baseball Team.

>Mr. Berkstresser (Daily) 7.

Track Team.

>Mr. Seymour (Daily) 7.

BULLETIN

OF THE

Iowa State Teachers College

CEDAR FALLS, IOWA

———

Courses of Study

and

Program of Recitations

FOR THE SCHOOL YEAR

1914-1915

———

XV

VOL. ~~XVI~~. NO. 2

JULY 1914

———

Issued Quarterly   Publisht by the Iowa State Teachers College.
Entered as second-class mail matter August 31, 1912,
at the post office at Cedar Falls, Iowa, under
the Act of Congress, August 24, 1912

Vol. XVI.   *JULY 1914*   *No. 2*

BULLETIN

OF THE

IOWA STATE TEACHERS COLLEGE

CEDAR FALLS, IOWA

COURSES OF STUDY

AND

PROGRAM OF RECITATIONS

FOR SCHOOL YEAR 1914-1915

The shorter forms of spelling found in this Bulletin are adopted for their simplicity and are accepted by either the Webster's New International Dictionary or the Funk & Wagnall's Standard Dictionary. They are supported by the best linguistic scholarship and are to be preferred by teachers in the public schools.

IOWA STATE TEACHERS COLLEGE

SCHOOL CALENDAR FOR 1914-1915.

Fall Term—Twelve Weeks

Wednesday, September 2, 1914,
Tuesday, November 24, 1914.

Winter Term—Twelve Weeks,

Wednesday, November 25, 1914,
Tuesday, December 22, 1914—four weeks.

Winter Vacation—two weeks.

Wednesday, January 6, 1915,
Tuesday, March 2, 1915—eight weeks.

Spring Term—Twelve Weeks,

Wednesday, March 3, 1915,
Tuesday, May 25, 1915.

Summer Term—Twelve Weeks,

First Half—Wednesday, May 26, 1915,
Tuesday, July 6, 1915—six weeks.

Second Half—Wednesday, July 7, 1915,
Tuesday, August 17, 1915—six weeks.

Summer Vacation—two weeks.

Note:—If the General Assembly does not approve of the extension of the Summer Term to twelve weeks the Summer Term Calendar will be six weeks—

Wednesday, June 9, 1915,
Tuesday, July 20, 1915.

IOWA STATE TEACHERS COLLEGE

COURSES OF STUDY.

(For full details see General Catalog)

I. THE DEGREE COURSE

Freshman Year—45 term hours

Rhetoric .... 5 term hours
Foreign Language .... 15 " "
Electives .... 25 " "
Literary Society
Physical Training

Note: With the consent of the adviser and the Registrar, Foreign Language may be delayd until the Sophomore year. The Electives must be chosen from Freshman studies designated in the outline of departments that follow.

Sophomore Year—45 term hours

Education I, II, and III. .... 15 term hours
English IX and II, III or VIII .... 10 " "
Electives .... 20 " "
Literary Society
Physical Training

Junior Year—45 term hours

Education IV, V, and VI. .... 15 term hours
Electives .... 30 " "

Senior Year—45 term hours

Teaching .... 10 term hours
Electives .... 35 " "

II. MASTER OF DIDACTICS DEGREE COURSES
FOR
COLLEGE GRADUATES

1. Professional Course—45 term hours

This course includes a full year's work in Education and Teaching and is pland to suit individual needs by the Head of

the Department of Education. With the facilities here for study-
ing rural and city school systems, this year's work is very rich in
development and training.

II. Professional Course with Electives—45 term hours

1. Education .... 15 term hours
2. Teaching .... 10 "   "
3. Elective with the approval of the adviser 20 "   "

III. Professional Course for Special Teachers

This course is pland by the Head of the Department of Education to give training to college graduates who wish to prepare in
the line of experts in rural education, in normal training in high
schools, in Public School Music, in Commercial Subjects, in Physical Education, in Manual Training, in Home Economics, in Drawing, in Kindergarten or in Primary Teaching.

III. THE DIPLOMA COURSES

THE GENERAL TEACHERS COURSE

This course is organized to give two years of instruction and
training to high school graduates who desire to become principals,
supervisors, or grade teachers. It is in conformity with the requirements for a second grade state certificate.

First Year—45 term hours

Education I, II, III. .... 15 term hours
Rhetoric 5   "   "
Electives 25   "   "
Literary Society
Physical Training

Second Year—45 term hours

Education IV. .... 5 term hours
Teaching 10   "   "
Electives 30   "   "
Literary Society
Physical Training

Note 1: The electives above indicated must be taken in Botany, Physiography or Geology, Advanced Physiology or Sanitation, Physics, American History, American Government, and Economics unless the corresponding subjects were presented and accepted for entrance.

6 IOWA STATE TEACHERS COLLEGE

Note 2: An additional requirement of 15 term hours must be met by election under the adviser from Penmanship, Vocal Music, Drawing, Orthography, Arithmetic, or English Grammar unless these subjects were taken in the secondary school.

THE PRIMARY TEACHERS COURSE

First Year—43 term hours

Primary Methods (12 hours) .... 6 term hours
Education I, II, and III. .... 15 " "
Rhetoric .... 5 " "
English Elective .... 5 " "
Nature Study .... 5 " "
Primary Theory and Observation (4 a week).... 2 " "
Drawing (two terms—5 a week) .... 5 " "
Manual Arts (5 a week)
Literary Society
Physical Training

Second Year—47 term hours

Education IV. .... 5 term hours
Hygiene and Sanitation (b) .... 3 " "
Criticism and Practise .... 15 " "
Kindergarten Theory and Observation (4 a week) 2 " "
Electives .... 22 " "
Vocal Music (two terms—5 a week)
Literary Society
Physical Training

THE KINDERGARTNERS COURSE

First Year—47½ term hours

Kindergarten Theory (one year, 5 a week) .... 7½ term hours
Education I, II, and III. .... 15 " "
Rhetoric and Elective in English .... 10 " "
Drawing (two terms, 5 a week) .... 5 " "
Nature Study .... 5 " "
Elective .... 5 " "
Literary Society
Physical Training

Second Year—42½ term hours

Kindergarten Theory (one term, 5 a week, one term, six a week) .... 5½ term hours
Kindergarten Practise, one year .... 15 " "

Education IV .... 5 term hours
Electives .... 15 " "
Primary Theory (4 a week) .... 2 " "
Music (two terms, 5 a week)
Literary Society
Physical Training

THE PUBLIC SCHOOL MUSIC TEACHERS COURSE

First Year—45 term hours

Education I, II, and III. .... 15 term hours
Rhetoric......... .... 5 " "
Harmony I (3 a week) .... 3 " "
History of Music I (2 a week) .... 2 " "
Music I (5 a week) .... 2½ " "
Music II (5 a week) .... 2½ " "
Sight Singing (lower grades, 3 a week)....... 2½ " "
Sight Singing (upper grades, 3 a week)...... 2½ " "
Conducting (3 a week) .... 2½ " "
Methods (lower grades, 3 a week) .... 2½ " "
Elective .... 5 " "
Literary Society
Physical Training

Second Year—45 term hours

Harmony II. (2 a week) .... 2 term hours
History of Music II. (3 a week) .... 3 " "
Teaching I and II. .... 10 " "
Methods (upper grades, 3 a week) .... 2½ " "
High School Music and Child Voice (3 a week) 2½ " "
Appreciation of Music (3 a week) .... 2½ " "
Theory of Music (3 a week) .... 2½ " "
Harmony III. (3 a week) .... 3 " "
Supervision (3 a week) .... 2 " "
Electives ...., ... 15 " "
Literary Society
Physical Training

THE DRAWING TEACHERS COURSE

First and Second Years—90 term hours

Education I, II, and III .... 15 term hours
Teaching I and II. .... 10 " "
Rhetoric .... 5 " "
History of Architecture .... 5 " "

History of Painting ...., ...   5   "   "
Cast Drawing (two terms, 5 a week) ....   2½ "   "
Still Life (one term, 5 a week) ....   2½ "   "
Perspective (one term, 5 a week) ....   2½ "   "
Design (one term, 5 a week)................   2½ "   "
Supervision in Art (one term, 5 a week) ......   2½ "   "
Water-Color (one term, 5 a week) ....   2½ "   "
Elective from Manual Training or Music (one
    term) ....   2½ "   "
Electives ....·...   30 "   "
Literary Society and Physical Training two years.
Other sub-collegiate electives possible ....   15 "   "

THE MANUAL ARTS TEACHERS COURSE

First and Second Years—90 term hours

Education I, II, and III.   15   "   "
Teaching ....   7½   "   "
Rhetoric....   5   "   "
Manual Training Methods I and II   8   "   "
Woodwork   12   "   "
Mechanical Drawing   8   "   "
Wood Turning   2   "   "
Metal Work ....   2½   "   "
Drawing and Design (each 5 a week)   5   "   "
Electives .... :.....   18   "   "
Special Elective   7   "   "
Literary Society and Physical Training each two
    years

THE HOME ECONOMICS TEACHERS COURSE

First Year—44 term hours

Chemistry IX, X, and XI. ....   15 term hours
Rhetoric   5   "   "
Education I and II ....   10 "   "
Elementary Food Theory (three terms)   6   "   "
Food Principles (two terms, 3 a week)   6   "   "
Household Management (2 a week) ....:   1   "   "
Household Methods   1   "   "
Sewing (three terms, 5 a week)
Literary Society
Physical Training

Second Year—46 term hours

Education III and IV .... ·........:	10	term hours
Teaching I and II	10	" "
Chemistry XIII	5	" "
Hygiene and Sanitation (a)	5	" "
Physiology I	5	" "
Dietetics (2 a week)	1	term hour
Advanced Cooking (2 a week)	1	" "
Serving (2 a week)...........................	1	" "
Household Architecture (2 a week)	2	term hours
Demonstrations	1	term hour
Elective	5	term hours
Literary Society		
Physical Training		

THE PHYSICAL EDUCATION TEACHERS COURSE

First Year—45 term hours

Anatomy I and II	10	term hours
Physiology I	5	" "
Education I, II, and III ....··..	15	" "
Rhetoric	5	" "
Public Speaking I or Elocution I	5	" "
English Literature	5	" "
Literary Society		
Double Work in Physical Training		

Second Year—45 term hours

Theory of Physical Education	5	term hours
Hygiene and Sanitation (a) ....,.	5	" "
Chemistry I, II, and III....	15	" "
Education IV ....··.........	5	" "
Play Ground Methods I	3	" "
First Aid to the Injured	2	" "
Genetic Psychology	5	" "
Play Ground Methods II	3	" "
Theory of Athletics I	2	" "
Literary Society		
Double Work in Physical Training		

Third Year—45 term hours

Anthropometry	3	term hours
Physical Diagnosis	2	" "
Theory of Athletics II	2	" "

Physiology of Exercise .... 5 term hours
Medical Gymnastics and Massage 3   "   "
Physical Department Administration 2   "   "
Teaching I and II .... 10 "   "
History of Physical Education 3   "   "
Electives .... 15 "   "
Physical Training and Officiating

THE COMMERCIAL TEACHERS COURSE

First Year—45 term hours

Education I, II, III .... 15 term hours
Rhetoric 5   "   "
Mathematical Elective   5   "   "
Commercial Correspondence 5   "   "
Commercial Law 5   "   "
Accounting I and II .... 10 "   "
Literary Society
Physical Training

Second Year—45 term hours

American Government ....·.... 5 term hours
Education IV ....·.. 5   "   "
General Economics ...._......... 5   "   "
Commercial Geography 5   "   "
Teaching I and II ....·.... 10 "   "
Electives .... 15 "   "
Shorthand and Typewriting, (three terms)
Literary Society
Physical Training

Note: The subjects Shorthand and Typewriting are additional to the 90 term hours required in diploma courses and must be taken not less than one year.

IV. NORMAL DIPLOMA COURSES

THE RURAL TEACHERS COURSE

The lowest admission is on the basis of the rural school diploma.

The recognition for graduation is the rural teacher diploma and the state certificate for five years.

The branches included in the course are as follows:

Second Grade Uniform County Certificate Subjects

Reading
Geography
Arithmetic
U. S. History
Orthography
English Language and Grammar
Physiology
Vocal Music
Penmanship

Note: Each subject represented here is given credit on the course when the student has received 85 per cent on a Uniform County Certificate. When 75 per cent has been received, one term's work is required in each subject. When less than 75 per cent has been received two term's work is required in Geography, Arithmetic, Language and Grammar, and United States History.

First Grade Uniform County Certificate Subjects

Elementary Civics
Elementary Economics
Algebra
Physics

Note: When 85 per cent has been obtaind in the uniform county examination that subject is given a credit on this course. When taken in class, one term's work is required in Civics and Economics, and two terms' work in Algebra and Physics.

Additional Subjects Required for the Diploma

(1)   Didactics, one term
(2)   Primary Methods, one term
(3)   The Country School, one term
(4)   Observation and Teaching, one term
(5)   Sewing, one term
(6)   Cooking, two terms
(7)   Agriculture, two terms
(8)   Handwork, one term
(9)   Woodwork, one term
(10) Elementary Psychology

Note: The Observation and Teaching here outlined consists of Illustrative Teaching work in the training department and

in work done in the demonstration rural schools maintaind
by the Teachers College. This term's work will be provided during each term of the college year so that the graduating class may
be divided into suitable sections.

The subjects of study represented by this course are all on the
program of recitations each term of the year so that a student can
come any time and get credit work. Uniform county certificate
examinations are given at the institution on the same dates as are
required by law at the county superintendents' offices.

THE GENERAL NORMAL COURSE FOR GRADE TEACHERS

Admission: First Grade Uniform County Certificate.
Recognition: The Normal Diploma and Second Grade State
Certificate.

Value of Credits: Each subject printed in this table represents 5 term hours, requiring five recitations a week of one hour
each.

First Year

Algebra, 2d and 3d	Two terms
Physics,	One term
*El. Sanitation,	One term
English Classics,	One term
Vocal Music,	One term
General History,	Two terms
*Bookkeeping,	One term
Drawing,	Two terms
*El. Elocution,	One term
Physical Training,	Three terms

Second Year

Physics,	One term
Plane Geometry,	Two terms
*Solid Geometry,	One term
Phychology,	Two terms
*Drawing,	One term
*El. Physiography,	One term
Elective,	One term
General Botany,	One term
School Management	One term
English Classics,	One term
Physical Training,	Three terms
Literary Society Work,	Three terms

*Latin or German Elective may be substituted.

Third Year

Rhetoric, ...	One term
College Algebra I or Trigonometry, ...	One term
History of Education, ...	One term
Special Elective, ...	Three terms
English Literature, ...	One term
Economics I., ...	One term .
Teaching, ..., ...	Two terms
American Government, ...	One term
American History, ... ·	One term
Literary Society Work, ...	Three terms

Notes: Students who have completed the vocational work, the Algebra or the Physics required in the Rural Teachers Course will be granted credit in proportion to the work accomplished, thus abridging the above requirements.

The Special Electives of the third year as designated are intended for Vocal Music and Drawing beyond the tabulated subjects in the same line, or in Manual Training, Home Economics, Commercial Studies, or Agriculture, as the student may elect.

THE VOCATIONAL NORMAL COURSE

For teachers of rural and consolidated schools.

Admission: First Grade Uniform County Certificate.

Recognition: The Normal Diploma and Second Grade State Certificate. ·

Value of Credits: Each subject represents 5 term hours, requiring five lessons a week of one hour each.

First Year

Sewing, ...	Two terms
Algebra, 2d and 3d ...... ·	Two terms
Vocal Music, ...	Two terms
English Classics, ...·..	Two terms
Drawing, ... '.........	Two terms
Penmanship and Bookkeeping, ...	One term
El. Sanitation, ...	One term
Cooking, ...	One term
General History, ...	One term
English Composition, ...	One term
Physical Training, ...	Three terms

Second Year

Cooking,	One term
General History,	One term
Plane Geometry,	Two terms
Psychology,	Two terms
El. Elocution,	One term
El. Physiography,	One term
Agriculture,	One term
Farm Botany,	One term
Rural School Management,	One term
American History,	One term
Physical Training,	Three terms
Literary Society Work,	Three terms

Third Year

Agriculture,	One term
Rhetoric	One term
Economics I,	One term
History of Education,	One term
English Literature,	One term
American Government,	One term
Manual Training,	Two terms
Physics,	Two terms
Teaching,	Two terms
Literary Society Work,	Three terms

Note:—This course is arranged for the giving of special qualifications of a superior kind in modern standards. None of these courses are to be the equivalent of College Courses as they will be taught so as to give the teacher in training more practical efficiency in educating the boys and girls of the farms of the state. The practise in teaching will be broad in its scope and notably efficient in its extent.

SPECIAL NORMAL COURSES

Preparation for the examination given by the State Educational Board of Examiners for special teacher certificates.

Teachers of twenty-one years of age and others that may be holders of first grade uniform county certificates are admitted to such classes in special courses in Primary, Kindergarten, Public School Music, Manual Training, Home Economics, Drawing, or Commercial studies as will properly prepare them for the examinations that are required by the state for the obtaining of such recognition. Such persons should make all arrangements with the Registrar before appearing for work in order to have their studies properly pland.

V. SPECIAL COURSES IN VOICE, PIANO, ORGAN, AND ORCHESTRAL INSTRUMENTS.

VOICE, PIANO AND ORGAN

These courses are pland to train students for capability as performers and for becoming special teachers.

The requirements for graduation are as follows:

1. Two lessons a week for at least two years in the major course, all this work to be done if possible under the instructor recommending for graduation.

2. Satisfactory public performance of a recital in the major study, the program to be of moderate difficulty.

3. Two years of a "minor" course in Music (Piano, Organ, Voice, or any of the Instruments taught in the Orchestra Department). It is understood that two lessons a week in the minor for one year shall not be the equivalent of two years' study.

4. Harmony equivalent to the texts of Chadwick or Bussler.

5. Two terms of Music History.

6. One five hour course of general culture each term, except the Senior year. This course to be selected by the personal adviser of the student, and to be of college grade in case the student has no entrance deficiencies.

7. To complete this course, a student must meet the college entrance requirements.

8. Literary Society work is recommended but not required.

VIOLIN AND OTHER ORCHESTRAL INSTRUMENTS

This course is pland to train a student for capability as a performer and for becoming a special teacher.

The requirements for graduation are as follows:

1. Violin instruction sufficient to enable the pupil to render a program the equivalent of a Beethoven Sonata, the Mendelssohn Concerto and similar modern works, to the satisfaction of the head of the department.

2.   Two years of piano (one lesson a week).

3.   Two years of Harmony—the equivalent of Chadwick or Bussler.

4.   Two years of ear training and dictation in relation to the Harmony.

5.   Orchestra and Ensemble during the course.

6.   Two terms of Music History.

The diploma of the college will be given when the student has satisfactorily completed this course, together with the requirements for college entrance. The certificate of Musical Proficiency to be granted those who finish the Violin course alone.

All students shall take at least one scholastic branch each term they are enrolled unless they are excused by the head of the department.

The courses for all other orchestral instruments, including Oboe, Flute, Clarinet, Bassoon, Cornet, French Horn, Trombone, Tuba, Cello, Double Bass and Harp are identical with the Violin Course. It is possible, however, to finish the courses of some of these instruments in less time than that of the Violin.

VI. DETAILS OF THE REQUIREMENTS FOR THE DEGREE OF BACHELOR OF ARTS IN EDUCATION.

The Major Study: Each student in the Degree Course must select a major study not later than the beginning of the Junior year. This selection assigns the head of the department in which the major is found as the adviser of said student during the pursuance of the course. The following are the major studies offerd.

1.   English
2.   Public Speaking
3.   Latin
4.   German
5.   French
6.   Mathematics
7.   Physics
8.   Chemistry
9.   Earth Science
10.   Biological Science
11.   History

12. Government
13. Economics
14. Education
15. Drawing
16. Manual Training
17. Home Economics
18. Physical Education

A major consists of 30 term hours work in the department chosen. The student may take 60 term hours in his major study, with the consent of the adviser.

The Minor Study: Under the direction of the adviser the student must select also a minor study which must include not less than 15 term hours nor more than 30 term hours. When the major and minor are chosen from the same group as hereafter outlined, not more than a total of 75 term hours can be taken in the two elections combined.

Groups of Courses: The following groups of courses are presented as plans for determining the standards that must be met in arranging an individual course of study leading to a degree:

I. The Professional Group.
II. The English Group.
III. The Foreign Language Group.
IV. The History, Government, and Economics Group.
V. The Science and Mathematics Group.
VI. The Home Economics, Drawing, Physical Education, or Manual Training Group.

Regulations Governing Groups

1. *The Professional Group.* When the Major is in the professional group the following other subjects are required: (1) The Minor of from 15 to 30 term-hours; (2) English, 15 term-hours; (3) Foreign Language, 15 term-hours; (4) History, Government, and Economics, 15 term-hours; (5) Science and Mathematics, 20 term-hours. The largest amount permitted in any subordinate major subject is 20 term-hours.

2. *The English Group.* When the Major is in the English group, the following other subjects are required: (1) The Minor of from 15 to 30 term-hours; (2) Professional, 40 term-hours; (3) Foreign Language, 15 term-hours; (4) History, Government, and Economics, 15 term-hours; (5) Science and Mathematics, 20 term-hours. The largest amount permitted in any subordinate major subject is 20 term-hours.

3. *The Foreign Language Group.* When the Major is in the Foreign Language group the following other subjects are required: (1) The Minor of from 15 to 30 term-hours; (2) Professional, 40 term-hours; (3) English, 15 term-hours; (4) History, Government, and Economics, 15 term-hours; (5) Science and Mathematics, 20 term-hours. The largest amount permitted in any subordinate major subject is 20 term-hours.

4. *The History, Government, and Economics Group.* When the Major is in the History, Government, and Economics group the following other subjects are required: (1) The Minor of from 15 to 30 term-hours; (2) Professional, 40 term-hours; (3) English, 15 term-hours; (4) Foreign Language, 15 term-hours; (5) Science and Mathematics, 20 term-hours. The largest amount permitted in any subordinate major subject is 20 term-hours.

5. *The Science and Mathematics Group.* When the Major is in the Science and Mathematics group, the following other subjects are required: (1) The Minor of from 15 to 30 term-hours; (2) Professional, 40 term-hours; (3) English, 15 term-hours; (4) Foreign Language, 15 term-hours; (5) History, Government, and Economics, 15 term-hours. The largest amount permitted in any subordinate major subject is 20 term-hours.

6. *The Home Economics, Drawing, Manual Arts, or Physical Education Group.* When the Major is in Home Economics, Drawing, Manual Training, or Physical Education, the following other subjects are required: (1) The Minor of from 15 to 30 term hours; (2) Professional, 40 term-hours; (3) English, 15 term-hours; (4) Foreign Language, 15 term-hours; (5) History, Government, and Economics, 15 term-hours; (6) Science and Mathematics, 30 term-hours. The largest amount permitted in any subordinate major subject is 20 term-hours.

DEPARTMENT COURSES

(All courses give 5 hours credit unless otherwise stated)

(For full details see General Catalog.)

Education.

(a) Degree Courses
  I.   Psychology I.
  II. Psychology II.
  III. School Management
  IV. History of Education
  V.   Philosophy of Education

VI. School Administration
VII. Logic—2 hr. cr.
VIII. Ethics—2 hr. cr.
IX. Experimental Psychology
X. Genetic Psychology
XI. Educational Classics
XII. Rural School Problems
(b) Diploma Courses
    1. Psychology I.
    2. Psychology II.
    3. Primary Methods I.—2½ hr. cr.
    4. Primary Methods II.—2½ hr. cr.
    5. Primary Methods III.—1 hr. cr.
(c) Normal Courses
    1. Didactics
    2. The Country School
    3. Elementary Psychology
    4. General Primary Methods

eaching

(a) Degree Courses
   I. Teaching I.
   II. Teaching II.
   III. Teaching III.
(b) Diploma Courses
Same as Degree Courses and
    1. Kindergarten Theory I. to IV.—each 2½ hr. cr.
    2. Kindergarten Theory V.—3 hr. cr.
    3. Kg. Theory for Primary Teachers— 2 hr. cr.
    4. Primary Theory for Kindergarten Teachers—2 hr. cr.
    5. Primary Criticism—3 terms with Teaching.
(c) Normal Courses
    1. Demonstration Teaching for Rural Teachers
    2. Teaching under Critic in Rural Schools

nglish

(a) Degree Courses
   I. College Rhetoric
   II. Theme Writing and Story Telling
   III. Advanced Exposition
   IV. Public Speaking I.
   V. Public Speaking II.—3 hr. cr.

    VI.   Argumentation I.—3 hr. cr.
   VII.   Argumentation II.—3 hr. cr.
  VIII.   The Oration
    IX.   English Literature
     X.   Anglo-Saxon—3 hr. cr.
    XI.   History of the English Language—2 hr. cr.
   XII.   Middle English
  XIII.   Shakespeare
  XIV.   Literary Criticism
   XV.   The History of the English Drama I.
  XVI.   The History of the English Drama II.
 XVII.   The Puritan Period (Milton)—3 hr. cr.
XVIII.   The English Romantic Movement
  XIX.   English Literature of the Nineteenth Century
   XX.   Tennyson—3 hr. cr.
  XXI.   American Literature
 XXII.   Recent American Literature—3 hr. cr.
XXIII.   The Development of the English Novel
XXIV.   Elocution I.
 XXV.   Elocution II.
XXVI.   Applied Drama
XXVII.   Repertoire I.
XXVIII.   Repertoire II.
XXIX.   The Teaching of English
 XXX.   Principles of Expression.

  (b) Diploma Courses

     Same as Degree Courses

  (c) Normal Courses

    1.   First half Language and Grammar
    2.   Second half Language and Grammar
    3.   Complete Language and Grammar
    4.   Reading
    5.   Elementary Elocution
    6.   First English Composition
    7.   Second English Composition
    8.   First English Classics
    9.   Second English Classics
   10.   Orthography (a)—5 hr. per week.
        Orthography (b)—2 hr. per week

Mathematics

  (a) Degree Courses
    I.   Solid Geometry I.
   II.   College Algebra I.

    III.   Plane Trigonometry
    IV.   College Algebra II.
     V.   Spherical Trigonometry—2 hr. cr.
    VI   Surveying—3 hr. cr.
    VII. History and Teaching of Mathematics
  VIII. Analytical Geometry
    IX. Differential Calculus
     X. Integral Calculus

  (b) Diploma Courses
      Same as Degree Courses

  (c) Normal Courses
     1. First half Arithmetic
     2. Second half Arithmetic
     3. Complete Arithmetic
     4. Commercial Arithmetic
     5. First Algebra
     6. Second Algebra
     7. Third Algebra
     8. First and Second Algebra
     9. Beginning Geometry
   10. Middle Geometry
   11. Solid Geometry

History

  (a) Degree Courses
     I. Greek History
    II. Roman History
   III. English History
   IV. Renaissance and Reformation
    V. American History (a)
   VI. Medieval History—3 hr. cr.
  VII. Eighteenth Century History (a)—2 hr. cr.
        Eighteenth Century History (b)—3 hr. cr.
 VIII. Nineteenth Century History (a)—3 hr. cr.
        Nineteenth Century History (b)—3 hr. cr.
   IX. Method History (a)—2 hr. cr.
        Method History (b)—2 hr. cr.
    X. American History (b)—3 hr. cr.

  (b) Diploma Courses
      Same as Degree Courses

  (c) Normal Courses
     1. First half U. S. History
     2. Second half U. S. History

3. Complete U. S. History
4. First General History
5. Second General History

Government

(a) Degree Courses
  I. American Government
  II. English Government—3 hr. cr.
  III. Municipal Government—3 hr. cr.
  IV. Local Government and Problems—3 hr. cr.
  V. Modern European Governments—3 hr. cr.
  VI. Political Parties—3 hr. cr.
  VII. American Constitutional History I.
  VIII. American Constitutional History II.
  IX. Constitutional Law
  X. International Law—3 hr. cr.
(b) Diploma Courses
  Same as Degree Courses
(c) Normal Courses
  1. Iowa Civics
  2. U. S. Civics
  3. Iowa and U. S. Civics (Not a credit course)

Economics

(a) Degree Course
  I. General Economics
  II. Social and Economic Problems (a)—3 hr. cr.
  III. Social and Economic Problems (b)—3 hr. cr.
  IV. Social and Economic Problems (c)—3 hr. cr.
  V. Sociology—2 hr. cr.
  VI. American Industrial History (a)—3 hr. cr.
  VII. American Industrial History (b)—3 hr. cr.
  VIII. American Industrial History (c)—3 hr. cr.
  IX. English Industrial History—2 hr. cr.
  X. Money and Banking (a)—2 hr. cr.
  XI. Money and Banking (b)—2 hr. cr.
  XII. Public Finance (a)—2 hr. cr.
  XIII. Public Finance (b)—2 hr. cr.
(b) Diploma Courses
  Same as Degree Courses
(c) Normal Courses
  1. Elementary Economics

atin and Greek

(a) Degree Courses
   I. Livy and Latin Composition
  II. Livy and Epodes of Horace
 III. The Odes of Horace
 IV. Latin Composition (a)—2 hr. cr.
  V. Latin Composition (b)—2 hr. cr.
 VI. Latin Composition (c)—2 hr. cr.
 VII. Roman Literature (a) (b) (c)—each 3 hr. cr.
VIII. Roman Literature (a) (b) (c)—each 3 hr. cr.
 IX. Roman Literature (a) (b) (c)—each 3 hr. cr.
  X. Historical Latin Grammar (a)—2 hr. cr.
 XI. Historical Latin Grammar (b)—2 hr. cr.
 XII. Historical Latin Grammar (c)—2 hr. cr.
XIII. Elementary Greek (a)—3 hr. cr.
XIV. Elementary Greek (b)—3 hr. cr.
 XV. Elementary Greek (c)—3 hr. cr.
XVI.—XVII.—XVIII. Seniors Electives—each 2 or 3 hr. cr.
XIX.—XX.—XXI. Beginning Latin and Caesar—each 5 hr. cr.
XXII.—XXIII. Cicero's Orations—each 5 hr. cr.
XXIV.—XXV. Virgil's Aeneid—each 5 hr. cr.
XXVI. Ovid

(b) Diploma Courses
   Same as Degree Courses

(c) Normal Courses
   1. First Latin Lessons
   2. Second Latin Lessons
   3 First Caesar
   4. Second Caesar

erman and French

(a) Degree Courses
   I. Die Jungfrau von Orleans
  II. German Prose Composition
 III. Emilia Galotti, Lyrics and Ballads
 IV. Nathan der Weise
  V. Ephigenie auf Tauris and Die Braut von Messina
 VI. Der dreissigjaerige Krieg
 VII. Modern German Prose
VIII. German Classics
 IX. German Lessons
  X. German Lessons

    XI.   Immense and Hoeher als die Kirche
   XII.   Die Journalisten
     I.   French Lessons
    II.   French Lessons
   III.   Le Voyage de M. Perrichon and L'Abbe Constantin.
   IV.   L'Histoire d'un jenne Homme and Le Conscrit de 1813
    V.   Le Bourgeois Gentilhomme and La Mare au Diable
   VI.   Le Gendre de M. Poirier and un Philosophe sous les Toits

(b) Diploma Courses
     Same as Degree Courses

(c) Normal Courses
   1. First German Lessons
   2. Second German Lessons
   3. Third German
   4. Fourth German

Physics and Chemistry

(a) Degree Courses
     I. Mechanics and Sound—3 hr. cr.
    II. Laboratory Work in Mechanics—2 hr. cr.
   III. Heat and Light—3 hr. cr.
   IV. Laboratory Work in Heat and Light—2 hr. cr.
    V. Electricity and Magnetism—3 hr. cr.
   VI. Laboratory Work in Electricity and Magnetism—2 hr. cr.
  VII. Advanced Mechanics—3 hr. cr.
 VIII. Advanced Course in Light—3 hr. cr.
   IX. Advanced Course in Electricity and Magnetism—3 hr. cr.
    X. Teachers Course in Physics
     I. Chemistry I.
    II. Chemistry II.
   III. Chemistry III.
   IV. Organic Chemistry
    V. Quantitive Analysis—Gravimetric
   VI. Quantitive Analysis—Volumetric
  VII. (a) Sanitary Water Analysis—2 hr. cr.
       (b) Mineral Water Analysis—3 hr. cr.
 VIII. Special Laboratory Course

(b) Diploma Courses
   1. Sound—3 or 5 hr. cr.
   2. Heat and Industrial Electricity—3 hr. cr.
   3. Laboratory Work in Heat and Industrial Electricity

—2 hr. cr.
4. Physics of Common Things—3 hr. cr.
5. Chemistry IX (Inorganic)
6. Chemistry X (Inorganic
7. Chemistry XI (Household)
8. Chemistry XIII (Food Analysis)
9. Chemistry XII (Food and Nutrition)
10. Chemistry XIV (a)—3 hr. cr.
Chemistry XIV. (b)—2 hr. cr.
(c) Normal Courses
1. First Physics—3 hr. cr.
2. First Physics Laboratory—2 hr. cr.
3. Second Physics—3 hr. cr
4. Second Physics Laboratory—2 hr. cr.

Natural Science

(a) Degree Courses
I. Zoology I.
II. Zoology II.
III. Zoology III.
IV. Nature Study
V. Physiology I.
VI. Hygiene and Sanitation (a)
VII. Hygiene and Sanitation (b)—3 hr. cr
VIII. Physiography I.
IX. Mineralogy
X. Influence of Geography upon American History
XI. Astronomy
XII. Geology I.
XIII. Geology II.
XIV. Agriculture I.
XV. Argiculture II.
XVI. Agriculture III.
XVII. Commercial and Economic Geography of North America
XVIII. Commercial Geography of Europe
XIX. Conservation of Natural Resources
XX. Botany I.
XXI. Botany II.
XXII. Botany III.
XXIII. Botany IV. 3 hr. cr.
XXIV. Botany V. (Bacteriology) 3 hr. cr.
(b) Diploma Courses
Same as Degree Courses

(c) Normal Courses
1. Elementary Zoology
2. Physiology
3. First Agriculture
4. Second Agriculture
5. Third Agriculture
6. First Geography
7. Second Geography
8. Complete Geography
9. Elementary Botany
10. Elementary Physiography

Manual Training

*(a) Degree Courses
I. Manual Training Methods I.
II. Manual Training Methods II.—3 hr. cr.
III. Organization and Economics of Manual Training—3 hr. cr.
IV. and VIII. Woodwork—each 3 hr. cr.
V. and VI. Woodwork—each 2 hr. cr.
VII. Woodwork—5 hr. cr.
IX. and XII. Mechanical Drawing—each 2 hr. cr.
X. and XI. Mechanical Drawing—each 3 hr. cr.
XIII. Wood Turning—2 hr. cr.
XIV. and XV. Sheet Metal Work—each 2½ hr. cr.

*Note: Not more than 20 hr. may be elected by a student who does not major in Manual Arts.

(b) Diploma Courses
Same as Degree Courses
(c) Normal Courses
1. Primary Handwork
2. Elementary Handwork
3. Handwork for Rural Schools
4. Woodwork for Rural Schools

Art

*(a) Degree Courses
I. History of Architecture and Sculpture
II. History of Painting
III. Cast Drawing I. 2½ hr. cr.
IV. Cast Drawing II.—2½ hr. cr.
V. Design—2½ hr. cr.

    VI.   Still Life—2½ hr. cr.
    VII.   Perspective—2½ hr. cr.
    VIII. Water Color—2½ hr. cr.
    IX.   Supervision in Art—2½ hr. cr.

  *Note: Not more than 10 hr. may be elected from courses III to IX by a student who does not major in Art.

    (b) Diploma Courses
        Same as Degree Courses and
        1. Kindergarten Drawing I.—2½ hr. cr.
        2. Kindergarten Drawing II.—2½ hr. cr.
        3. Primary Drawing I—2½ hr. cr.
        4. Primary Drawing II.—2½ hr. cr.

    (c) Normal Courses
        1. First Drawing
        2. Second Drawing

Home Economics

    (a) Degree Courses
      I.   Elementary Food Theory I.—2 hr. cr.
      II.   Elementary Food Theory II.—2 hr. cr.
      III. Elementary Food Theory III.—2 hr. cr.
      IV. Principles and Preparations of Foods I.—3 hr. cr.
      V.   Principles and Preparations of Foods II.—3 hr. cr.
      VI. Advanced Cooking—1 hr cr.

    (b) Diploma Courses
        Same as Degree Courses and
        1. Household Architecture—2 hr. cr.
        2. Household Management—1 hr. cr.
        3. Methods, Home Economics—1 hr. cr.
        4. Dietetics—1 hr. cr.
        5. Serving—1 hr. cr.
        6. Demonstrations—1 hr. cr.
        7. Sewing, three terms—Sub-collegiate

    (c) Normal Courses
        1. First Sewing
        2. Second Sewing
        3. First Cooking and Household Management
        4. Second Cooking and Household Management

Public School Music

  *(a) Degree Courses
      I.   Music I.—2½ hr. cr.

   II.   Music II.—2½ hr cr.
  III. History of Music I.—2 hr. cr.
  IV. History of Music II.—3 hr. cr.
   V. Harmony I.—3 hr. cr.
  VI. Harmony II.—2 hr. cr.
 VII. Harmony III.—3 hr. cr.
VIII. Harmony IV.—2 hr. cr.

  * Note: Not more than 10 hr. may be elected by a student who does not major in Music.

   (b) Diploma Courses

      Same as Degree courses and—

1. Sight Singing (Lower grades)—2½ hr. cr.
2. Sight Singing (Upper Grades)—2½ hr. cr.
3. Methods (Lower grades)—2½ hr. cr.
4. Methods (Upper grades)—2½ hr. cr.
5. High School Music and Child Voice—2½ hr. cr.
6. Appreciation of Music—2½ hr. cr.
7. Theory of Music—2½ hr. cr.
8. Supervision—2 hr. cr.
9. Voice, Piano and Organ—Sub-collegiate

   (c) Normal Courses

1. First term Music
2. Second term Music

Commercial

   (b) Diploma Courses

1. Accounting I.
2. Accounting II.
3. Commercial Correspondence
4. Commercial Law
5. Shorthand, three terms—Sub-collegiate
6. Typewriting, three terms—Sub-collegiate

   (c) Normal Courses

1. Elementary Bookkeeping
2. Shorthand, three terms
3. Typewriting, three terms
4. Penmanship, six terms

Physical Education

  *(a) Degree Courses

    I. Anatomy I.
   II. Anatomy II.
  III. Theory of Physical Education

IV. Playground Methods I, II—each 3 hr. cr.
V. History of Physical Education—3 hr. cr.
VI. First Aid to the Injured—2 hr. cr.
VII Theory of Athletics I, II—each 2 hr. cr.

*Note.: Not more than 20 hr. cr. may be elected by students who do not major in Physical Education.

(b) Diploma Courses

Same as Degree Courses and—
1. Anthropometry—3 hr. cr.
2. Physical Diagnosis—2 hr. cr
3. Physiology of Exercise
4. Medical Gymnastics and Massage—3 hr. cr.
5. Physical Department Administration—2 hr. cr.

Violin and Other Orchestral Instruments

(b) Diploma Courses

1. Violin, Oboe, Flute, Clarinet, Bassoon, Cornet, French Horn, Trombone, Tuba, Cello, Double Bass, Harp—Sub-collegiate
2. Orchestra and Ensemble
3. Harmony
4. Ear Training

PROGRAM OF RECITATIONS.

EXPLANATORY NOTE:

The program of recitations is for Fall, Winter, and Spring terms 1914-15. Changes may be made and the program extended, if the number enrolled makes this necessary.

The arabic numerals following the teachers' names indicate the periods in which the subjects are given, i.e. 3-4 shows two sections (one reciting the third period and the other the fourth period) ; while 3 and 4 means one section extending over the third and fourth periods.

The periods are as follows:

First .... · 8:00 to 9:00
Second .... 9:00 to 10:00
Chapel .... 10:00 to 10:20
Third .... 10:25 to 11:25
Fourth ... . 11:25 to 12:25
Fifth .... 1:30 to 2:30

Sixth .... 2:30 to 3:30
Seventh .... 3:30 to 4:30
Eighth .... 4:30 to 5:30

FALL TERM

EDUCATION:

COLLEGE COURSES

Psychology I., Mr. Samson 3-7.
Psychology II., Mr. Samson 2.
School Management, Mr. Colegrove 2-7.
History of Education, Mr. Walters 1-2-4.
Experimental Psychology, Mr. Mount 7.
School Administration, Mr. Colegrove 1.
Philosophy of Education, Mr. Walters 5.
Ethics, Mr. Samson 6.

DIPLOMA COURSES

Psychology I., Miss Buck 1-3-4-5; Mr. Mount 2-6.
Psychology II., Mr. Mount 3.
Primary Methods, 1st term, Miss McGovern 1-2-3.

NORMAL COURSES.

Elementary Psychology, Mr. Campbell 3.
The Country School, Mr. Campbell 1.
Didactics, Mr. Campbell 4.
General Primary Methods, Miss McGovern 5.

TEACHING:

COLLEGE COURSES

Illustrative Teaching, 2-5-6.
Teaching as arranged.

DIPLOMA COURSES

Kindergarten Theory I, Miss Ward 3.
Criticism, (Mon. Tues. Wed. Thurs.), Miss Hatcher 6.
Teaching as arranged.

NORMAL COURSES.

Rural Demonstration Teaching, 3.
Teaching as arranged.

ENGLISH.

COLLEGE COURSES

Rhetoric, Mr. Lynch 3-5; Mr. Gist 1-4; Miss Lambert 2; Mr. Barnes 1-3; Miss Gregg 5; Miss Hearst 6; Miss Siner 6.
Theme Writing & Story Telling, Miss Carpenter 2.
Public Speaking II., Mr. Barnes 5.
Argumentation II., Mr. Barnes 6.
English Literature, Miss Carpenter 1.
Shakespeare, Mr. Gist 3.
Literary Criticism, Miss Carpenter 4.
The Puritan Period (Milton), Mr. Lynch 7.
Recent American Literature, Miss Lambert 4.
Elocution I., Miss Martin 1; Miss Falkler 2-3; Miss Shanewise 4-5.
Elocution II., Miss Martin 2; Miss Shanewise 3.
The History of the English Drama I., Miss Lambert 1.
Repertoire II., Miss Martin 3.

DIPLOMA COURSES

Same as College Courses.

NORMAL COURSES.

1st half Language and Grammar, Miss Gregg 4; Miss Hearst 2.
2nd half Language and Grammar, Miss Hearst 3.
Complete Language and Grammar, Miss Gregg 2-3.
Reading, Miss Falkler 6.
Elementary Elocution, Miss Falkler 4.
First .English Composition, Miss Siner 2-4.
First English Classics, Miss Oliver 4.
Second English Classics, Miss Hearst 5.
Orthography (a), Miss Oliver 1-2.

MATHEMATICS:

COLLEGE COURSES

Solid Geometry, Mr. Wright 4.
College Algebra I., Mr. Condit 5-6.
Plane Trigonometry, Mr. Condit 7.
Analytical Geometry, Mr. Condit 3.

DIPLOMA COURSES

Same as College Courses.

Normal Courses.

First half Arithmetic, Miss Lambert 4-5; Mr. Daugherty 1.
Second half Arithmetic, Miss Allen 6.
Complete Arithmetic, Mr. Daugherty 3-5; Mr. Cory 4.
First Algebra, Miss Allen 1-2.
Second Algebra, Miss Allen 5.
Third Algebra, Miss Lambert 1-2.
Beginning Geometry, Mr. Wright 2.
Middle Geometry, Mr. Wright 3.
First and Second Algebra, Mr. Daugherty 4.

LATIN AND GREEK:

College Courses

Latin I., (Livy and Latin Composition), Mr. Merchant 1.
Latin IV., (Latin Composition), Mr. Merchant 3.
Latin VII., (Roman Literature), Mr. Merchant 2.
Latin X., (Historical Latin Grammar), Mr. Merchant 2.
Latin XIX., (First Beginning Latin), Mr. Merchant 6.
Greek XIII., (First Elementary Greek), Mr. Merchant 3.
Latin XXIV., (Virgil's Aeneid), Miss Call 5.

Diploma Courses

Same as College Courses.

Normal Courses.

First Latin Lessons, Miss Call 2.
First Caesar, Miss Call 4.
Second Caeser, Miss Call 3.

GERMAN AND FRENCH:

College Courses

German I., (Die Jungfrau von Orleans), Miss Lorenz 5.
German II., (German Prose Composition), Miss Lorenz 2.
German III., (Emilia Galotti, Lyrics and Ballads), Miss Lorenz 1.
German VI., (Der dreissigjaehrige Krieg), Mr. Knoepfler 3.
German IX., (German Lessons), Mr. Knoepfler 5.
German XII., (Die Journalisten), Miss Lorenz 6.
French I. (French Lessons), Mr. Knoepfler 1.
French IV. (L'Histoire d'un jenne Homme and Le Conscrit de 1813), Mr. Knoepfler 2.

Same as College Courses.

NORMAL COURSES.

First German Lessons, Miss Nolte 4.
Second German Lessons, Miss Nolte 2.
Third German, Miss Nolte 3.
Fourth German, Miss Nolte 6.

PHYSICS AND CHEMISTRY:

COLLEGE COURSES

Mechanics and Sound, (Mon. Wed. Fri.), Mr. Begeman 2.
Laboratory Work in Mechanics, (Mon. Wed.), Mr Begeman 7 and 8.
Advanced Mechanics, Mr. Begeman 5.
Chemistry I., Mr. Getchell 3.
Organic Chemistry, Mr. Bond 5.

DIPLOMA COURSES

Chemistry IX (Inorganic), Mr. Getchell 5-7; Mr. Read 2-4.
Chemistry XIII. (Food Analysis), Mr. Bond 1-3.
Physics of Common Things, Mr. Perrine 5.
Sound, Mr. Begeman 4.

NORMAL COURSES.

First Physics (Mon. Wed. Fri.), Mr. Perrine 3; Mr. Hersey 1.
First Physics (Tues. Thurs. Fri.), Mr. Perrine 4; Mr. Hersey 2.
First Physics Laboratory (Mon. Wed.), Mr. Perrine 7 and 8; Mr. Hersey 5 and 6.
First Physics Laboratory (Tues. and Thurs.), Mr. Perrine 7 and 8; Mr. Hersey 5 and 6.
Second Physics (Mon. Wed. Fri.), Mr. Hersey 3.
Second Physics Laboratory (Tues. Thurs.), Mr Hersey 3 and 4.

HISTORY:

COLLEGE COURSES

Greek History, Miss Rice 1-2.
Renaissance and Reformation, Miss Riggs 5.
American History, Miss Riggs 3.
Method History, (Tues. Thurs), Miss Riggs 6.

DIPLOMA COURSES

Same as College Courses.

NORMAL COURSES.

First half U. S. History, Miss Rice 5; Mr. Peterson 1.
Second half U. S. History, Miss Rice 3.
Complete U. S. History, Miss Riggs 4; Mr. Morgan 2.

GOVERNMENT:

COLLEGE COURSES

American Government, Mr Meyerholz 2.
English Government, Mr. Peterson 5.
Municipal Government, Mr. Meyerholz 4.
American Constitutional History I., Mr. Meyerholz 6.

DIPLOMA COURSES

Same as College Courses.

NORMAL COURSES.

Iowa Civics, Mr. Peterson 3.
U. S. Civics, Mr. Peterson 2.
Iowa and U. S. Civics, Mr. Meyerholz 1

ECONOMICS:

COLLEGE COURSES

General Economics, Mr. McKitrick 6; Mr. Morgan 1.
Social and Economic Problems, (Mon. Wed. Fri.), Mr. McKitrick 7.
Sociology (Tues. Thurs.), Mr. McKitrick 7.
American Industrial History (Mon. Wed. Fri.), Mr. Morgan 3.
English Industrial History (Tues. Thurs.), Mr. Morgan 3.

DIPLOMA COURSES

Same as College Courses.

NORMAL COURSES.

Elementary Economics, Mr. McKitrick 4; Mr. Morgan 5.

NATURAL SCIENCE:

COLLEGE COURSES

Zoology I., Mr. Arey 1-3.
Zoology I. Laboratory, (Mon. Wed. and Tues. Thurs.), Mr. Arey 7 and 8.
Physiology I., Mr. Newton 1.
Hygiene and Sanitation (a), Mr. Newton 3.
Hygiene and Sanitation (b), Mr. Newton 4-5.
Physiography I., Mr. Cable 2.
Mineralogy, Mr. Cable 4.
Agriculture I., Mr. Davis 1.
Agriculture I. Laboratory, Mr. Davis 7 and 8.
Commercial and Economic Geography of North America, Miss Aitchison 4.
Botany I., Mr. Palmer 3.
Botany I. Laboratory, (Tues.) Mr. Palmer 7 and 8.

DIPLOMA COURSES

Same as College Courses.

NORMAL COURSES.

Elementary Zoology, Mr. Arey 5.
Elementary Physiology, Mr. Newton 2.
Elementary Physiography, Mr. Cable 1-5.
First Agriculture, Mr. Davis 2; ....1-3-4.
Agriculture Laboratory, (Mon. Wed.) ....7 and 8.
Second Agriculture, Mr. Davis 3.
First half Geography, Miss Aitchison 1.
Second half Geography, Miss Aitchison 2.
Complete Geography, Miss Aitchison 3.
Elementary Botany, Mr. Palmer 1-2.

MANUAL TRAINING:

COLLEGE COURSES

Manual Training Methods I., Mr. Bailey 2.
Woodwork, Advanced, Mr. Brown 3 and 4.
Woodwork IV., (Mon. Wed. Fri.), Mr. Brown 7 and 8.
Mechanical Drawing X and XI. (Mon. Wed. Fri.), Mr. Bailey 3 and 4.
Mechanical Drawing IX and XII. (Tues. Thurs.), Mr. Bailey 7 and 8.
Wood Turning, Mr. Brown 3 and 4.

DIPLOMA COURSES

Same as College Courses.

NORMAL COURSES.

Primary Handwork, Mrs. McMahon 1-2-3.
Handwork for Rural Schools, Mrs. McMahon 5.
Woodwork for Rural Schools, Mr. Brown 6.

ART:

COLLEGE COURSES

Cast Drawing I., Miss Patt 5.
Still Life, Miss Thorton 2.
Perspective, Miss Thornton 1.
Water Color, Miss Thornton 6.

DIPLOMA COURSES

Same as College Courses and
Kindergarten Drawing I., Miss Schuneman 2.
Primary Drawing I., Miss Schuneman 4-5.

NORMAL COURSES.

First Drawing, Miss Patt 1-4; Miss Thornton 3.
Second Drawing, Miss Patt 2.

PUBLIC SCHOOL MUSIC:

COLLEGE COURSES

Music I., Mr. Fullerton 1.
Music II., Mr. Fullerton 3.
History of Music II., (Mon. Wed. Thurs.), Miss Childs 6.
Harmony I., (Mon. Wed. Fri.), Miss Thomson 3.

DIPLOMA COURSES

Same as College Courses and
Methods (Lower Grades), (Mon. Wed. Thrus.), ...1.
Methods (Upper Grades), (Mon. Wed. Fri.), Miss Stenwall 5.
High School Music (Tues. Thurs.) Mr. Fullerton 5.

NORMAL COURSES.

First term Music, Miss Stenwall 1-2; Miss Thomson 4-6.
Second term Music, ...3-4.

COMMERCIAL:

DIPLOMA COURSES

Commercial Correspondence, Mr. Coffey 1.
Commercial Law, Mr. Coffey 5.
First Typewriting, Mr. Coffey 4.
First Shorthand, Mr. Coffey 3.

NORMAL COURSES

First Bookkeeping, Mr. Cummins 2.
First Penmanship, Mr. Cummins 3-5-6.
Advanced Penmanship, Mr. Cummins 4.

HOME ECONOMICS:

COLLEGE COURSES

Elementary Food Theory I. (Mon. Wed.), Miss Young 1 and
    2; 3 and 4; Miss Goff 1 and 2; 5 and 6; Miss Stallman
    3 and 4; 5 and 6.
Principles and Preparation of Foods I. (Tues. Thurs. Fri.),
    Miss Young 1; Miss Stallman 3-5.

DIPLOMA COURSES

Same as College Courses and
Dietetics, (Tues. Thurs.), Miss Young 5 and 6; Miss Goff 3
    and 4; 5 and 6; 7 and 8; Miss Stallman 7 and 8.
First Sewing (Daily) 1, Miss Heinz.
First Sewing (Mon. Wed.) 1 and 2, (Fri.) 2, Miss Freer.
First Sewing (Mon. Wed.) 3 and 4, (Fri.) 3, Miss Heinz,
    Miss Freer.
First Sewing (Tues. Thurs.) 3 and 4, (Fri.) 4, Miss Heinz,
    Miss Freer.
First Sewing (Tues. Thurs.) 5 and 6, (Fri.) 5, Miss Freer,
First Sewing (Mon. Wed.), 5 and 6, (Fri.) 5, Miss Heinz.

NORMAL COURSES

First Sewing, Miss Hurd 1-2-7.
Second Sewing, Miss Hurd 4.
First Cooking (Mon. Wed. and Tues. Thurs.), Miss Hurd 3
    and 4.
First Cooking (Tues. Thurs.), Miss Hurd 5 and 6.
Second Cooking (Mon. Wed.), Miss Hurd 5 and 6.

PHYSICAL EDUCATION:

COLLEGE COURSES

Anatomy I., Mr. Seymour 3.
Theory of Physical Education, Mr. Seymour 4; Miss
Hussey 4.
Theory of Atheletics I. (Tues. Thurs.), Mr. Seymour 6.

DIPLOMA COURSES

Same as College Courses, and
Anthropometry, (Mon. Wed. Fri.), Mr. Seymour 2.
Physical Diagnosis, (Tues. Thurs), Mr. Seymour 2.

PRACTICAL WORK

First term Physical Training (Primary), Miss Hussey 5;
Miss Wild 4.
First Physical Training, (Tues. Thurs.), Miss Hussey 6;
Miss Wild 3; Miss Nisbet 4-6.
First Physical Training, (Mon. Wed.), Miss Hussey 3; Miss
Wild 5.
Second Physical Training (Tues. Thurs.), Miss Wild 6.
Third Physical Training, (Mon. Wed.), Miss Nisbet 6.
Gymnastics, Miss Hussey 7.
Tennis, (Mon. Wed.), Mr. Berkstresser 4-5.
Tennis, (Tues. Thurs.), Mr. Berkstresser 5.
Swimming, (Mon. Wed.), Miss Hussey 6; Miss Wild 3-7;
Miss Nisbet 4.
Swimming, (Tues. Thurs.), Miss Wild 5; Miss Nisbet 3-7;
Mr. Berkstresser 4-6.
Cricket (Tues. Thurs.), Miss Nisbet 5.
Rhythm II., (Mon. Wed.), Miss Wild 6.
Folk Dancing, (Mon. Wed.), Miss Nisbet 3-5.
Rhythm I., (Tues. Thurs.), Miss Wild 7.
Golf, (Mon. Wed.), Mr. Seymour 5.
Golf, (Tues. Thurs.), Mr. Seymour 5.
Football, (Mon. Wed.), Mr. Berkstresser 6.
Cross Country (Mon. Wed.), Mr. Seymour 6.
Hockey, (Mon. Wed.), Miss Nisbet 7.
Athletics, Miss Hussey 8.
Football Team, Mr. Berkstresser 7 and 8.
Football Squad, Mr. Seymour 7 and 8.

WINTER TERM

EDUCATION:

COLLEGE COURSES

Psychology I., Mr. Samson 2-5.
Psychology II., Mr. Samson 1-4.
School Management, Mr. Colegrove 2-3-5.
History of Education, Mr. Walters 3-4-7.
Experimental Psychology, Mr. Mount 7.
Educational Classics, Mr. Walters 6.

DIPLOMA COURSES

Psychology I., Miss Buck 1-2-3.
Psychology II., Mr. Colegrove 4; Mr. Mount 1-2-3; Miss Buck 7.
Primary Methods II., Miss McGovern 1-2.
Primary Methods I., Miss McGovern 3.

NORMAL COURSES

Didactics, Mr. Campbell 3-4.
The Country School, Mr. Campbell 1.
Elementary Psychology, Mr. Campbell 2.
General Primary Methods, Miss McGovern 5.

TEACHING:

COLLEGE COURSES

Illustrative Teaching, 6.
Teaching as arranged.

DIPLOMA COURSES

Same as College Courses and
Kindergarten Theory II, Miss Ward 2.
Kindergarten Theory IV., Miss Ward 4.
Primary Criticism, (Tues. Thurs.), Miss Hatcher 6.
Teaching as arranged.

NORMAL COURSES

Rural Demonstration Teaching, 3.
Teaching as arranged.

ENGLISH:

COLLEGE COURSES

Rhetoric, Mr. Lynch 5; Mr. Gist 4; Miss Siner 2.
Advanced Exposition, Mr. Lynch 2.

Public Speaking I., Mr. Barnes 3.
Public Speaking II., Mr. Barnes 5.
Argumentation I., Mr. Barnes 2.
Argumentation II., Mr. Barnes 6.
English Literature, Miss Carpenter 1-3; Miss Lambert 2-4.
Anglo-Saxon, Mr. Gist 5.
History of the English Language, Mr. Gist 5.
The History of the English Drama II., Miss Lambert 1.
Tennyson, Mr. Gist 2.
American Literature, Mr. Lynch 7.
Elocution I., Miss Falkler 4-5; Miss Shanewise 3-4.
Elocution II., Miss Martin 1; Miss Shanewise 5.
Applied Drama, Miss Martin 4.
Repertoire I., Miss Martin 2.
The English Romantic Movement, Miss Carpenter 4.

DIPLOMA COURSES

Same as College Courses.

NORMAL COURSES

First half Language and Grammar ,Miss Gregg   5;   Miss
    Hearst 1-4.
Second half Language and Grammar, Miss Hearst 5.
Complete Language and Grammar, Miss Gregg 3-4.
Reading, Miss Falkler 2.
Elementary Elocution, Miss Falkler 3.
First English Composition, Miss Gregg 2; Miss Siner 3.
Second English Composition, Miss Siner 5.
First English Classics, Miss Oliver 4.
Second English Classics, Miss Hearst 3.
Orthography (a), Miss Oliver 1-2.

MATHEMATICS:

· COLLEGE COURSES

Solid Geometry, Mr. Wright 1.
College Algebra I., Miss Lambert 2.
Plane Trigonometry, Mr. Daugherty 6-7.
College Algebra II., Mr. Condit 2.
Spherical Trigonometry, (Tues. Thurs.), Mr. Condit 7.
Differential Calculus, Mr. Condit 3.

DIPLOMA COURSES

Same as College Courses.

NORMAL COURSES

First half Arithmetic, Mr. Daugherty 3-4.
Second half Arithmetic, Miss Lambert 3-4.
Complete Arithmetic, Mr. Condit 5; Mr. Cory 4.
First Algebra, Miss Lambert 6.
Second Algebra, Miss Allen 3.
Third Algebra, Miss Allen 1-5.
First and Second Algebra, Miss Allen 2.
Beginning Geometry, Mr. Wright 4.
Middle Geometry, Mr. Wright 2.

HISTORY:

COLLEGE COURSES

American History (b), (Mon. Wed. Fri.), Miss Riggs 5.
Eighteenth Century History, (Tues. Thurs.), Miss Riggs 4.
Nineteenth Century History (Mon. Wed. Fri.), Miss Riggs 4.
Roman History, Miss Rice 2-3.

DIPLOMA COURSES

Same as College Courses.

NORMAL COURSES

First half U. S. History, Miss Rice 4-5.
Second half U. S. History, Mr. Morgan 2.
Complete U. S. History, Miss Riggs 2-3.
First General History, Mr. Peterson 2.

GOVERNMENT:

COLLEGE COURSES

American Government, Mr. Peterson 3.
Modern European Government, Mr. Meyerholz 5.
American Constitutional History II., Mr. Meyerholz 6.
International Law, Mr. Meyerholz 2.

DIPLOMA COURSES

Same as College Courses.

NORMAL COURSES

Iowa Civics, Mr. Peterson 1.
U. S. Civics, Mr. Peterson 4.
Iowa and U. S. Civics, Mr. Meyerholz 3.

ECONOMICS:

COLLEGE COURSES

General Economics, Mr McKitrick 6; Mr. Morgan 1.
Social and Economic Problems (b) (Mon. Wed. Fri.), Mr.
McKitrick 7.
American Industrial History (b) (Mon. Wed. Fri.), Mr.
Morgan 3.
Sociology, (Tues. Thurs.), Mr. McKitrick 7.
Money and Banking (a) (Tues. Thurs.), Mr. McKitrick 3.

DIPLOMA COURSES

Same as College Courses.

NORMAL COURSES

Elementary Economics, Mr. McKitrick 4; Mr. Morgan 5.

LATIN AND GREEK:

COLLEGE COURSES

Latin II., (Livy and the Epodes of Horace), Mr. Merchant 1.
Latin V., (Latin Composition), Mr. Merchant 3.
Latin VIII., (Roman Literature), Mr. Merchant 2.
Latin XI., (Historical Latin Grammar), Mr. Merchant 2.
Latin XX., (Second Beginning Latin), Mr. Merchant 6.
Latin XXII., (Cicero's Orations), Miss Call 3
Latin XXV., (Virgil's Aeneid), Miss Call 5.
Greek XIV., (Second Elementary Greek), Mr. Merchant 3.

DIPLOMA COURSES

Same as College Courses.

NORMAL COURSES

Second Latin Lessons, Miss Call 2.
Second Caesar, Miss Call 4.

GERMAN AND FRENCH:

COLLEGE COURSES

German I., (Die Jungfrau von Orleans), Miss Lorenz 5.
German II., (German Prose Composition), Miss Lorenz 2.
German IV., (Nathan der Weise), Miss Lorenz 3.
German VII., (Modern German Prose), Mr. Knoepfler 3.

German X., (German Lessons), Mr. Knoepfler 5.
German XII., (Die Journalisten), Miss Lorenz 6.
French II., (French Lessons), Mr. Knoepfler 1.
French V., (Le Bourgeois Gentilhomme and La Mare au
Diable), Mr. Knoepfler 2.

DIPLOMA COURSES

Same as College Courses.

NORMAL COURSES

First German Lessons, Miss Nolte 4.
Second German Lessons, Miss Nolte 2.
Third German, Miss Nolte 3.
Fourth German, Miss Nolte 6.

PHYSICS AND CHEMISTRY:

COLLEGE COURSES

Mechanics and Sound (Mon. Wed. Fri.), Mr. Begeman 2.
Laboratory Work in Mechanics, (Mon. Wed.), Mr. Begeman
7 and 8
Electricity and Magnetism, (Tues. Thurs. Fri.), Mr. Bege-
man 4.
Laboratory Work in Electricity and Magnetism, (Mon. Wed.)
Mr. Begeman 4 and 5.
Advanced Course in Light, Mr. Begeman 5.
Chemistry II., Mr. Getchell 3.
Quantitive Analysis—Gravimetric, Mr. Bond 1.

DIPLOMA COURSES

Chemistry X., (Inorganic), Mr. Getchell 5-7; Mr. Read 2-4.
Chemistry XII., (Food and Nutrition), Mr. Bond 5.

NORMAL COURSES

First Physics, (Mon. Wed. Fri.), Mr. Perrine 1; Mr. Her-
sey 3.
First Physics, (Tues. Thurs. Fri.), Mr. Perrine 2.
First Physics Laboratory, (Tues. Thurs.), Mr. Perrine 5
and 6.
First Physics Laboratory, (Mon. Wed.), Mr. Perrine 5 and 6;
Mr. Hersey 7 and 8.
Second Physics (Mon. Wed. Fri.), Mr. Perrine 3; Mr. Her-
sey 5.

Second Physics, (Tues. Thurs. Fri.), Mr. Hersey 4.
Second Physics Laboratory (Tues. Thurs.), Mr. Perrine 3
    and 4; Mr. Hersey 7 and 8.

NATURAL SCIENCE:

COLLEGE COURSES

Zoology II., Mr. Arey 1.
Zoology II. Laboratory, (Mon. Wed.), Mr. Arey 7 and 8.
Hygiene and Sanitation (a) Mr. Newton 2-4-5.
Agriculture II., Mr. Davis I.
Agriculture II. Laboratory, Mr. Davis 7 and 8.
Commercial Geography of Europe, Miss Aitchison 5.
Geology I., Mr. Cable 2.
Botany II., Mr. Palmer 3.
Botany II. Laboratory (Tues. Thurs.), Mr. Palmer 4.
Botany IV., Mr. Palmer 5.
Botany IV. Laboratory (Tues. Thurs.), Mr. Palmer 5 and 6.
Botany V. (Bacteriology), Mr. Palmer 1.
Influence of Geography upon American History, Mr. Cable 4.

DIPLOMA COURSES

Same as College Courses.

NORMAL COURSES

Elementary Physiology, Mr. Newton 3.
First Agriculture, Mr. Davis 3.
Second Agriculture, Mr. Davis 2; ....2-3-4.
Agriculture Laboratory, (Mon. Wed.), Mr. Davis 7 and 8.
First half Geography, Miss Aitchison 1.
Second half Geography, Miss Aitchison 2.
Complete Geography, Miss Aitchison 3.
Elementary Botany, Mr. Palmer 2.
Elementary Physiography, Mr. Cable 1-3.

MANUAL TRAINING:

COLLEGE COURSES

Manual Training Methods II., (Mon. Wed. Fri.), Mr.
    Bailey 3.
Woodwork IV., (Mon. Wed. Fri.), Mr. Brown 3 and 4.
Wood Turning, Mr. Brown 5 and 6.
Mechanical Drawing IX and XII. (Tues. and Thurs.), Mr.
    Bailey 3 and 4.

Mechanical Drawing X and XI. (Mon. Wed. Fri.), Mr. Bailey 5 and 6.
Sheet Metal Work, Mr. Bailey 2.
Woodwork, Advanced, Mr. Brown 5 and 6.

DIPLOMA COURSES

Same as College Courses.

NORMAL COURSES

Primary Handwork, Mrs. McMahon 1-4.
Elementary Handwork, Mrs. McMahon 2.
Handwork for Rural Schools, Mrs. McMahon 5.
Woodwork for Rural Schools, Mr. Brown 7.

ART:

COLLEGE COURSES

History of Architecture and Sculpture, Miss Thornton 5.
Cast Drawing II., Miss Patt 6.
Still Life, Miss Thornton 3.
Perspective, Miss Thornton 4.
Water Color, Miss Thornton 6.

DIPLOMA COURSES

Same as College Courses and
Kindergarten Drawing II., Miss Schuneman 3.
Primary Drawing I., Miss Patt 2; Miss Schuneman 5-6.
Primary Drawing II., Miss Schuneman 2.

NORMAL COURSES

First Drawing, Miss Patt 1-4.

HOME ECONOMICS:

COLLEGE COURSES

Elementary Food Theory II. (Mon. Wed.), Miss Young 1 and 2; Miss Goff 1 and 2; 5 and 6; Miss Stallman 3 and 4; 5 and 6.
Elementary Food Theory II. (Tues. Thurs.), Miss Goff 3 and 4.
Principles and Preparations of Foods II., (Tues. Thurs. Fri.), Miss Young 1; Miss Stallman 3-5.

DIPLOMA COURSES

Same as College Courses and
Household Architecture (Tues. Thurs.), Miss Young 2
   and 3.
Second Sewing (Daily), 1, Miss Heinz.
Second Sewing (Daily), 2, Miss Freer.
Second Sewing (Mon. Wed.) 3 and 4, (Fri) 3, Miss Heinz,
   Miss Freer.
Second Sewing (Mon. Wed.), 5 and 6, (Fri.) 5, Miss Heinz,
   Miss Freer.
Second Sewing (Tues. Thurs.), 3 and 4, (Fri.) 4, Miss
   Heinz, Miss Freer.
Second Sewing (Tues. Thurs.) 5 and 6, (Fri.) 5; Miss Freer.
Serving, Miss Young 7; Miss Goff 7; Miss Stallman 7.

NORMAL COURSES

First Sewing, Miss Hurd 1-2.
Second Sewing, Miss Hurd 4-6.
First Cooking (Mon. Wed.), Miss Hurd 3 and 4; 5 and 6.
Second Cooking (Tues. Thurs.), Miss Hurd 3 and 4; 5 and 6.

PUBLIC SCHOOL MUSIC:

COLLEGE COURSES

Music I., Mr. Fullerton 2.
Music II., Mr. Fullerton 1.
History of Music I. (Tues. Thurs), Miss Childs 4.
Harmony I., (Mon. Wed. Fri), Miss Thomson 4.
Harmony III., (Mon. Wed. Thurs.), Miss Thomson 6.   (

DIPLOMA COURSES

Same as College Courses and
Sight Singing (Upper grades) (Mon. Wed. Fri.), Miss Sten-
   wall 5.
Sight Singing (Lower Grades) (Tues. Wed. Fri.),........3.
Theory of Music (Tues. Wed. Fri.), Mr. Fulerton 5.

NORMAL COURSES

First Term Music, Miss Stenwall 1-2; Miss Thomson 3.
Second Term Music, ... 1-4.

COMMERCIAL:

DIPLOMA COURSES

Accounting I:, Mr. Cummins 1.
Commercial Correspondence, Mr. Coffey 4.

First Shorthand, Mr. Coffey 3.
Second Shorthand, Mr. Coffey 5.
First Typewriting, Mr. Coffey 1.
Second Typewriting, Mr. Coffey 2.

NORMAL COURSES

Elementary Bookkeeping, Mr. Cummins 2.
First Penmanship, Mr. Cummins 3-5-6.
Advanced Penmanship, Mr. Cummins 4.

PHYSICAL EDUCATION:

COLLEGE COURSES

Anatomy II, Mr. Seymour 3.
Playground Methods I., (Mon. Wed. Fri.), Mr. Seymour 6.
History of Physical Education (Mon. Wed. Fri.), Mr. Seymour 4.
First Aid to the Injured (Tues. Thurs), Mr. Seymour 4.
Theory of Athletics II. (Tues. Thurs.), Mr. Seymour 5.

PRACTICAL WORK

Second term Physical Training (Mon. Wed.), Miss Hussey 5; Miss Wild 3; Miss Nisbet 4.
First term Physical Training (Mon. Wed.), Miss Nisbet 5.
Second term Physical Training (Tues. Thurs.), Miss Hussey 4; Miss Wild 6; Miss Nisbet 7.
Third term Physical Training (Tues. Thurs.), Miss Nisbet 6.
Second term Physical Training (Primary), (Mon. Wed.), Miss Hussey 3.
Second term Physical Training (Primary), (Tues. Thurs.), Miss Wild 4.
Gymnastics, Miss Hussey 7.
First Gymnastics, (Mon. Wed.), Mr. Berkstresser 4-6.
Second Gymnastics (Tues. Thurs.), Mr. Berkstresser 5.
Third Gymnastics, (Tues. Thurs.), Mr. Seymour 7.
Basket Ball (Mon. Wed.), Miss Hussey 4; Miss Nisbet 3; Mr. Berkstresser 7.
Basket Ball (Tues. Thurs.), Miss Wild 5; Miss Nisbet 4; Mr. Berkstresser 6.
Advanced Basket Ball, (Mon. Wed.), Miss Nisbet 7.
Rhythm First, (Tues. Thurs.), Miss Wild 4-7.
Rhythm Second, (Mon. Wed.), Miss Wild 6.
Advanced Gymnastics (Mon. Wed.), Miss Wild 7.

Aesthetic Dancing, Miss Hussey 8.
Folk Dancing (Mon. Wed.), Miss Wild 5; Miss Nisbet 6.
Folk Dancing (Tues. Thurs.), Miss Nisbet 3.
Swimming (Mon. Wed.), Mr. Berkstresser 5.
Swimming (Tues. Thurs.), Mr. Berkstresser 7.
Games (Tues. Thurs.), Miss Hussey 6.
Gymnastic Team, Mr. Seymour 8.
Basketball Team, Mr. Berkstresser 8.

SPRING TERM

EDUCATION:

COLLEGE COURSES

Psychology I., Mr. Samson 1.
Psychology II., Mr. Samson 2-5.
School Management, Mr. Colegrove 1-2-3-5.
History of Education, Mr. Walters 1-2.
Philosophy of Education, Mr. Walters 6.
Logic, Mr. Walters 7.
Experimental Psychology, Mr. Mount 6.
Genetic Psychology, Mr. Mount 3.
Rural School Problems, Mr. Hart 1.

DIPLOMA COURSES

Psychology I., Miss Buck 1-2.
Psychology II., Mr. Mount 1-2; Miss Buck 3-5.
Primary Methods II., Miss McGovern 2.
Primary Methods III., (Mon. Wed. and Tues. Thurs.), Miss
McGovern 1.

NORMAL COURSES

Didactics, Mr. Campbell 4.
The Country School, Mr. Campbell 1.
Elementary Psychology, Mr. Campbell 3.
General Primary Methods, Miss McGovern 3-4.

TEACHING:

COLLEGE COURSES

Illustrative Teaching, 6.
Teaching as arranged.

Diploma Courses

Same as College Courses and
Kindergarten Theory III., Miss Ward 2.
Kindergarten Theory IV., Miss Ward 4.
Primary Theory for Kindergarten Teachers, Miss Hatcher 2-5.
Kindergarten Theory for Primary Teachers, Miss Ward 3.
Primary Criticism (Tues. Thurs.), Miss Hatcher 6.
Teaching as arranged.

Normal Courses

Rural Demonstration Teaching, 3.
Teaching as arranged.

ENGLISH:

College Courses

Rhetoric, Mr. Lynch 5; Mr. Gist 1; Miss Siner 2.
Public Speaking I., Mr. Barnes 1.
Public Speaking II., Mr. Barnes 5.
Argumentation I., Mr. Barnes 2.
The Oration, Mr. Barnes 4.
English Literature, Miss Carpenter 1-3; Miss Lambert 2-4.
Anglo-Saxon and Middle English, Mr. Gist 4.
English Literature of the Nineteenth Century, Miss Lambert 1.
American Literature, Mr. Lynch 3.
The Development of the English Novel, Miss Carpenter 4.
Elocution I., Miss Falkler 3; Miss Shanewise 1-4.
Elocution II., Miss Martin 1; Miss Shanewise 2.
Repertoire I., Miss Martin 2.
The Teaching of English, Mr. Lynch 7.
Shakespeare, Mr. Gist 3.

Diploma Courses

Same as College Courses.

Normal Courses

First half Language and Grammar, Miss Hearst 5.
Second half Language and Grammar, Miss Hearst 3-4.
Complete Language and Grammar, Miss Gregg 2-3-4.
Reading, Miss Falkler 2.
Elementary Elocution, Miss Falkler 4-5.
First English Composition, Miss Siner 4.

Second English Composition, Miss Gregg 5; Miss Siner 1.
First English Classics, Miss Oliver 4.
Second English Classics, Miss Hearst 1.
Orthography (a), Miss Oliver 1-3.
Orthography (b), Miss Oliver 5.

MATHEMATICS:

COLLEGE COURSES

Solid Geometry, Mr. Wright 4.
College Algebra I., Miss Lambert 5.
College Algebra II., Mr. Condit 2.
Plane Trigonometry, Mr. Daugherty 3.
Surveying (Mon. Wed. Fri.), Mr. Daugherty 6.
History and Teaching of Mathematics, Mr. Condit 5.
Integral Calculus, Mr. Condit 3.

DIPLOMA COURSES

Same as College Courses.

NORMAL COURSES

First half Arithmetic, Miss Lambert 2.
Second half Arithmetic, Mr. Daugherty 5.
Complete Arithmetic, Mr. Daugherty 2; Miss Allen 4; Mr.
    Cory 3.
First Algebra, Miss Allen 5.
Second Algebra, Miss Lambert 3.
Third Algebra, Miss Allen 1-3.
First and Second Algebra, Miss Lambert 4.
Beginning Geometry, Mr. Wright 1.
Middle Geometry, Mr. Wright 5.
Solid Geometry, Mr. Wright 2

HISTORY:

COLLEGE COURSES

English History, Miss Rice 2-5.
Medieval History (Mon. Wed. Fri.), Miss Riggs 6.
Eighteenth Century History (Mon. Wed. Fri.), Miss Riggs 2.
Nineteenth Century History (Mon. Wed. Fri.), Miss Riggs 5.
Method History (Tues. Thurs.), Miss Riggs 5.

DIPLOMA COURSES

Same as College Courses.

NORMAL COURSES

First half U. S. History, Miss Rice 4.
Second half U. S. History, Miss Rice 3.
Complete U. S. History, Miss Riggs 3; Mr. Morgan 2.
Second General History, Mr. Peterson 1.

GOVERNMENT:

COLLEGE COURSES

American Government, Mr. Meyerholz 2.
Local Government and Problems, Mr. Meyerholz 4.
Political Parties, Mr. Peterson 6.
Constitutional Law, Mr. Meyerholz 5.

DIPLOMA COURSES

Same as College Courses

NORMAL COURSES

Iowa Civics, Mr. Peterson 2.
U. S. Civics, Mr. Peterson 5.
Iowa and U. S. Civics, Mr. Meyerholz 1.

ECONOMICS:

COLLEGE COURSES

General Economics, Mr. Morgan 1; Mr. McKitrick 6.
Social and Economic Problems (Mon. Wed. Fri.), Mr. Mc-
    Kitrick 7.
Sociology, (Tues. Thurs.), Mr. McKitrick 7.
American Industrial History (Mon. Wed. Fri.), Mr. Mor-
    gan 3.
Money and Banking (Tues. Thurs.), Mr. McKitrick 3.

DIPLOMA COURSES

Same as College Courses

NORMAL COURSES

Elementary Economics, Mr. McKitrick 4; Mr. Morgan 5.

LATIN AND GREEK:

COLLEGE COURSES

Latin III. (The Odes of Horace), Mr. Merchant 1.
Latin IX. (Roman Literature), Mr. Merchant 2.
Latin VI. (Latin Composition), Mr. Merchant 3.

Latin XII. (Historical Latin Grammar), Mr. Merchant 3.
Latin XXI. (Third Beginning Latin), Mr. Merchant 6.
Latin XXIII. (Cicero's Orations), Miss Call 3.
Latin XXII. (Cicero's Orations), Miss Call 4.
Latin XXVI. (Ovid), Miss Call 5.
Greek XV. (Third Elementary Greek), Mr. Merchant 3.

DIPLOMA COURSES

Same as College Courses.

NORMAL COURSES

First Caesar, Miss Call 2.

GERMAN AND FRENCH:

COLLEGE COURSES

German I. (Die Jungfrau von Orleans), Miss Lorenz 5.
German II. (German Prose Composition), Miss Lorenz 2.
German V. (Ephigenie auf Tauris, and Die Braut von Messina), Miss Lorenz 3.
German XII. (Die Journalisten), Miss Lorenz 6.
German VIII. (German Classics), Mr. Knoepfler 3.
German XI. (Immensee and Hoeher als die Kirche), Mr. Knoepfler 5.
French III. Le Voyage de M. Perrichon and L'Abbe Constantin), Mr. Knoepfler 1.
French VI. (Le Gendre de M. Poirier, and un Philosophe sous les Toits), Mr. Knoepfler 2.

DIPLOMA COURSES

Same as College Courses.

NORMAL COURSES

First German Lessons, Miss Nolte 4.
Second German Lessons, Miss Nolte 2.
Third German, Miss Nolte 3.
Fourth German, Miss Nolte 6.

PHYSICS AND CHEMISTRY:

COLLEGE COURSES

Mechanics and Sound (Mon. Wed. Fri.), Mr. Begeman 2.
Laboratory Work in Mechanics (Mon. Wed.), Mr. Begeman 7 and 8.

Heat and Light (Tues. Thurs. Fri.), Mr. Begeman 4.
Advanced Course in Electricity and Magnetism (Mon. Wed.), Mr. Begeman 3-4-5.
Chemistry I., Mr. Bond 4.
Quantitive Analysis—Volumetric, Mr. Bond 1.
Chemistry III., Mr. Getchell 3.

DIPLOMA COURSES

Heat and Industrial Electricity (Mon. Wed. Fri.), Mr. Perrine 5.
Laboratory Work in Heat and Industrial Electricity (Tues. Thurs.), Mr. Perrine 5 and 6.
Chemistry XI. (Household), Mr. Getchell 7; Mr. Read 2-4.
Chemistry XIII. (Food Analysis), Mr. Bond 5.

NORMAL COURSES

First Physics, (Mon. Wed. Fri.), Mr. Perrine 3; Mr. Hersey 1.
First Physics (Tues. Thurs. Fri.), Mr. Hersey 2.
First Physics Laboratory (Mon. Wed.), Mr. Perrine 7 and 8; Mr. Hersey 5 and 6.
First Physics Laboratory (Tues. Thurs.), Mr. Hersey 3 and 4.
Second Physics (Tues. Thurs. Fri.), Mr. Perrine 4
Second Physics (Mon. Wed. Fri.), Mr. Hersey 3.
Second Physics Laboratory (Tues. Thurs.), Mr. Perrine 7 and 8; Mr. Hersey 5 and 6.

NATURAL SCIENCE:

COLLEGE COURSES

Zoology III., Mr. Arey 1.
Nature Study, Mr. Arey 3-5.
Zoology Laboratory (Mon. Wed.), Mr. Arey 7 and 8.
Physiology I., Mr. Newton 1-3-4.
Astronomy, Mr Cable 4.
Agriculture III., Mr. Davis 1.
Agriculture III. Laboratory, Mr. Davis 7 and 8.
Conservation of Natural Resources, Miss Aitchison 1.
Botany III., Mr. Palmer 2-3.
Botany III. Laboratory, (Tues. Thurs.), Mr. Palmer 7 and 8.
Geology II., Mr. Cable 2

DIPLOMA COURSES

Same as College Courses.

Normal Courses

Elementary Zoology, Mr. Arey 4.
Physiology, Mr. Newton 2.
Third Agriculture, Mr. Davis 2-3; ....2-3-4.
Agriculture Laboratory, (Mon. Wed.), Mr. Davis 7 and 8.
First half Geography, Miss Aitchison 2.
Second half Geography, Miss Aitchison 3.
Complete Geography, Miss Aitchison 4.
Elementary Botany, Mr. Palmer 1.
Elementary Physiography, Mr. Cable 1-5.

MANUAL TRAINING:

College Courses

Organization and Economics of Manual Training (Mon. Wed.
    Fri.), Mr. Bailey 1.
Woodwork, Advanced, Mr. Brown 3 and 4.
Woodwork IV. (Mon. Wed. Fri.), Mr. Brown 7 and 8.
Mechanical Drawing IX and XII. (Tues. Thurs.), Mr.
    Bailey 7 and 8.
Mechanical Drawing X. and XI. (Mon. Wed. Fri.), Mr.
    Bailey 3 and 4.
Wood Turning, Mr. Brown 3 and 4.
Sheet Metal Work, Mr. Bailey 2.

Diploma Courses

Same as College Courses.

Normal Courses

Primary Handwork, Mrs. McMahon 1-4.
Handwork for Rural Schools, Mrs. McMahon 2-5.
Woodwork for Rural Schools, Mr. Brown 6.

ART:

College Courses

History of Painting, Miss Thornton 4.
Design, Miss Patt 1-5.
Still Life, Miss Patt 3.
Perspective, Miss Thornton 3.
Water Color, Miss Thornton 1.
Supervision in Art, Miss Thornton 2.

Diploma Courses

Primary Drawing II., Miss Schuneman 1-2-3.

NORMAL COURSES

First Drawing, Miss Patt 2; Miss Schuneman 5.

HOME ECONOMICS:

COLLEGE COURSES

Elementary Food Theory III. (Mon. Wed.), Miss Young 1 and 2; Miss Goff 1 and 2; 5 and 6; Miss Stallman 3 and 4; 5 and 6.
Elementary Food Theory III., (Tues. Thurs.), Miss Goff 3 and 4.

DIPLOMA COURSES

Same as College Courses and
Household Management (Tues. Thurs. Fri.), Miss Young **1-3-5.**
Third Sewing (Daily), 2, Miss Heinz.
Third Sewing (Mon. Wed) 3 and 4, (Fri.) 3, Miss Heinz, Miss Freer.
Third Sewing, (Mon. Wed.), 1 and 2, (Fri.), 2, Miss Freer.
Third Sewing (Mon. Wed.), 5 and 6, (Fri.), 5, Miss Heinz.
Third Sewing (Tues. Thurs.) 3 and 4, (Fri.) 4, Miss Heinz, **Miss Freer.**
Third Sewing (Tues. Thurs.), 5 and 6, (Fri.) 6, Miss Freer.
Demonstrations (Mon. Wed.), Miss Young 7 and 8.
Demonstrations (Tues. Thurs. Fri.), Miss Stallman 5 and 6; Miss Goff 5 and 6.
Demonstrations (Mon. Wed. Fri.), Miss Stallman 7 and 8.

NORMAL COURSES

First Sewing, Miss Hurd 1-2.
Second Sewing, Miss Hurd 4-6.
First Cooking and Household Management (Mon. Wed.), Miss Hurd 3 and 4; 5 and 6.

PUBLIC SCHOOL MUSIC:

COLLEGE COURSES

Music II, Mr. Fullerton 3.
History of Music I., (Tues. Fri.), Miss Childs 1.
Harmony I., (Mon. Wed. Thurs.), Miss Thomson 1.

DIPLOMA COURSES

Same as College Courss and
Methods (Lower grades), (Mon. Wed. Thurs.), ... 3.
Appreciation of Music (Mon. Wed. Thurs.), Miss Thomson 5.
Supervision, (Mon. Wed. Fri.), Mr. Fullerton and Miss Stenwall 1.
Conducting (Tues. Wed. Fri.), Mr. Fullerton 4.

NORMAL COURSES

First term Music, Miss Stenwall 2-5.
Second term Music, ... 1-4.

COMMERCIAL:

DIPLOMA COURSES

Accounting II., Mr. Cummins 1.
Commercial Law, Mr. Coffey 4.
Second Typewriting, Mr. Coffey 1.
Third Typewriting, Mr. Coffey 3.
Second Shorthand, Mr. Coffey 5.
Third Shorthand, Mr. Coffey 2.

NORMAL COURSES

Elementary Bookkeeping, Mr. Cummins 2.
First Penmanship, Mr. Cummins 3-5-6.
Advanced Penmanship, Mr. Cummins 4.

PHYSICAL EDUCATION:

COLLEGE COURSES

Playground Methods II., (Mon. Wed. Fri.), Mr. Seymour 6.
Theory of Athletics I., (Tues. Thurs.), Mr. Seymour 6.

DIPLOMA COURSES

Same as College Courses and
Physiology of Exercise, Mr. Seymour 3.
Medical Gymnastics and Massage (Mon. Wed. Fri.), Mr. Seymour 4.
Physical Department Administration (Tues. Thurs.), Mr. Seymour 4.

PRACTICAL WORK

First term Physical Training (Mon. Wed.), Miss Nisbet 6.
Second term Physical Training (Mon. Wed.), Miss Wild 5.

Third term Physical Training (Tues. Thurs.), Miss Hussey 3-6; Miss Nisbet 5-7.

Third term Physical Training (Mon. Wed.), Miss Hussey 5: Miss Wild 4.

Gymnastics, Miss Hussey 7.

Tennis (Mon. Wed.), Mr. Berkstresser 5.

Tennis (Tues. Thurs.), Mr. Berkstresser 5.

Swimming (Tues. Thurs.), Miss Wild 4-5; Miss Nisbet 3.

Swimming (Mon. Wed.), Miss Hussey 3; Miss Wild 6; Miss Nisbet 4-7.

First Rhythm (Tues. Thurs.), Miss Wild 6.

Second Rhythm (Mon. Wed.), Miss Wild 7.

Folk Dancing (Tues. Thurs.), Miss Wild 7.

Folk Dancing (Mon. Wed.), Miss Nisbet 3-5.

Baseball (Mon. Wed.), Mr. Berkstresser 6.

Baseball (Tues. Thurs.), Miss Nisbet 4-6; Mr. Berkstresser 6.

Golf (Mon. Wed.), Mr. Seymour 5.

Golf (Tues. Thurs.), Mr. Seymour 5.

Corrective Work, Miss Hussey 4.

Athletics, etc., Miss Hussey 8.

Track Team, Mr. Seymour 7 and 8.

Baseball team, Mr. Berkstresser 7 and 8.

C

XVI.   *JULY 1915*   No. 2.

BULLETIN

DEC 9

OF THE

IOWA STATE TEACHERS COLLEGE

CEDAR FALLS, IOWA

1915-16

·COURSES OF STUDY

AND

PROGRAM OF RECITATIONS

FOR SCHOOL YEAR 1915-1916

Issued Quarterly.   Published by the Iowa State Teachers College.
Entered as second-class mail matter August 31, 1912,
at the post office at Cedar Falls, Iowa, under
the Act of Congress, August 24, 1912.

IOWA STATE TEACHERS COLLEGE

SCHOOL CALENDAR FOR 1915-1916

FALL TERM—TWELVE WEEKS

1915

Sept. 15—Wednesday, Enrollment, without penalty, 8:00 A. M. to 4:00 P. M. One dollar penalty for later dates.

Sept. 16—Thursday, Recitations begin 8:00 A. M., class periods as on program. Training Schools open 9:00 A. M.

Oct. 27, 28, 29—Wednesday, Thursday, Friday, Examination for Uniform County Certificates, beginning Wednesday, 8:00 A. M. Examination for State Certificates if arranged in advance.

Dec. 7—Tuesday, Recitations close at noon.

Winter Term—Twelve Weeks.

Dec. 8—Wednesday, Enrollment, without penalty, 8:00 A. M. to 4:00 P. M. One dollar penalty for later dates.

Dec. 9—Thursday, Recitations begin 8:00 A. M., class periods as on the program.

Dec. 21—Tuesday, Holiday Recess, beginning at noon and continuing two weeks.

1916

Jan. 5—Wednesday, Recitations resumed, 8:00 A. M.

Jan. 26, 27, 28—Wednesday, Thursday, Friday, Examination for Uniform County Certificates, beginning Wednesday, 8:00 A. M. Examination for State Certificates if arranged in advance.

March 14—Tuesday, Recitations close at noon.

Spring Term—Twelve Weeks.

March 15—Wednesday, Enrollment, without penalty, 8:00 A. M. to 4:00 P. M. One dollar penalty for later dates.

March 16—Thursday, Recitations begin 8:00 A. M. Class periods as on the program.

June 2—Friday, Recitations close at noon.

June 2 to 6—Commencement Exercises.

Summer Term—Twelve Weeks.

June 7—Wednesday, Enrollment, without penalty, 8:00 A. M. to 4:00 P. M.

June 8—Thursday, Recitations begin 7:00 A. M., class periods as on the program.

June 28, 29, 30—Wednesday, Thursday, Friday, Examination for Uniform County Certificates. Examination for State Certificates if arranged in advance.

July 26, 27, 28—Wednesday, Thursday, Friday, Examination for Uniform County Certificates. Examination for State Certificates if arranged in advance.

August 29—Tuesday, Recitations close at noon.

REQUIREMENTS FOR ADMISSION

Applicants for unconditional admission to the Degree or Diploma Courses must be at least sixteen years of age and must present 15 units of satisfactory work from accredited high schools or the equivalent as hereafter printed in detail.

I. The Degree Course (Bachelor of Arts in Education).

1. English	3	units
2. One Foreign Language	2	units
3. History, Civics, Economics	1	unit
4. Algebra	1½	units
5. Plane Geometry	1	unit
6. Electives	6½	units

Total 15   units

II. The Diploma Courses (Two-Year Courses in Kindergarten, Primary, Grade Teacher, Music, Manual Training, Home Economics, Drawing, Commercial and a three-year course in Physical Education).

1. English	3	units
2. Algebra thru quadratics	1	unit
3. Plane Geometry	1	unit
4. History, Civics, Economics	1	unit
5. Electives	9	units

Total 15   units

III. Elementary Normal Courses—Three Years.
A first Grade Uniform County Certificate or its equivalent.

IV. The Rural Teachers Course—Two Years.
Completion of the Eighth Grade work in Town or Rural School.

Notes.—1. Students from High Schools should file official statements showing the work completed in high school.
2. Those who have had no high school work should file the County Certificate or an official statement from the City Superintendent or the County Superintendent showing the completion of the Eighth Grade work.
3. Graduates of Four Year Courses in Non-Accredited high schools need to take entrance examinations in one-third of each group of high school subjects presented or they may validate the high school credits by taking work here in secondary subjects selected by the College Examiner. Those who have not completed a four year course in high school may make up the remaining units by taking secondary work offerd in the Elementary Normal Courses and in the Rural Teachers Course.

Electives.

The constants and electives in the above requirements may be accepted from the following subjects (For full details see Bulletin

No. 1 of the Board on Secondary School Relations):

I. Foreign Language.
    1. Latin .... 2 to 4 units
    2. German .... 2 to 4 units
    3. Greek .... 2 to 4 units
    4. French .... 2 to 4 units
    5. Spanish .... 2 to 4 units

II. English (Not to exceed 4 units).

III. History, Civics, Economics (Not to exceed 4 units).
    1. Ancient History .... ½ to 1 unit
    2. Medieval and Modern History...... ½ to 1 unit
    3. Civil Government .... ½ to 1 unit
    4. Economics .... ½ unit
    5. General History in place of 1 and
       2 above .... 1 unit
    6. U. S. History in 3rd or 4th year.... ½ to 1 unit
    7. English History .... ½ to 1 unit

IV. Mathematics (Not to exceed 4 units).
    1. Algebra .... 1 to 1½ units
    2. Plane Geometry .... 1 unit
    3. Solid Geometry .... ½ unit
    4. Trigonometry .... ½ unit
    5. Adv. Algebra in 4th year......... ½ unit
    6. Adv. Arithmetic (See below)...... ½ unit

V. Science, Commercial, and Industrial Subjects.
    A. (Not to exceed 4½ units in this list.)
       1. Physics .... 1 unit
       2. Chemistry .... 1 unit
       3. Agriculture .... ½ to 1 unit
       4. Physiography .... ½ to 1 unit
       5. Botany .... ½ to 1 unit
       6. Physiology .... ½ unit
       7. Zoology .... ½ to 1 unit
       8. Geology .... ½ unit
       9. Astronomy .... ½ unit

    B. (Not to exceed 2 units in this list.)
       1. Bookkeeping .... ½ to 1 unit
       2. Commercial Geography .... ½ unit
       3. Commercial Law .... ½ unit
       4. Industrial History .... ½ unit
       5. Adv. Arithmetic after Algebra.... ½ unit

    C. (Not to exceed 2 units in this list.)
       1. Freehand and Mechanical Drawing.. ½ to 1 unit
       2. Manual Training, i. e., Shop Work.. ½ to 2 units
       3. Domestic Science .... ½ to 1 unit
       4. Stenography .... ½ to 1 unit

Note: Credit is not given for English Grammar or U. S. History unless taken in the last half of the course, nor for Arithmetic unless taken after Algebra.

THE COLLEGE DEGREE COURSES

Details of the Requirements For The Degree Bachelor Of Arts In Education.

The Plan of the Course.—This degree course requires credit for 180 term hours distributed thru four years, each divided into three twelve week terms. A term hour consists of one hour a week for twelve weeks. A student's work for a term consists of 15 term hours. An additional hour a day is permitted in vocal music, instrumental music, drawing, elementary manual training, elementary domestic science, penmanship, or other art subject.

The Major Study.—Each student in the course must select a major study not later than the beginning of the Junior year. A major consists of 30 term hours of work in the study chosen, but the student may elect up to 60 term hours in the major. When the major is selected, the head of the department becomes the adviser of said student during the pursuance of the course. The following are the major studies offerd:

1. English.
2. Public Speaking.
3. Latin.
4. German.
5. French.
6. Mathematics.
7. Physics.
8. Chemistry.
9. Earth Science.
10. Biological Science.
11. History.
12. Government.
13. Economics.
14. Education.
15. Drawing.
16. Manual Arts.
17. Home Economics.
18. Physical Education.

The Minor Study.—After consulting the student, the adviser selects a minor study which must include not less than 15 term hours nor more than 30 term hours in the study selected. When the major and minor are chosen from the same group as hereafter outlined, not more than a total of 75 term hours can be taken in the two elections combined.

Groups of Subjects Recognized.

The following groups of subjects are recognized in arranging the work for an individual course of study leading to a degree.

I. The Professional Group.
II. The English Group.
III. The Foreign Language Group.
IV. The History, Government, and Economics Group.
V. The Science and Mathematics Group.

VI. The Home Economics, Drawing, Physical Education or Manual Arts Group.

VII. The Primary, Kindergarten, Public School Music, or Commercial Group.

Regulations Governing Groups And The Arrangement Of Studies In The Course.

When the Major study is determined by the student, the head of the department becomes the adviser and the entire course is pland. The adviser decides the minor study. The student decides the quantity taken in both major and minor studies beyond the minimum. The possible maximum varies with the amount of work offerd by the several departments. No combination of Major and Minor studies can exceed 75 term hours if both are selected from the same group.

I. The Professional Group.

1. The Major study—Education.
    Minimum ....30 term hours
    Maximum ....54 "   "
2. The Minor Study—Minimum...............15 term hours
    Maximum...............30 "   "
3. Constant requirements.
    (1) English ....15 term hours
    (2) Foreign Language ....15 "   "
    (3) History, Government, and Economics...15 "   "
    (4) Science and Mathematics.............20 "   "
    (5) Teaching ....10 "   "
4. Elective requirements.
    (1) Enough additional term hours to make at least a total of 180 term hours.
    (2) Outside of the Major study, the Minor study, and the Professional work, the total credit in any other Major study can not exceed 20 term hours.

II. The English Group.

1. The Major study—English or Public Speaking.
    Minimum ....30 term hours
    Maximum, English......................60 "   "
    Public Speaking ....49 "   "
2. The Minor study—Minimum...............15 "   "
    Maximum...............30 "   "
3. Constant Requirements.
    (1) Professional ....40 term hours
    (2) Foreign Language ....15 "   "
    (3) History, Government, and Economics..15 "   "
    (4) Science and Mathematics.............20 "   "
4. Elective Requirements.
    (1) Enough additional term hours to make at least a total of 180 term hours.
    (2) Outside of the Major study, the Minor study, and the Professional work, the total credit in any other major study can not exceed 20 term hours.

III. The Foreign Language Group.

 1. The Major study—Latin or German.
 Minimum....................30 term hours (See catalog)
 Maximum, Latin ....60 term hours
      German ....45 "   "
 2. The Minor Study—Minimum...............15 term hours
                 Maximum................30 "   "
 3. Constant Requirements.
     (1) Professional work ....40 term hours
     (2) English ....15 "   "
     (3) History, Government, and Economics...15 "   "
     (4) Science and Mathematics..............20 "   "
 4. Elective Requirements.
     (1) Enough additional term hours to make at least a total of 180 term hours.
     (2) Outside of the Major Study, the Minor study, and the Professional work, the total credit in any other major study can not exceed 20 term hours.

IV. The History, Government, and Economics Group.

 1. The Major study—History or Government or Economics.
 Minimum ....30 term hours
 Maximum, History ....46 "   "
      Government ....38 "   "
      Economics ....35 "   "
 2. The Minor study—Minimum...............15 term hours
                 Maximum................30 "   "
 3. Constant Requirements.
     (1) Professional ....40 term hours
     (2) English ....15 "   "
     (3) Foreign Language ....15 "   "
     (4) Mathematics and Science..............20 "   "
 4. Elective Requirements.
     (1) Enough additional term hours to make at least a total of 180 term hours.
     (2) Outside of the Major study, the Minor study, and the Professional work, the total credit in any other major study can not exceed 20 term hours.

V. Science and Mathematics Group.

 1. The Major—Physics or Chemistry or Earth Science or Biological Science or Mathematics.
 Minimum ....30 term hours
 Maximum, Chemistry ....40 "   "
      Physics ....31 "   "
      Earth Science ....45 "   "
      Biological Science ....60 "   "
      Mathematics ....45 "   "
 2. The Minor—Minimum.....................15 term hours
               Maximum.....................30 "   "
 3. Constant Requirements.
     (1) Professional ....40 term hours
     (2) English ....15 "   "

        (3)   Foreign Language 15   "   "
        (4)   History, Government, and Economics..15   "   "
    4. Elective Requirements.
        (1)   Enough additional term hours to make at least a total of 180 term hours.
        (2)   Outside of the Major study, the Minor study, and the Professional work, the total credit in any other major study can not exceed 20 term hours.

  VI.   The Home Economics, Drawing, Manual Arts, or Physical Education Group.

    1. The Major study—Home Economics, or Drawing, or Manual Arts, or Physical Education.
        Minimum ....30 term hours
        Maximum, *Home Economics...............20 "   "
               *Drawing ....27½ "   "
               Manual Arts ....43 "   "
               Physical Education ....45 "   "
    2. The Minor Study—Minimum................15 term hours
                     Maximum................30 "   "
    3. Constant Requirements.
        (1)   Professional ....40 term hours
        (2)   English 15   "   "
        (3)   Foreign Language 15   "   "
        (4)   History, Government, and Economics..15   "   "
        (5)   Science and Mathematics..............30   "   "
    4. Elective Requirements.
        (1)   Enough additional term hours to make at least a total of 180 term hours.
        (2)   Outside of the Major study, the Minor study, the required Science work, and the Professional work, the total credit in any other Major study can not exceed 20 term hours.

REQUIREMENTS FOR B. A. DEGREE AFTER COMPLETING THE TWO YEAR COURSES REPRESENTED IN GROUP VI.

    1. Home Economics.

1st and 2nd years			Junior and Senior.		
Home Economics.20	term hours		**Professional 15	term hours	
Professional 30	"	"	***English 10	"	"
English 5	"	"	***Foreign Lan-		
Science 30	"	"	guage 15	"	"
Elective 5	"	"	***History, Etc.....15	"	"
			***Chemistry 10	"	"
Total 90	"	"	Electives 25	"	"
			Total 90	"	"

*These are combined with Education in making the Major.

**This includes 5 term hours of Teaching for which substitution may be made at the discretion of the Department.

***If part of this work is taken as Elective on the Diploma Course, the student may substitute other Electives in the Junior and Senior years.

2. Art.

1st and 2nd years			Junior and Senior.		
Art	27½	term hours	**Professional 15	term hours	
Manual Training			***English 10	"	"
or Music	2½	" "	***Science & Math.30	"	"
Professional	30	" "	***Foreign Lan-		
English	5	" "	guage 15	"	"
History	5	" "	***History, Etc.....10	"	"
Electives	20	" "	Elective 10	"	"
Total	90	" "	Total 90	"	"

3. Manual Arts.

1st and 2nd years			Junior and Senior.		
Manual Arts.....	32½	term hours	**Professional 15	term hours	
Art	5	" "	***English 10	"	"
Professional	30	" "	***Foreign Lan-		
English	5	" "	guage 15	"	"
Special Elect.....	5	" "	***Science & Math.30	"	"
Electives	12½	" "	***History, Etc.....15	"	"
			Electives 5	".."	".."
Total	90	" "			
			Total 90	"	"

4. Physical Education.

1st, 2nd, and 3rd years			Senior Year		
Physical Educa-			**Professional 15	term hours	
cation	45	term hours	***Foreign Lan-		
Professional	35	" "	guage 15	"	"
English	15	" "	***Science & Math. 5	"	"
Schience &			***History, Etc.....15	"	"
Math.	25	" "			
Electives	15	" "	Total ****50	"	"
Total	135	" "			

VII. The Primary Teacher, Kindergarten Teacher, Public School
Music Teacher, or Commercial Teacher Group.

1. The Major Study—Primary School work, or Kindergarten,
or Public School Music, or Commercial.
Minimum ....30 term hours
Maximum, *Primary & Drawing...........15 "   "
*Kindergarten & Drawing.......20 "   "
Public School Music.............42 "   "
*Commercial ....20 "   "

*See previous page.
**See previous page.
***See previous page.
****At least 5 term hours of this should be taken as Elective on the
Diploma Course so as to leave only 45 term hours for the Senior Year.

2. The Minor study—Minimum................15 term hours
               Maximum................30   "   "

3. Constant Requirements.

    (1) Professional ....40 term hours
    (2) English 15   "   "
    (3) Foreign Language....................15   "   "
    (4) Science and Math....................20   "   "
    (5) History, Government, and Economics..15   "   "

4. Elective Requirements.

    (1) Enough additional term hours to make at least a total of 180 term hours.
    (2) Outside of the Major Study, the Minor study, and the Professional work, the total credit in any other Major study can not exceed 20 term hours.

Requirements For The B. A. Degree After Completing The Two Year Courses Represented In Group VII.

1. Primary Teacher.

1st and 2nd years	Junior and Senior
Primary & Drawing 15 term hours	Professional ......10 term hours
Professional ......35 " "	***English .... 5 " "
English ....10 " "	***Foreign Language ....15 " "
Science & Math.... 8 " "	***Science & Math.12 " "
Electives ....22 " "	***History, Govt., & Econ. ....15 " "
Total ....90 " "	Elective ....33 " "
	Total ....90 " "

2. Kindergarten Teacher.

1st and 2nd years	Junior and Senior
Kindergarten & Drawing ....20 term hours	Professional ......10 " "
Professional ......35 " "	***English 5
English ....10 " "	***Foreign Language ....15 " "
Science & Math.... 5 " "	***Science & Math.15 " "
Elective ....20 " "	***History, Govt., & Econ. ....15 " "
Total ....90 " "	Elective ....30 " "
	Total ....90 " "

**See previous page.
***See previous page.

3. Public School Music Teacher.

1st and 2nd years		Junior and Senior	
Public School Music 40 term hours		**Professional ....15 term hours	
Professional ......30 " "		***English ....10 " "	
English .... 5 " "		***Foreign Lan-	
Elective ... .15 " "		guage ....15 " "	
		***Science & Math.20 " "	
Total ....90 " "		***History, Govt.,	
		and Economics.15 " . "	
		Elective ....15 " "	
		Total ....90 " "	

4. Commercial Teacher.

1st and 2nd years		Junior and Senior	
Commercial ....20 term hours		**Professional ....15 term hours	
Professional ...:..30 " "		***English ....10 " "	
English .... 5 " "		***Foreign Lan-	
Science & Math....10 " "		guage ....15 " "	
History, Govt., &		***Science & Math.10 " "	
Economics ....10 " "		***History, Govt.,	
Electives ....15 " "		and Economics. 5 " "	
		Electives ....35 " "	
Total ....90 " "			
		Total ....90 " "	

Outline Of The Degree Course By Years Showing the Location Of Constants.

Freshman Year—45 term hours.

Rhetoric .... 5 term hours
Foreign Language ....15 " "
Electives ....25 " "

Literary Society Work.
Physical Training.

Note.—With the consent of the Adviser and the Registrar, foreign language may be delayed until the Sophomore year. The Electives must be chosen from Freshman studies.

Sophomore Year—45 term hours.

Education I, II, and III................................15 term hours
English IX, and II, III, or VIII........................10 " "
Electives ....20 " "

Literary Society Work.
Physical Training.

Junior Year—45 term hours.

Education IV, V, and VI...............................15 term hours
Electives ....30 " "

**See previous page.
***See previous page.

Senior Year—45 term hours.

Teaching ....10 term hours
Electives 35   "   "

The Master of Didactics Degree Course For College Graduates.

I. Professional Course—45 term hours.

This course includes a full year's work in Education and Teaching and is pland to suit individual needs by the Head of the Department of Education, who becomes the student's adviser. With the facilities here for a study of the rural and city school systems this year's work is very rich in development and training.

II. Professional Course with Electives—45 term hours.

1. Education, 15 term hours.
2. Teaching, 10 term hours.
3. Elective with the approval of the adviser, 20 term hours.

III. Professional Course as Special Teachers—45 term hours.

This course is pland by the Head of the Department of Education to give training to college graduates who wish to prepare in the line of experts in rural education, in normal training in high schools, in public school music, in physical education, in manual training, in home economics, in drawing, in commercial, in kindergarten, or in primary teaching.

The Critic Teachers Course.

This course is pland for the special development, education, and training of critic teachers for normal training high schools and for work as teachers in the training department of state normal schools. The following conditions govern the admission, study, and graduation from this course.

I. The Entrance Requirements.—The applicant must have completed a diploma course of this college, or its equivalent.

II. Required work for the Critic Teachers Certificate.—

1. Time—Two years.
2. Satisfactory completion of 15 term hours of critic training credit (college credit on this course only) and 30 term hours of other college work approved by the Director of the Training School.
3. During these two years, critics in training are allowd to carry 5 term hours each term in addition to the critic training work.

III. Required Work for the Degree Bachelor of Arts in Education.—

1. Enough credit to make a total of 180 term hours distributed in accordance with the requirements of the B. A. Course outlined on previous pages, except that the major shall consist of Teaching—15 term hours, and Critic Training—15 term hours.
   NOTE.—Students taking this course are selected by the department for work as Critics in Training.

THE DIPLOMA COURSES

The Plan Presented.—These courses represent the latest conception of organization to meet the needs of special training for different fields of public school work and yet place regard upon collegiate scholarship as an essential to efficient preparation. Graduates of these courses are admitted to the Junior class in the Degree Course without conditions, provided they have complied with all the entrance conditions demanded in that course.

Conditions of Admission.—Admission to diploma courses requires 15 units, as follows: 3 units of English, 1 unit of Algebra (thru quadratics), 1 unit of Plane Geometry, 1 unit from the History, Government, and Economics group, and 9 units Elective, selected from those outlined for admission to the Degree Course.

Honors Conferd.—Appropriate diplomas granted by the Faculty are conferd for completing the courses outlined. These diplomas will show the special qualifications of the graduates and will commend them as traind teachers. The Educational Board of Examiners agrees to grant second grade state certificates to all graduates who complete one of these courses and who show credit for 10 term hours in Psychology, 5 term hours in School Management, 5 term hours in History of Education, and 10 term hours in Teaching as required at the Teachers College. These state certificates authorize the possessor to teach in any school in Iowa and give the teacher's specialization. For persons who may graduate from any of these diploma courses without having met all these requirements in Psychology,. Education, and Teaching, a third grade state certificate will be granted, the second grade state certificate being obtainable whenever the deficiencies occurring have been removed.

THE GENERAL TEACHERS COURSE.

This course is organized to give two years of instruction and training to high school graduates who desire to become principals, supervisors, or grade teachers. It is in conformity with the requirements for the second grade state certificate.

First Year.—45 term hours.

Education I, II, and III..............................15 term hours
Rhetoric 5   "   "
Electives 25   "   "
    Literary Society.
    Physical Training.

Second Year—45 term hours.

Education IV... 5 term hours
Teaching 10   "   "
Electives 30   "   "
    Literary Society.
    Physical Training.

Note 1: The electives above indicated must be of College grade and must include Botany, Physiography or Geology, Advanced Physiology or Sanitation, Physics, American History, American Government, and Economics unless the corresponding subjects were presented and accepted for entrance.

Note 2: An additional requirement of 3 term credits must be met by election under the adviser from Penmanship, Vocal Music, Drawing, Orthography, Arithmetic, or English Grammar, unless these subjects were taken in the secondary school.

PRIMARY TEACHERS COURSE.

First Year—43 term hours.

Primary Methods (12 hours of recitation)................6 term hours
Education I, II, and III................................15 "   "
Rhetoric .... 5 "   "
English Elective 5
Nature Study .... 5 "   "
Primary Theory and Observation (4 a week)............. 2 "   "
Drawing (2 terms—5 a week)............................ 5 "   "
Manual Arts (1 term—5 a week).........................
    Literary Society.
    Physical Training.

Second Year—47 term hours.

Education IV .... 5 term hours
Hygiene and Sanitation (b)............................. 3 "   "
Criticism and Practice................................15 "   "
Kindergarten Theory and Observation (4 a week)....... 2
Electives ....22 "   "
Vocal Music (2 terms-5 a week)........................
    Literary Society.
    Physical Training.

KINDERGARTNERS COURSE.

First Year—47½ term hours.

Kindergarten Theory (1 year-5 a week)............... 7½ term hours
Education I, II, and III...............................15 "   "
Rhetoric and Elective in English.....................10 "   "
Drawing (2 terms—5 a week)............................ 5 "   "
Nature Study .... 5 "   "
Elective .... 5 "   "
    Literary Society.
    Physical Training.

Second Year—42½ term hours.

Kindergarten Theory (1 term—5 a week and 1 term—6
    a week) .... 5½ term hours
Kindergarten Practice (1 year—5 a week)............15 "   "
Education IV 5

Primary Theory (1 term—4 a week)................. 2   "   "
Electives 15   "   .   "
Vocal Music (2 terms—5 a week)....................
   Literary Society.
   Physical Training.

PUBLIC SCHOOL MUSIC TEACHERS COURSE.

First .Year—45 term hours.

Education I, II, and III..............................15   term hours
Rhetoric 5   "   "
Harmony I 3   "   "
History of Music I.................................. 2   "   "
Music I (5 a week)................................. 2½   "   "
Music II (5 a week)................................ 2½   "   "
Sight Singing (Lower grades—3 a week)............. 2½   "   "
Sight Singing (Upper grades—3 a week)............. 2½   "   "
Conducting (3 a week) .... 2½   "   "
Methods (Lower grades—3 a week)................... 2½   "   "
Elective 5   "   "
   Literary Society.
   Physical Training.

Second Year—45 term hours.

Education IV 5   term hours
Harmony II 2   "   "
History of Music II................................ 3   "   "
Teaching 10   "   "
Methods (Upper grades—3 a week).................. 2½   "   "
High School Music and Child Voice (3 a week)........ 2½   "   "
Appreciation of Music (3 a week)................... 2½   "   "
Theory of Music (3 a week)......................... 2½   "   "
Harmony III 3   "   "
Supervision (3 a week)............................. 2   "   "
Electives 10   "   "
   Literary Society.
   Physical Training.

ART TEACHERS COURSE.

First Year—45 term hours.

Education I, II, III...............................15   term hours
Rhetoric 5   "   "
History Elective 5   "   "
Cast Drawing I and II.............................. 5   "   "
Design .... 2½   "   "
History of Architecture............................ 5   "   "
History of Painting................................ 5   "   "
Elective .... 2½   "   "
   Literary Society.
   Physical Training.

Second Year—45 term hours.

Education IV 5   term hours
Teaching 10   "   "
Still Life ....2½   "   "
Perspective ....2½   "   "
Art Supervision ....2½   "   "
Water-Color ....2½   "   "
Manual Training or Music.............................2½   "   "
Elective ....17½   "   "
   Literary Society.
   Physical Training.

MANUAL ARTS TEACHERS COURSE.

First Year—44 term hours.

Education I, II, III.................................15   term hours
Rhetoric 5   "   "
Mechanical Drawing I, II, III........................ 8   "   "
Woodwork I, II, III.................................. 7   "   "
Freehand Drawing (5 a week).........................2½   "   "
Design (5 a week)...................................2½   "   "
Illustrative Teaching ....1½   "   "
Elementary Handwork (5 a week)....................
Special Elective ....2½   "   "
   Literary Society.
   Physical Training.

Second Year—46 term hours.

Education IV 5   term hours
Manual Training I and II............................ 8   "   "
Woodwork IV 5   "   "
Sheet Metal Work...................................2½   "   "
Woodturning 2   "   "
Teaching ....8½   "   "
Special Elective ....2½   "   "
Elective ....12½   "   "
   Literary Society.
   Physical Training.

HOME ECONOMICS TEACHERS COURSE.

First Year—44 term hours.

Chemistry IX, X, and XI.............................15 term hours
Rhetoric ....: 5   "   "
Education I and II..................................10   "   "
Elementary Food Theory (3 terms).................... 6
Food Principles (2 terms)........................... 6
Household Management (1 term—2 a week)............ 1
Household Methods (1 term)........................ 1
Sewing (3 terms)...................................
   Literary Society.
   Physical Training.

Second Year—46 term hours.

```
Education III and IV.................................10 term hours
Teaching ..........................................10   "      "
Chemistry XII .....................................  5   "      "
Hygiene and Sanitation (a).........................  5
Physiology I ......................................  5
Dietetics (2 a week)...............................  1
Advanced Cooking (2 a week)........................  1
Serving (2 a week).................................  1
Household Architecture ............................  2
Demonstrations ....................................  1
Elective ..........................................  5
```
  Literary Society.
  Physical Training.

PHYSICAL EDUCATION TEACHERS COURSE.

First Year—45 term hours.

```
Anatomy I and II...................................10 term hours
Physiology I ......................................  5   "      "
Education I, II, and III...........................15   "      "
Rhetoric ..........................................  5
Public Speaking I or Elocution I...................  5
English Literature ................................  5
```
  Literary Society.
  Double work in Physical Training.

Second Year—45 term hours.

```
Theory of Physical Education.......................  5 term hours
Hygiene and Sanitation (a).........................  5    "      "
Chemistry I, II, and III...........................15    "      "
Education IV ......................................  5    "      "
Playground Methods I and II........................  6
First Aid to the Injured...........................  2    "      "
Theory of Athletics I..............................  2    "      "
Genetic Psychology ................................  5
```
  Literary Society.
  Double work in Physical Training.

Third Year—45 term hours.

```
Anthropometry .....................................  3 term hours
Physical Diagnosis ................................  2    "      "
Theory of Athletics II.............................  2    "      "
Physiology of Exercise.............................  5
Medical Gymnastics and Massage ....................  3
Physical Department Administration ................  2
Teaching ..........................................10    "      "
History of Physical Education......................  3
Electives .........................................15    "      "
```
  Physical Training and Officiating.

COMMERCIAL TEACHERS COURSE.

First Year—45 term hours.

```
Education I, II, III..................................15 term hours
Rhetoric ............................................... 5   "    "
Mathematical Elective ............................... 5   "    "
Commercial Correspondence.......................... 5
Commercial Law .................................... 5
Accounting I and II.................................10   "    "
```
Literary Society.

Physical Training.

Second Year—45 term hours.

```
American Government ............................... 5 term hours
Education IV ......................................... 5   "    "
General Economics ................................. 5   "    "
Commercial Geography ............................. 5   "    "
Teaching ..............................................10   "    "
Electives .............................................15   "    "
Shorthand and Typewriting (three terms).............
```
Literary Society.

Physical Training.

NORMAL DIPLOMA COURSES

THE RURAL TEACHERS COURSE.

1. Admission is made on the basis of the rural school diploma.

2. The recognition for graduation is the rural teacher diploma and the state certificate for five years.

3. The branches included in the course are as follows:

I. Second Grade Uniform County Certificate Subjects:

Reading	English Language and Grammar
Geography	Physiology
Arithmetic	Vocal Music
U. S. History	Penmanship
Orthography	

Note: Each subject represented here is given credit on the course when the student has received 85 per cent on the Uniform County Certificate. When 75 per cent has been received, one term's work is required in each subject. When less than 75 per cent has been received two term's work is required in geography, arithmetic, language and grammar, and United States history.

II. First Grade Uniform County Certificate Subjects:

Elementary Civics	Algebra
Elementary Economics	Physics

Note: When 85 per cent has been obtained in the Uniform County Examination that subject is given credit on this course. When taken in class one term's work is required in civics and economics and two term's work in algebra and physics.

III. **Additional Subjects Required for the Diploma:**
(1) Didactics, one term.
(2) General Primary Methods, one term.
(3) The Country School, one term.
(4) Observation and Teaching, one term.
(5) *Domestic Science, two terms.
(6) Agriculture, two terms.
(7) Handwork, one term.
(8) Woodwork, one term.
(9) Elementary Psychology, one term.
(10) Drawing, one term.

Notes: The observation and Teaching here outlined consists of demonstration teaching in the training department and in work done in the demonstration rural schools maintaind by the Teachers College. This term's work will be provided during each term of the college year so that the graduating class may be divided into suitable sections.

The subjects of study represented by this course are all on the program of recitations each term of the year so that a student can come any term and get credit work.

Uniform county certificate examinations are given at the institution on the same dates as are required by law at the county superintendents' offices.

THE GENERAL NORMAL COURSE FOR GRADE TEACHERS.

Admission.—First Grade Uniform County Certificate.

Recognition.—The Normal Diploma and Second Grade State Certificate.

Value of Credits.—Each subject, except physical training and literary society work, printed in this table requires five recitations a week of one hour each.

First Year.

Algebra, 2nd and 3rd	two terms
General History	two terms
First English Classics	one term
**Bookkeeping	one term
**Elementary Elocution	one term
First English Composition	one term
Physiography	one term
Vocal Music	one term
Drawing	two terms
Physical Training	three terms

Second Year.

Second English Classics	one term
Physics	two terms
Plane Geometry	two terms

*Additional work in Manual Arts and Agriculture may be substituted for this.
**Latin or German electives may be substituted.

Elementary Botany ....one term
*Manual Arts or Elementary Agriculture...................two terms
Second English Composition................................one term
*Solid Geometry...one term
Psychology ....two terms
Physical Training.......................................three terms
Literary Society Work...................................three terms

Third Year.

School Management...one term
College Algebra I or Trigonometry.........................one term
History of Education......................................one term
Rhetoric ....one term
General Economics...one term
American Government.......................................one term
American History..one term
Teaching ....two terms
Special Electives.......................................three terms
Literary Society Work...................................three terms

Notes: Students who have completed the vocational work, the algebra, or physics required in the Rural Teachers Course will be granted credit in proportion to the work accomplished, thus abridging the above requirements.

The special electives of the third year are intended for Manual Arts, Home Economics, Commercial studies, or Elementary Agriculture, as the student may elect.

THE VOCATIONAL NORMAL COURSE.

For rural and consolidated school teachers.

Admission.—First Grade Uniform County Certificate.

Recognition.—The Normal Diploma and Second Grade State Certificate.

Value of Credits.—Each subject, except physical training and literary society work, printed in this table requires five recitations a week of one hour each.

First Year.

Algebra, 2nd and 3rd......................................two terms
General History...two terms
First English Classics....................................one term
Bookkeeping ....one term
Physiography ....one term
First English Composition.................................one term
Elementary Elocution......................................one term
Vocal Music...one term
Domestic Science ....two terms
Physical Training.......................................three terms

*Latin or German electives may be substituted.

Second Year.

Plane Geometry ....two terms
Physics ....two terms
Elementary Agriculture......................................two terms
Second English Classics.....................................one term
Elementary Botany...one term
Psychology ....two terms
Drawing ....two terms
Physical Training...three terms
Literary Society Work.......................................three terms

Third Year.

Second English Composition..................................one term
School Management...one term
American History..one term
General Economics...one term
History of Education..one term
American Government...one term
Rhetòric ....one term
Teaching ....two terms
Manual Arts ....two terms
Special Elective..one term
Literary Society Work.......................................three terms

Note: This course is arranged for the giving of special qualifications of a superior kind in modern standards. These courses will be taught so as to give the teacher in training practical efficiency in educating the boys and girls of the farms of the state. The practice in teaching will be broad in its scope and notably efficient in its extent.

Special Students.

Preparation for the examination given by the State Educational Board of Examiners for special teacher certificates.

Teachers of twenty-one years of age and those who may be holders of a first grade uniform county certificate are admitted to such classes in special courses in primary, kindergarten, public school music, manual training, home economics, drawing, or commercial studies as will probably prepare them for the examinations that are required by the state for the obtaining of such recognition. Credits earnd in this way do not count on a course toward graduation. Such persons should make all arrangements with the Registrar before appearing for work in order to have their studies properly adjusted.

SPECIAL COURSE IN VOICE, PIANO, ORGAN AND ORCHESTRAL INSTRUMENTS

Conditions of Admission.—Students are admitted to these special music courses on liberal terms as to preparatory training and are encouraged to begin early enough to develop the skill and capability for professional artistic success that are so notably demanded in teachers of these kinds.

To become a candidate for graduation, the student must have attaind to the scholastic qualification required of secondary schools for full college entrance. These scholastic conditions may be acquired in any good secondary school or may be accomplished in the normal courses at the College.

Conditions of Graduation.—A special Music Diploma will be awarded to such persons as complete satisfactorily any one of the courses here outlined, it being understood that skill and capability as musicians are also qualities to be attaind. On account of these conditions the exact time required to complete any one of these courses can not be stated in school years. The candidate must have sufficient proficiency in the special line chosen to secure the recommendation of the professors in charge of the work in order to apply for graduation. The courses as here mapped out, outside of the attainment in capability as a musician, can be satisfactorily completed in two years.

VOICE, PIANO AND ORGAN COURSES.

Piano—Professor: John Ross Frampton

Instructors: Elizabeth Platner
Grace C. Thomson

Voice—Professors: Anna Gertrude Childs
Lowell E. M. Welles
Harriet Case

Organ—Professor: John Ross Frampton

These courses are pland to train students for capability as performers and for becoming special teachers.

The requirements for graduation are as follows:

1. Two lessons a week for at least two years in the major course, all this work to be done if possible under the instructor recommending for graduation.

2. Satisfactory public performance of a recital in the major study, the program to be of moderate difficulty.

3. Two years of a "minor" course in music (Piano, organ, voice or any of the instruments taught in the orchestral department). It is understood that two lessons a week in the minor for one year shall not be the equivalent of two years' study.

4. Harmony equivalent to the texts of Chadwick or Bussler.

5. Two terms of Music History.

6. One five hour course of general culture each term, except the Senior year. This course to be selected by the personal adviser of the student, and to be of college grade in case the student has no entrance deficiencies.

7. Literary Society work is recommended but not required.

8. A certificate of Musical Proficiency will be granted to those who complete the piano, voice, or organ work alone.

VIOLIN AND OTHER ORCHESTRAL INSTRUMENTS.

Professor: B. Winfred Merrill

Assistants: Alma Cutler
            Frank Lynn McCreary

This course is pland to train a student for capability as a performer and for becoming a special teacher.

The requirements for graduation are as follows:

1. Violin instruction sufficient to enable the pupil to render a program the equivalent of a Beethoven Sonata, the Mendelssohn Concerto and similar works, to the satisfaction of the head of the department.

2. Two years of piano (one lesson a week).

3. Two years of harmony—the equivalent of Chadwick or Bussler.

4. Two years of ear training and dictation in relation to the harmony.

5. Orchestra and Ensemble during the course.

6. Two terms of Music History.

The diploma of the College will be given when the student has satisfactorily completed this course, together with the requirements for college entrance. A certificate of Musical Proficiency will be granted to those who complete the violin work alone.

All students shall take at least one scholastic branch each term they are enrolled unless they are excused by the head of the department.

The courses for all other orchestral instruments including Oboe, Flute, Clarinet, Bassoon, Cornet, French Horn, Trombone, Tuba, Cello, Double Bass, and Harp are identical with the violin course. It is possible, however, to finish the courses of some of these instruments in less time than that of the violin.

PROGRAM OF RECITATIONS

EXPLANATORY NOTE

The program of recitations is for Fall, Winter and Spring terms, 1915-1916. Changes may be made and program extended, if the number enrolled makes this necessary.

The arabic numerals following the teachers' names indicate periods in which the subjects are given, i. e., 3-4 shows two sections (one reciting the third period and the other the fourth period); while 3 and 4 means one section extending over the third and fourth periods.

The periods are as follows:

```
First ................................ 8:00 to  9:00
Second .............................. 9:00 to 10:00
Chapel ..............................10:00 to 10:20
Third ...............................10:25 to 11:25
Fourth ..............................11:25 to 12:25
Fifth ............................... 1:30 to  2:30
Sixth ............................... 2:30 to  3:30
Seventh ............................. 3:30 to  4:30
Eighth .............................. 4:30 to  5:30
```

FALL TERM

EDUCATION:

COLLEGE COURSES

Psychology I., Mr. Sampson 1-4-5.
Psychology II., Mr. Sampson 2.
School Management, Mr. Colegrove, 2-3; Mr. Buffum 3-5.
History of Education, Mr. Walters 2-4-5.
Philosophy of Education, Mr. Walters 1.
School Administration, Mr. Colegrove 1.
Experimental Psychology, Mr. Mount 5.

DIPLOMA COURSES

Same as College Courses and
Psychology I., Mr. Mount 1-2; Miss Buck 3-4-5-6; Mr. Buffum 6.
Psychology II., Mr. Mount 3.
Primary Methods I. (2½ hrs.), Miss McGovern 1-2-3-5.

RURAL EDUCATION:

NORMAL COURSES

Didactics, Mr. Campbell 1.
Elementary Psychology, Mr. Campbell 3.
General Methods, Mr. Hart 1.
Observation and Teaching, Mr. Hart, 2.
The Country School, Mr. Campbell 4.

TEACHING

COLLEGE COURSES

Illustrative Teaching (1½ hrs), Mr. Stone, Miss Fesenbeck, Miss
    Hughes, Miss Luse, Miss Correll, Miss Cresswell, 4-5-6.
Practice Teaching as arranged.
Conference Teaching (½ hr.) as arranged.

Same as College Courses and
Kindergarten Theory I. (2½ hrs.), Miss Brown 3.
Criticism (Mon., Tues., Wed., Thurs.), Miss Scofield 6.

NORMAL COURSES
Rural Demonstration Teaching, Mr. Stone and training school
    critics 2.

ENGLISH:

COLLEGE COURSES
College Rhetoric, Mr. Lynch 1; Mr. Gist 2-5; Miss Carpenter 4;
    Miss Lambert 4; Mr. Barnes 1-3; Mr. Fagan 2-3-6; Miss Siner 6.
Theme Writing and Story Telling, Miss Carpenter 3.
Argumentation I. (3 hrs.), Mr. Barnes 6.
Argumentation II. (3 hrs.), Mr. Barnes 6.
English Literature, Mr. Lynch 4.
Shakespeare, Mr. Gist 3.
Literary Criticism, Miss Carpenter 1.
The History of the English Drama I., Miss Lambert 1.
Milton (3 hrs.), Mr. Lynch 3.
Recent American Literature (3 hrs.) (M. W. F.), Miss Lambert 3.
Elocution I., Miss Martin 1-4; Miss Falkler 2; Miss Shanewise 3.
Elocution II., Miss Martin 2; Miss Shanewise 4.
Repertoire II., Miss Martin 3.

DIPLOMA COURSES
Same as College Courses.

NORMAL COURSES
First Half Language and Grammar, Miss Hutchison 2-3-4.
Second Half Language and Grammar, Miss Hutchison 6.
Complete Language and Grammar, Miss Gregg 2-3-4.
Reading, Miss Falkler, 3-6.
Elementary Elocution, Miss Falkler 4.
First Term English Composition, Miss Siner 2-4.
First Term English Classics, Miss Oliver 5.
Second Term English Classics, Miss Gregg 5.
Orthography (a), Miss Oliver 1-2.

MATHEMATICS:

COLLEGE COURSES
Solid Geometry, Mr. Wright 4.
College Algebra I., Mr. Condit 5-6.
Plane Trigonometry, Mr. Daugherty 5.
Analytical Geometry, Mr. Condit 3.

DIPLOMA COURSES
Same as College Courses.

NORMAL COURSES
First Half Arithmetic, Miss Lambert 3-4; Mr. Daugherty 1.
Second Half Arithmetic, Miss Allen 6.
Complete Arithmetic, Mr. Condit 2; Mr. Daugherty 4.

First Term Algebra, Miss Allen 1-2.
Second Term Algebra, Miss Allen 5.
Third Term Algebra, Miss Lambert 2-5.
First and Second Term Algebra, Mr. Daugherty 3.
Beginning Geometry, Mr. Wright 2.
Middle Geometry, Mr. Wright 1.

HISTORY:

COLLEGE COURSES

Greek History, Miss Rice 4.
Renaissance and Reformation, Miss Riggs 3.
American History I., Miss Riggs 5.
Method History I. (2 hrs.). (Tu. Th.), Miss Riggs 6.

DIPLOMA COURSES

Same as College Courses.

NORMAL COURSES

First Half United States History, Miss Rice 1-2.
Second Half United States History, Miss Rice 5.
Complete United States History, Miss Riggs 4; Mr. Mitchell 2.

GOVERNMENT:

COLLEGE COURSES

American Government, Mr. Meyerholz 2; Mr. Peterson 4.
English Government (3 hrs.) (M.W. F.), Mr. Peterson 6.
Municipal Government (3 hrs.). (M. W. F.), Mr. Meyerholz 3.
American Constitutional History I., Mr. Meyerholz 6.

DIPLOMA COURSES

Same as College Courses.

NORMAL COURSES

Elementary Civics of Iowa, Mr. Peterson 3.
Elementary Civics of the United States, Mr. Peterson 2.
Review of Iowa and U. S. Civics (non-credit), Mr. Meyerholz 1.

ECONOMICS:

COLLEGE COURSES

General Economics, Mr. McKitrick 6; Mr. Mitchell 1.
Social and Economic Problems I. (3 hrs.), Mr. McKitrick 1.
Sociology (2 hrs.), Mr. McKitrick 1.
American Industrial History I. (3 hrs.), Mr. Mitchell 7.
English Industrial History (2 hrs.), Mr. Mitchell 7.

DIPLOMA COURSES

Same as College Courses.

NORMAL COURSES

Elementary Economics, Mr. McKitrick 2; Mr. Mitchell 4.

LATIN:

COLLEGE COURSES

Latin I. (Livy and Latin Composition), Mr. Merchant 1.
Latin IV. (Latin Composition) (2 hrs.) (Tu. Th.), Mr. Merchant 3.
Latin VII. (Roman Literature) (3 hrs.) (M. W. F.), Mr. Merchant 2.
Latin X. (Historical Latin Grammar) (2 hrs.) (Tu. Th.), Mr.
    Merchant 4.
Greek I. (3 hrs.) (M. W. F.), Mr. Merchant 3.
Greek IV. (2 hrs.) (Tu. Th.), Mr. Merchant 2.
Vergil I. (Vergil's Aeneid), Miss Call 5.
College Ele. Latin I., Mr. Merchant 6.

DIPLOMA COURSES

Same as College Courses.

NORMAL COURSES

First Term Latin Lessons, Miss Call 2.
First Term Caesar and Latin Composition, Miss Call 4.
Second Term Caesar and Latin Composition, Miss Call 3.

GERMAN AND FRENCH:

COLLEGE COURSES

German I. (Die Jungfrau von Orleans), Miss Lorenz 5.
German II. (Emilia Galotti and Lyrics and Ballads), Miss Lorenz 2.
German III. (Nathan der Weise), Miss Lorenz 1.
German VI. (Der dreissigjaehrige Krieg), Mr. Knoepfler 3.
German IX. (German Lessons), Mr. Knoepfler 5.
German XII. (Die Journalisten), Miss Lorenz 6.
French I. (French Lessons), Mr. Knoepfler 1.
French IV. (L'historie d'un jeune Homme pauvre and Colomba),
    Mr. Knoepfler 2.

DIPLOMA COURSES

Same as College Courses.

NORMAL COURSES

First Term German, Miss Nolte 6.
Second Term German, Miss Nolte 2.
Third Term German, Miss Nolte 3.
Fourth Term German, Miss Nolte 4.

PHYSICS AND CHEMISTRY:

COLLEGE COURSES

Physics I. (Mechanics and Sound) (3 hrs.) (M. W. F.), Mr. Bege-
    man 2.
Physics II. (Laboratory Physics in Mechanics) (2 hrs.) (Tu. Th.),
    Mr. Begeman 7 and 8.
Physics VII. (Advanced Mechanics) (3 hrs.) (M. W. F.), Mr. Bege-
    man 6 and 7.

DIPLOMA COURSES

Same as College Courses and
Physics XI. (Sound) (3 hrs. or 5 hrs.), Mr. Begeman 4.
Physics XIV. (Physics or Common Things) (3 hrs.), Mr. Begeman 5.

NORMAL COURSES

First Term Physics, Mr. Hersey 1-2; Mr. Read 3-4.
First Term Physics Laboratory, Mr. Read 7 and 8.
Second Term Physics, Mr. Hersey 3.
Second Term Physics Laboratory, Mr. Hersey 5 and 6.

CHEMISTRY:

COLLEGE COURSES

Chemistry I. (General Inorganic Chemistry), Mr. Getchell 3.
Chemistry II. (General Inorganic Chemistry), Mr. Getchell 6.
Quantitative Analysis, Mr. Getchell 5.
Chemistry IX. (Inorganic), Mr. Getchell 7; Mr. Bond 4; Mr. Read 1.
Chemistry XII. (Chemistry of Food and Nutrition), Mr. Bond 5.
Chemistry XIII. (Food Analysis), Mr. Bond 1.
Chemistry Laboratory as arranged (under each division).

NATURAL SCIENCE:

COLLEGE COURSES

Zoology I. Mr. Arey 1-3.
Zoology I. Laboratory (M. W. or Tu. Th.), Mr. Arey 7 and 8.
Physiology I., Mr. Newton 1.
Hygiene and Sanitation (a), Mr. Newton 3.
Hygiene and Sanitation (b) (3 hrs.), Mr. Newton 4-5.
Physiography I., Mr. Cable 2.
Mineralogy I., Mr. Cable 4.
Agriculture I., Mr. Oldenburg 1.
Commercial and Economic Geography of North America, Miss
    Aitchison 6.
Botany I., Mr. Palmer 3.
Botany Laboratory, Mr. Palmer 3 and 4.

DIPLOMA COURSES

Same as College Courses.

NORMAL COURSES

Elementary Zoology, Mr. Arey 5.
Elementary Physiology, Mr. Newton 2.
First Elementary Agriculture, Mr. Oldenburg 2-5; Mr. ...... 3-4.
Agriculture Laboratory, Mr. Oldenburg 6 and 7; Mr......7 and 8.
First Half Geography, Miss Aitchison 1.
Second Half Geography, Miss Aitchison 2.
Complete Geography, Miss Aitchison 3.
Elementary Botany, Mr. Palmer 1-2.
Elementary Physiography, Mr. Cable 1-5.

MANUAL ARTS:

COLLEGE COURSES

Manual Training Methods I., Mr. Bailey 2.
Woodwork I. (3 hrs.) (M. W. F.), Mr. Brown 7 and 8.
Mechanical Drawing I. (2 hrs.) (Tu. Th.), Mr. Bailey 7 and 8.
Mechanical Drawing IV. (2 hrs.) (Tu. Th.), Mr. Bailey 7 and 8.
Mechanical Drawing II. (3 hrs.) (M. W. F.), Mr. Bailey 3 and 4.
Mechanical Drawing III. (3 hrs.) (M. W. F.), Mr. Bailey 3 and 4.
Wood Turning (2 hrs.), Mr. Brown 3 and 4.
Advanced Woodwork, Mr. Brown 3 and 4.

DIPLOMA COURSES

Same as College Courses.

NORMAL COURSES

Primary Handwork, Miss Dandliker 1-2.
Handwork for Rural Schools, Miss Schuneman 3-4.
Woodwork for Rural Schools, Mr. Brown 5-6.
Elementary Woodwork, Mr. Brown 3 and 4.
Elementary Mechanical Drawing, Mr. Bailey 7 and 8.

ART:

COLLEGE COURSES

Cast Drawing I. (2½ hrs.), Miss Patt 5.
Still-life (2½ hrs.), Miss Thornton 2.
Perspective (2½ hrs.), Miss Thornton 1.
Water-Color (2½ hrs.), Miss Thornton 4.

DIPLOMA COURSES

Same as College Courses and
Kindergarten Drawing I. (2½ hrs.), Miss Patt 2.
Primary Drawing I. (2½ hrs.), Miss Patt 3-4.

NORMAL COURSES

Drawing for Rural Schools, Miss Schuneman 1-2.

HOME ECONOMICS:

COLLEGE COURSES

Elementary Food Theory I. (2 hrs.) (Tu. Th.), Miss Young 1 and
    2; 3 and 4; 5 and 6.
Principles of the Selection and Preparation of Foods I. (3 hrs.)
    (M. W. F.), Miss Young 3-4-5.
Advanced Cookery (1 hr.) (Wed.), Miss Young 1 and 2; 7 and 8;
    (Thurs.) Miss Roberts 3 and 4.

DIPLOMA COURSES

Same as College Courses and
Dietetics (1 hr.) (Mon.), Miss Young 1 and 2; 7 and 8; (Tues.)
    Miss Roberts 3 and 4.
First Term Sewing (Sub-collegiate)
    Sections A and B (M. W. F. 1 and M. W. 2), Miss Roberts
        and Miss Freer.
    Section C (M. W. F. 3 and M. W. 4), Miss Roberts.
    Section D (Tu. Th. 3 and Tu. Th. F. 4), Miss Freer.
    Sections E and F (M. W. 5 and M. W. F. 6), Miss Roberts
        and Miss Freer.

NORMAL COURSES

First Domestic Science:
    Section A (Daily 1 and Tu. Th. 2), Miss Osborne and Miss
        Hurd.
    Section B (Daily 3 and M. W. 4), Miss Osborne and Miss
        Hurd.
    Section C (Daily 5 and Tu. Th. 6), Miss Osborne and Miss
        Hurd.

Second Domestic Science:
  Section A (Daily 2 and M. W. 1), Miss Osborne and Miss
    Hurd.
  Section B (Daily 3 and Tu. Th. 4), Miss Osborne and Miss
    Hurd.

COMMERCIAL EDUCATION:

DIPLOMA COURSES

Commercial Correspondence, Mr. Coffey 5.
First Term Shorthand (Sub-collegiate), Mr. Coffey 3.
Second Term Shorthand (Sub-collegiate), Mr. Coffey 2.
Typewriting (Sub-collegiate), Mr. Coffey 4.

NORMAL COURSES

Elementary Bookkeeping, Mr. Cummins 2.
First Term Shorthand, Mr. Coffey 3.
Second Term Shorthand, Mr. Coffey 2.
Typewriting, Mr. Coffey 4.
First Term Penmanship, Mr. Cummins 1-3-5-6.
Advanced Penmanship, Mr. Cummins 4.

MUSIC:

COLLEGE COURSES

Music I. (2½ hrs.), Miss Barr 1.
Music II. (2½ hrs.), Mr. Fullerton 3.
History of Music I. (2 hrs.) (Tu. Th.), Miss Childs 2.
History of Music II. (3 hrs.) (M. W. F.), Miss Childs 6.
Harmony I. (3 hrs.) (M. W. F.), Miss Thomson 2.
Harmony II. (2 hrs.) (Tu. Th.), Miss Thomson 6.
Harmony III. (3 hrs.) (M. W. F.), Miss Thomson 4.

DIPLOMA COURSES

Same as College Courses and
Methods (Upper Grades) (2½ hrs.) (M. W. F.), Miss Hooper 4.
High School Music and Child Voice (2½ hrs.), Mr. Fullerton 1.

DIPLOMA COURSES

First Term Music, Mr. Fullerton 2-4; Miss Barr 4; Miss Hooper
  1; Miss Thomson 5.
Second Term Music, Miss Barr 3.

PHYSICAL EDUCATION:

COLLEGE COURSES

Anatomy I., Mr. Seymour 3.
Theory of Physical Education, Mr. Seymour 4; Miss Hussey 4.
Theory of Athletics I. (2 hrs.) (M. W.), Mr. Seymour 5.

DIPLOMA COURSES

Same as College Courses and
Anthropometry (3 hrs.), Mr. Seymour 2.
Physical Diagnosis (2 hrs.), Mr. Seymour 2; Miss Hussey 2.

PRACTICAL WORK

First Physical Training (Primary), Miss Wild 4-5.
First Physical Training (M. W.), Miss Hussey 5; Miss Nisbet 6;
  Miss Grantham 3.

First Physical Training (Tu. Th.), Miss Nisbit 4-7.
Second Physical Training (Tu. Th.), Miss Wild 6.
Third Physical Training (Tu. Th.), Miss Nisbet 8.
Third Physical Training (M. W.), Miss Grantham 6.
Gymnastics, Miss Hussey 7.
Tennis (Tu. Th.), Miss Nisbet 3; Mr. Berkstresser 5; Miss Wild 7.
Tennis (M. W.), Mr. Berkstresser 3-4-5; Miss Nisbet 5.
Swimming (Tu. Th.), Mr. Berkstresser 4; Miss Wild 8; Miss
   Nisbet 6; Miss Grantham 3-7.
Swimming (M. W.), Miss Wild 6; Miss Nisbet 3; Miss Gran-
   tham 4-5.
Tennis, Mr. Seymour 6.
Esthetic Dancing (Tu. Th.), Miss Hussey 6.
Folk Dancing (Tu. Th.), Miss Nisbet 5.
Folk Dancing (M. W.), Miss Grantham 7-8.
Athletics (M. W.), Miss Hussey 8.
First Rhythm (M. W.), Miss Wild 7.
Hockey (M. W.), Miss Nisbet 7.
Baseball (Tu. Th.), Miss Grantham 6.
Advanced Gymnastics (M. W.), Mr. Seymour 8.
Plays and Games (Tu. Th.), Mr. Seymour 5; Mr. Berkstresser 3.
Elementary Football, Mr. Berkstresser 6.
Football, Mr. Berkstresser 7 and 8.
Corrective Work, Miss Hussey 8; Miss Grantham 5.

WINTER TERM
EDUCATION:

COLLEGE COURSES

Psychology I., Mr. Samson 4.
Psychology II., Mr. Samson 1-2-5.
School Management, Mr. Colegrove 3; Mr. Buffum 3.
History of Education, Mr. Walters 1-2; Mr. Buffum 6.
Philosophy of Education, Mr. Walters 4.
Logic (2 hrs.) (Tu. Th.), Mr. Walters 6.
Experimental Psychology, Mr. Mount 7.
Genetic Psychology, Mr. Mount 1.

DIPLOMA COURSES

Same as College Courses and
Psychology I., Miss Buck 3-4-5.
Psychology II., Mr. Colegrove 1-2; Mr. Mount 3-4; Miss Buck 6;
   Mr. Buffum 1-2.
Primary Methods I. (2½ hrs.), Miss McGovern 5.
Primary II. (2½ hrs.), Miss McGovern 1-2-3.

RURAL EDUCATION:

COLLEGE COURSES
Rural School Problems, Mr. Hart 3.

NORMAL COURSES
Didactics, Mr. Campbell 1.
Elementary Psychology, Mr. Campbell 3.
General Methods, Mr. Hart 1.
Observation and Teaching, Mr. Hart 2.
The Country School, Mr. Campbell 4.

TEACHING:

COLLEGE COURSES

Illustrative Teaching (1½ hrs.), Mr. Stone, Miss Fesenbeck, Miss Hughes, Miss Luse, Miss Correll, Miss Cresswell 5.

Practice Teaching as arranged.

Conference Teaching (½ hr.) as arranged.

DIPLOMA COURSES

Same as College Courses and

Kindergarten Theory II. (2½ hrs.), Miss Brown 2.

Kindergarten Theory IV. (2½ hrs.), Miss Brown 4.

Criticism (M. T. W. Th.), Miss Scofield 6.

NORMAL COURSES

Rural Demonstration Teaching, Mr. Stone and Training School Critics 2.

ENGLISH:

COLLEGE COURSES

College Rhetoric, Mr. Fagan 2-3-5; Miss Siner 3.

Advanced Exposition, Mr. Lynch 2.

Public Speaking I., Mr. Barnes 3.

Public Speaking II. (3 hrs.), Mr. Barnes 5.

Argumentation I. (3 hrs.), Mr. Barnes 2.

Argumentation II. (3 hrs.), Mr. Barnes 2.

English Literature, Mr. Gist 3; Miss Carpenter 1-3; Miss Lambert 2-4.

Anglo-Saxon (3 hrs.) (M. W. F.), Mr. Gist 5.

History of the English Language (2 hrs.) (Tu. Th.), Mr. Gist 5.

The History of the English Drama II., Miss Lambert 1.

Tennyson (3 hrs.), Mr. Gist 2.

American Literature, Mr. Lynch 3.

The English Romantic Movement, Miss Carpenter 4.

Elocution I., Miss Martin 2; Miss Falkler 3; Miss Shanewise 4.

Elocution II., Miss Martin 1; Miss Shanewise 3.

Applied Drama, Miss Martin 4.

Repertoire I., Miss Martin 3.

The Teaching of English, Mr. Lynch 7.

DIPLOMA COURSES

Same as College Courses.

NORMAL COURSES

First Half Language and Grammar, Miss Hutchison 1-4-5.

Second Half Language and Grammar, Miss Gregg 5.

Complete Language and Grammar, Miss Gregg 3-4.

Reading, Miss Falkler 4-5.

Elementary Elocution, Miss Falkler 2.

First Half English Composition, Miss Siner 1.

Second Half English Composition, Miss Siner 5.

First Term English Classics, Miss Oliver 4.

Second Term English Classics, Miss Gregg 2.

Orthography (a), Miss Oliver 1-2.

MATHEMATICS:

COLLEGE COURSES

Solid Geometry, Mr. Wright 1.
College Algebra I., Miss Lambert 3-6.
Plane Trigonometry, Mr. Condit 2.
Differential Calculus, Mr. Condit 3.

DIPLOMA COURSES

Same as College Courses.

NORMAL COURSES

First Half Arithmetic, Mr. Daugherty 2-4.
Second Half Arithmetic, Miss Lambert 2-5; Mr. Daugherty 6.
Complete Arithmetic, Mr. Condit 5-6.
First Term Algebra, Miss Allen 4.
Second Term Algebra, Miss Allen 1-2.
Third Term Algebra, Miss Allen 5.
First and Second Term Algebra, Mr. Daugherty 1.
Beginning Geometry, Mr. Wright 4.
Middle Geometry, Mr. Wright 3.

HISTORY:

COLLEGE COURSES

Roman History, Miss Rice 3.
American History I., Miss Riggs 2.
18th Century History I. (2 hrs.) (Tu. Th.), Miss Riggs 5.
19th Century History I. (3 hrs.) (M. W. F.), Miss Riggs 4.
American History II. (3 hrs.) (M. W. F.), Miss Riggs 5.

DIPLOMA COURSES

Same as College Courses.

NORMAL COURSES

First Half United States History, Miss Rice 4.
Second Half United States History, Miss Rice 5.
Complete United States History, Miss Riggs 3; Mr. Mitchell 1.
First Term General History, Miss Rice 2.

GOVERNMENT:

COLLEGE COURSES

American Government, Mr. Meyerholz 2; Mr. Peterson 3.
Modern European Governments (3 hrs.), Mr. Meyerholz 5.
American Constitutional History II., Mr. Meyerholz 6.

DIPLOMA COURSES

Same as College Courses.

NORMAL COURSES

Elementary Civics of Iowa, Mr. Peterson 5.
Elementary Civics of the United States, Mr. Peterson 4.
Review of Iowa and U. S. Civics (non-credit), Mr. Meyerholz 3;
    Mr. Peterson 1.

ECONOMICS:

COLLEGE COURSES

General Economics, Mr. McKitrick 6; Mr. Mitchell 2.
Social and Economic Problems II. (3 hrs.), Mr. McKitrick 1.
Sociology (2 hrs.), Mr. McKitrick 1.
American Industrial History II. (3 hrs.), Mr. Mitchell 7.
Public Finance I. (2 hrs.), Mr. McKitrick 7.

DIPLOMA COURSES

Same as College Courses.

NORMAL COURSES

Elementary Economics, Mr. McKitrick 2; Mr. Mitchell 4.

LATIN:

COLLEGE COURSES

Latin II. (Livy and the Epodes of Horace), Mr. Merchant 1.
Latin V. (Latin Composition) (2 hrs.), Mr. Merchant 3.
Latin VIII. (Roman Literature) (3 hrs.), Mr. Merchant 2.
Latin XI. (Historical Latin Grammar) (2 hrs.), Mr. Merchant 4.
Greek II. (3 hrs.), Mr. Merchant 3.
Greek V. (2 hrs.), Mr. Merchant 2.
College Ele. Latin II., Mr. Merchant 6.
Cicero I., Miss Call 3.
Vergil II., Miss Call 5.

DIPLOMA COURSES

Same as College Courses.

NORMAL COURSES

Second Term Latin Lessons, Miss Call 2.
Second Term Caesar and Latin Composition, Miss Call 4.

GERMAN AND FRENCH:

COLLEGE COURSES

German I. (Die Jungfrau von Orleans), Miss Lorenz 5.
German II. (Emilia Galotti and Lyrics and Ballads), Miss Lorenz 2.
German IV. (German Prose Composition), Miss Lorenz 3.
German VII. (Modern German Prose, or Scientific German), Mr. Knoepfler 3.
German X (German Lessons), Mr. Knoepfler 5.
German XII (Die Journalisten), Miss Lorenz 6.
French II. (French Lessons), Mr. Knoepfler 1.
French V. (Le Bourgeois Gentilhomme and La Mare au Diable), Mr. Knoepfler 2.

DIPLOMA COURSES

Same as College Courses.

NORMAL COURSES

First Term German, Miss Nolte 4.
Second Term German, Miss Nolte 6.
Third Term German, Miss Nolte 3.
Fourth Term German, Miss Nolte 2.

PHYSICS AND CHEMISTRY:

Physics I. (Mechanics and Sound) (3 hrs.) (M. W. F.), Mr. Bege-
man 2.
Physics II. (Laboratory Physics in Mechanics) (2 hrs.), Mr. Bege-
man 7 and 8.
Physics V. (Electricity and Magnetism) (3 hrs.) (Tu. Th. F.)
Mr. Begeman 4.
Physics VI. (Laboratory Physics in Electricity and Magnetism)
(2 hrs.) (M. W.), Mr. Begeman 5 and 6.
Physics VIII. (Advanced Course in Light) (3 hrs.), Mr. Begeman
5 and 6.

DIPLOMA COURSES

Same as College Courses.

NORMAL COURSES

First Term Physics, Mr. Hersey 3; Mr. Read 1-2.
First Term Laboratory Physics, Mr. Hersey 7 and 8; Mr. Read 5
and 6.
Second Term Physics, Mr. Hersey 4-5; Mr. Read 3.
Second Term Laboratory Physics, Mr. Hersey 7 and 8.

CHEMISTRY:

COLLEGE COURSES

Chemistry II. (General Inorganic Chemistry), Mr. Getchell 3.
Chemistry III. (Chemistry of Metals and Qualitative Analysis),
Mr. Getchell 6.
Quantitative Analysis, Mr. Getchell 7 and 8.
Chemistry X., Mr. Bond 4-7; Mr. Getchell 1.
Chemistry XIII. (Food Analysis), Mr. Bond 5.
Chemistry XIV. (Textiles) (3 hrs. or 2 hrs.), Mr. Bond 6.
Chemical Laboratory as arranged (under each division).

NATURAL SCIENCE:

COLLEGE COURSES

Zoology II., Mr. Arey 1.
Hygiene and Sanitation (a), Mr. Newton 2-4-5.
Influence of Geography upon American History, Mr. Cable 4.
Geology I., Mr. Cable 2.
Agriculture II., Mr. Oldenburg 1.
Commercial Geography of Europe, Miss Aitchison 5.
Botany II., Mr. Palmer 3.
Botany II. Laboratory (Tu. Th.), Mr. Palmer 4.
Botany IV. (3 hrs.) (Tu. W. Th.), Mr. Palmer 5-6.
Bacteriology (2 hrs.) (Tu. Th.), Mr. .... 6 and 7.
Zoology II. Laboratory (M. W.), Mr. Arey 7 and 8.
Agriculture Laboratory as arranged.

DIPLOMA COURSES

Same as College Courses.

NORMAL COURSES

Elementary Physiology, Mr. Newton 3.
First Elementary Agriculture, Mr. ....2-3-5.

Second Elementary Agriculture, Mr. Oldenburg 2-3.
First Half Geography, Miss Aitchison 1.
Second Half Geography, Miss Aitchison 2.
Complete Geography, Miss Aitchison 3.
Elementary Botany, Mr. Palmer 2.
Elementary Physiography, Mr. Cable 1-3.
Agriculture Laboratory as arranged.

MANUAL ARTS:

COLLEGE COURSES

Manual Training Methods II (3 hrs.) (M. W. F.), M. Bailey 4.
Woodwork I. (3 hrs.) (M. W. F.), Mr. Brown 3 and 4.
Advanced Woodwork, Mr. Brown 5 and 6.
Mechanical Drawing I. (2 hrs.) (Tu. Th.), Mr. Bailey 3 and 4.
Mechanical Drawing IV. (2 hrs.) (Tu. Th.), Mr. Bailey 3 and 4.
Mechanical Drawing II. (3 hrs.) (M. W. F.), Mr. Bailey 5 and 6.
Mechanical Drawing III. (3 hrs.) (M. W. F.), Mr. Bailey 5 and 6.
Wood Turning (2 hrs.), Mr. Brown 5 and 6.
Sheet Metal Work I. (2½ hrs.), Mr. Bailey 2.

DIPLOMA COURSES

Same as College Courses.

NORMAL COURSES

Primary Handwork, Miss Dandliker 1.
Elementary Handwork, Miss Dandliker 2.
Handwork for Rural Schools, Miss Schuneman 2-3.
Woodwork for Rural School, Mr. Brown 1-7.
Elementary Woodwork, Mr. Brown 3 and 4.
Elementary Mechanical Drawing, Mr. Bailey 3.

ART:

COLLEGE COURSES

History of Architecture and Sculpture, Miss Thornton 5.
Cast Drawing II. (2½ hrs.), Miss Patt 5.
Still-life (2½ hrs.), Miss Thornton 4.
Perspective (2½ hrs.), Miss Thornton 6.

DIPLOMA COURSES

Same as College Courses and
Kindergarten Drawing II. (2½ hrs.), Miss Thornton 3.
Primary Drawing I. (2½ hrs.), Miss Patt 1-2-3.
Primary Drawing II. (2½ hrs.), Miss Schuneman 1.

NORMAL COURSES

Drawing for Rural Schools, Miss Schuneman 4.

HOME ECONOMICS:

COLLEGE COURSES

Elementary Food Theory II. (2 hrs.) (Tu. Th.), Miss Young 1 and
    2; 3 and 4; 5 and 6.
Principles of the Selection and Preparation of Foods II. (3 hrs.)
    (M. W. F.), Miss Young 3-4-5.

DIPLOMA COURSES

Same as College Courses and
Household Architecture (2 hrs.) (M. W.), Miss Young 3.
Dietetics (1 hr.) (Tues.), Miss Roberts 3 and 4.
Serving (1 hr.), Miss Young 7 and 8.
Second Term Sewing (Sub-collegiate):
  Sections A and B (M. W. F. 1 and M. W. 2), Miss Roberts
    and Miss Freer.
  Section C (M. W. F. 3 and M. W. 4), Miss Roberts.
  Section D (Tu. Th. 3 and Tu. Th. F. 4), Miss Freer.
  Sections E and F (M. W. 5 and M. W. F. 6), Miss Roberts
    and Miss Freer.

NORMAL COURSES

First Domestic Science:
  Section A (Daily 1 and Tu. Th. 2), Miss Osborne and Miss
    Hurd.
  Section B (Daily 3 and M. W. 4), Miss Osborne and Miss
    Hurd.
  Section C (Daily 5 and Tu. Th. 6), Miss Osborne and Miss
    Hurd.
Second Domestic Science:
  Section A (Daily 2 and M. W. 1), Miss Osborne and Miss
    Hurd.
  Section B (Daily 4 and Tu. Th. 3), Miss Osborne and Miss
    Hurd.

COMMERCIAL EDUCATION:.

DIPLOMA COURSES

Accounting I., Mr. Cummins 1.
First Term Shorthand (Sub-collegiate), Mr. Coffey 2.
Second Term Shorthand (Sub-collegiate), Mr. Coffey 1.
Third Term Shorthand (Sub-collegiate), Mr. Coffey 3.
Typewriting (Sub-collegiate), Mr. Coffey 4.

NORMAL COURSES

Elementary Bookkeeping, Mr. Cummins 2.
First Term Shorthand, Mr. Coffey 2.
Second Term Shorthand, Mr. Coffey 1.
Third Term Shorthand (Sub-collegiate), Mr. Coffey 3.
Typewriting, Mr. Coffey 4.
First Term Penmanship, Mr. Cummins 3-5-6.
Advanced Penmanship, Mr. Cummins 4.

MUSIC:

COLLEGE COURSES

Music I. (2½ hrs.), Mr. Fullerton 2.
History of Music I. (2 hrs.) (Tu. Th.), Miss Childs 4.
History of Music II. (3 hrs.) (M. W. F.), Miss Childs 3.
Marmony I. (3 hrs.) (M. W. F.), Miss Thomson 4.
Harmony III. (3 hrs.) (M. W. F.), Miss Thomson 6.

DIPLOMA COURSES

Same as College Courses and
Sight Singing—Upper Grades (2½ hrs.), Mr. Fullerton 3.
Sight Singing—Lower Grades (2½ hrs.), Miss Hooper 2.
Theory of Music (2½ hrs.), Miss Thomson 1.

NORMAL COURSES

First Term Music, Mr. Fullerton 1-4; Miss Barr 4; Miss Hooper 5.
Second Term Music, Miss Barr 3-6.

PHYSICAL EDUCATION:

COLLEGE COURSES

Anatomy II., Mr. Seymour 3.
Playground Methods I. (3 hrs.) (M. W. F.), Mr. Seymour 5.
History of Physical Training (3 hrs.) (M. W. F.), Mr. Seymour 4.
First Aid to the Injured (2 hrs.) (Tu. Th.), Mr. Seymour 4.

PRACTICAL WORK

First Physical Training (M. W.), Miss Nisbet 6.
Second Physical Training (M. W.), Miss Hussey 4-5; Miss Grantham 3.
Second Physical Training (Tu. Th.), Miss Hussey 5-6; Miss Grantham 4-7.
Third Physical Training (M. W.), Miss Wild 4.
Third Physical Training (Tu. Th.), Miss Wild 4-6; Miss Nisbet 5.
Department Gymnastics (M. W. F.), Miss Hussey 7.
Advanced Gymnastics (Fri.), Mr. Seymour 6.
First Gymnastics (M. W.), Mr. Berkstresser 4-6.
Esthetic Dancing (Tu. Th.), Miss Hussey 7.
Athletics (Tu. Th.), Hiss Hussey 8.
Basketball (M. W.), Miss Wild 3.
Basketball (Tu. Th.), Miss Nisbet 6-7.
Basketball League, Mr. Berkstresser 7.
Basketball Team, Mr. Berkstresser 8.
Folk Dancing (M. W.), Miss Wild 5; Miss Grantham 7.
Folk Dancing (Tu. Th.), Miss Nisbet 4; Miss Grantham 3-5.
Advanced Folk Dancing (M. W.), Miss Nisbet 8.
First Rhythm (Tu. Th.), Miss Wild 5.
First Rhythm (M. W.), Miss Grantham 6.
Plays (M. W.), Miss Wild 7.
Games (Tu. Th.), Miss Wild 8.
Indoor Games (M. W.), Miss Nisbet 4-5.
Swimming (M. W.), Mr. Berkstresser 5.
Swimming (Tu. Th.), Mr. Berkstresser 4.
Second Gymnastics (Tu. Th.), Mr. Berkstresser 6.
Plays and Games (Tu. Th.), Mr. Seymour 5.
Gymnastic Team, Mr. Seymour 8.
Corrective Work (M. W.), Miss Nisbet 3-7.
Corrective Work (Tu. Th.), Miss Grantham 6-8.
Dancing, Miss Grantham 5.

SPRING TERM

EDUCATION:

COLLEGE COURSES

Psychology I., Mr. Samson 5.
Psychology II., Mr. Samson 2-3

School Management, Mr. Colegrove 1-2-3; Mr. Buffum 3-5-6.
History of Education, Mr. Walters 1-2.
Philosophy of Education, Mr. Walters 4.
Ethics (2 hrs.), Mr. Samson 6.
Experimental Psychology, Mr. Mount 5.
Genetic Psychology, Mr. Mount 4.
Educational Classics, Mr. Walters 5

DIPLOMA COURSES

Same as College Courses and
Psychology I., Miss Buck 1-2.
Psychology II., Mr. Mount 1-2; Miss Buck 3-5.
Primary Methods I. (2½ hrs.), Miss McGovern 4.
Primary Methods II. (2½ hrs.), Miss McGovern 3.
Primary Methods- III. (1 hr.) (M. W. or Tu. Th.), Miss McGovern 1-2.

RURAL EDUCATION:

NORMAL COURSES

Didactics, Mr. Campbell 1.
Elementary Psychology, Mr. Campbell 3.
General Methods, Mr. Hart 1.
Observation and Teaching, Mr. Hart 2.
The County School, Mr. Campbell 4.

TEACHING:

COLLEGE COURSES

Illustrative Teaching (1½ hrs.), Mr. Stone, Miss Fesenbeck, Miss
    Hughes, Miss Luse, Miss Correll, Miss Cresswell 5-6.
Practice Teaching as arranged.
Conference Teaching (½ hr.) as arranged.

DIPLOMA COURSES

Same as College Courses and
Kindergarten Theory and Observation (2 hrs.), Miss Brown 3.
Kindergarten Theory III. (2½ hrs.), Miss Brown 2.
Kindergarten Theory V. (3 hrs.), Miss Brown 4.
Primary Theory and Observation (2 hrs.), Miss Scofield 2-5.
Criticism, Miss Scofield 6.

NORMAL COURSES

Rural Demonstration Teaching, Mr. Stone and Training School
    Critics 2.

ENGLISH:

COLLEGE COURSES

College Rhetoric, Mr. Fagan 2-3-6.
Public Speaking I., Mr. Barnes 1.
Public Speaking II., (3 hrs.), Mr. Barnes 5.
Argumentation I. (3 hrs.), Mr. Barnes 2.
The Oration, Mr. Barnes 3.
English Literature, Mr. Gist 1; Miss Carpenter 1; Miss Lambert
    4; Miss Siner 2.
Middle English, Mr. Gist 4.
Shakespeare, Mr. Gist 3.

English Literature of the Nineteenth Century, Miss Lambert 1.
American Literature, Miss Carpenter 3.
Recent American Literature (3 hrs.), Miss Lambert 2.
The Development of the English Novel, Miss Carpenter 4.
Elocution I, Miss Falkler 2-3; Miss Shanewise 2.
Elocution II., Miss Shanewise 3-4.
Repertoire I., Miss Martin 1. .
Principles of Expression, Miss Martin 2.

DIPLOMA COURSES

Same as College Courses.

NORMAL COURSES

First Half Language and Grammar, Miss Hutchison 2-4.
Second Half Language and Grammar, Miss Hutchison 3-5.
Complete Language and Grammar, Miss Gregg 2-3-5.
Reading, Miss Falkler 5.
Elementary Elocution, Miss Falkler 4.
First Half English Composition, Miss Siner 1.
Second Half English Composition, Miss Siner 4.
First Term English Classics, Miss Oliver 4.
Second Term English Classics, Miss Gregg 4.
Orthography (a), Miss Oliver 1-3.
Orthography (b) (Tu. Th.), Miss Oliver 5.

MATHEMATICS:

COLLEGE COURSES

Solid Geometry, Mr. Wright 4.
College Algebra I., Miss Lambert 5.
Plane Trigonometry, Mr. Daugherty 3.
College Algebra II., Mr. Condit 2.
Spherical Trigonometry (2 hrs.), Mr. Daugherty 6.
Surveying (3 hrs.), Mr. Daugherty 6.
History and Teaching of Mathematics, Mr. Condit 5.
Integral Calculus, Mr. Condit 3.

DIPLOMA COURSES

Same as College Courses.

NORMAL COURSES

First Half Arithmetic, Miss Lambert 2.
Second Half Arithmetic, Mr. Daugherty 4.
Complete Arithmetic, Mr. Condit 1; Miss Allen 4; Mr. Daugherty 2.
First Term Algebra, Miss Lambert 3.
Second Term Algebra, Miss Allen 3-6.
First and Second Term Algebra, Miss Lambert 1.
Third Term Algebra, Miss Allen 1.
Beginning Geometry, Mr. Wright 6.
Middle Geometry, Mr. Wright 5.
Solid Geometry, Mr. Wright 2.

HISTORY:

COLLEGE COURSES

English History, Miss Rice 4.
Renaissance and Reformation, Miss Riggs 1.
19th Century History II. (3 hrs.) (M. W. F.), Miss Riggs 5.
Method History II. (2 hrs.) (Tu. Th.), Miss Riggs 5.
18th Century History II. (3 hrs.) (M. W. F.), Miss Riggs 2.

Same as College Courses.

NORMAL COURSES
First Half United States History, Miss Rice 1-2.
Complete United States History, Miss Rice 3; Mr. Mitchell 2.
Second Term General History, Miss Riggs 3.

GOVERNMENT:

COLLEGE COURSES
American Government, Mr. Meyerholz 1; Mr. Peterson 4.
Local Government and Problems (3 hrs.), Mr. Meyerholz 5.
Political Parties (3 hrs.), Mr. Peterson 5.
Constitutional Law, Mr. Meyerholz 3.

DIPLOMA COURSES
Same as College Courses.

NORMAL COURSES
Elementary Civics of Iowa, Mr. Peterson 2.
Elementary Civics of the United States, Mr. Peterson 6.
Review of Iowa and U. S. Civics (non-credit), Mr. Meyerholz 2.

ECONOMICS:

COLLEGE COURSES
General Economics, Mr. McKitrick 6; Mr. Mitchell 1.
Social and Economic Problems III. (3 hrs.), Mr. McKitrick 1.
Sociology (2 hrs.), Mr. McKitrick 1.
American Industrial History III. (3 hrs.), Mr. Mitchell 7.
Public Finance II. (2 hrs.), Mr. McKitrick 7.

DIPLOMA COURSES
Same as College Courses.

NORMAL COURSES
Elementary Economics, Mr. McKitrick 2; Mr. Mitchell 4.

LATIN:

COLLEGE COURSES
Latin III. (The Odes of Horace), Mr. Merchant 1.
Latin VI. (Latin Composition) (2 hrs.), Mr. Merchant 3.
Latin IX. (Roman Literature) (3 hrs.), Mr. Merchant 2.
Latin XII. (Historical Latin Grammar) (2 hrs.), Mr. Merchant 4.
Greek III. (3 hrs.), Mr. Merchant 3.
Greek VI. (2 hrs.), Mr. Merchant 2.
College Ele. Latin III., Mr. Merchant 6.
Cicero I., Miss Call 3.
Cicero II., Miss Call 4.
Ovid, Miss Call 5.

DIPLOMA COURSES
Same as College Courses.

NORMAL COURSES
First Term Caesar and Latin Composition, Miss Call 2.

GERMAN AND FRENCH:

German I. (Die Jungfrau von Orleans), Miss Lorenz 5.
German II. (Emilia Galotti and Lyrics and Ballads), Miss Lorenz 2.
German V. (Iphigenie auf Tauris and Die Braut von Messina),
    Miss Lorenz 3.
German VIII. (German Classics, or History of German Language
    and Literature), Mr. Knoepfler 3.
German XI. (Immensee and Hoeher als die Kirche), Mr. Knoep-
    fler 5.
German XII. (Die Journalisten), Miss Lorenz 6.
French III. (Le Voyage de M. Perrichon and L'Abbe Constantin),
    Mr. Knoepfler 1.
French VI. (Le Gendre de M. Poirier and Un Philosophe sous les
    Toits) Mr. Knoepfler 2.

DIPLOMA COURSES

Same as College Courses.

NORMAL COURSES

First Term German, Miss Nolte 4.
Second Term German, Miss Nolte 2.
Third Term German, Miss Nolte 6.
Fourth Term German, Miss Nolte 3.

PHYSICS AND CHEMISTRY.

COLLEGE COURSES

Physics I. (Mechanics and Sound) (3 hrs.) (M. W. F.), Mr. Bege-
    man 2.
Physics II. (Laboratory Physics in Mechanics) (M. W.) (2 hrs.),
    Mr. Begeman 7 and 8.
Physics III. (Heat and Light) (3 hrs.) (Tu. Th. F.), Mr. Bege-
    man 4.
Physics IV. (Laboratory Physics in Heat and Light) (2 hrs.) (M.
    W.), Mr. Begeman 5 and 6.
Physics IX. (Advanced Course in Electricity and Magnetism), Mr.
    Begeman 3 and 4.

NORMAL COURSES

First Term Physics, Mr. Hersey 1; Mr. Read 3.
First Term Laboratory Physics, Mr. Hersey 7 and 8; Mr. Read
    5 and 6.
Second Term Physics, Mr. Hersey 3-4.
Second Term Laboratory Physics, Mr. Hersey 5 and 6.

CHEMISTRY:

COLLEGE COURSES

Chemistry I. (General Inorganic Chemistry), Mr. Getchell 2.
Chemistry III. (Chemistry of Metals and Qualitative Analysis),
    Mr. Getchell 3.
Chemistry IV. (Organic Chemistry), Mr. Bond 5.
Quantitative Analysis, Mr. Getchell 5 and 6.
Chemistry VI. (Water Analysis), Mr. Bond 1.
Chemistry XI. (Household Chemistry), Mr. Bond 4-6; Mr. Getchell
    7; Mr. Read 1.
Chemistry Laboratory as arranged (under each division).

NATURAL SCIENCE:

COLLEGE COURSES

Zoology III., Mr. Arey I.
Zoology Laboratory (M. W.), Mr. Arey 7 and 8.
Nature Study, Mr. Arey 3-5.
Physiology I., Mr. Newton 1-3-4.
Astronomy, Mr. Cable 4.
Geology II.   Mr. Cable 2.
Agriculture III., Mr. Oldenburg 1.
Agriculture Laboratory, Mr. Oldenburg 5 and 6.
Conservation of Natural Resources, Miss Aitchison 1.
Botany III., Mr. Palmer 2-3.
Botany III. Laboratory (Tu., Th.), Mr. Palmer 7 and 8.

DIPLOMA COURSES

Same as College Courses.

NORMAL COURSES

Elementary Zoology, Mr. Arey 4.
Elementary Physiology, Mr. Newton 2.
First Ele. Agriculture, Mr............. 2-3-5.
Second Ele. Agriculture, Mr. Oldenburg 2-4.
Agriculture Laboratory, Mr. .... 7 and 8.
First Half Geography, Miss Aitchison 2.
Second Half Geography, Miss Aitchison 3.
Complete Geography, Miss Aitchison 4.
Elementary Botany, Mr. Palmer 1.
Elementary Physiography, Mr. Cable 1-5.

MANUAL ARTS:

COLLEGE COURSES

Organization and Economics of Manual Training (3 hrs.) (M. W.
    F.), Mr. Bailey 1.
Woodwork 1 (3 hrs.)' (M. W. F.), Mr. Brown 7 and 8.
Advanced Woodwork, Mr. Brown 3 and 4.
Mechanical Drawing I. (2 hrs.) (Tu. Th.), Mr. Bailey 7 and 8.
Mechanical Drawing IV. (2 hrs.) (Tu. Th.), Mr. Bailey 7 and 8.
Mechanical Drawing II. (3 hrs.) (M. W. F.), Mr. Bailey 3 and 4.
Mechanical Drawing III. (3 hrs.) (M. W. F.), Mr. Bailey 3 and 4.
Wood Turning (2 hrs.), Mr. Brown 3 and 4.
Sheet Metal Work (2½ hrs.), Mr. Bailey 2.

DIPLOMA COURSES

Same as College Courses.

NORMAL COURSES

Primary Handwork, Miss Dandliker 1-2.
Handwork for Rural Schools, Miss Schuneman 3-4.
Woodwork for Rural Schools, Mr. Brown 5-6.
Elementary Woodwork, Mr. Brown 3 and 4; 7 and 8.
Elementary Mechanical Drawing, Mr. Bailey 7 and 8.

ART:

COLLEGE COURSES

History of Painting, Miss Thornton 4.
Design (2½ hrs.), Miss Patt 1-6.

Perspective (2½ hrs.), Miss Thornton 3.
Water-Color (2½ hrs.), Miss Thornton 1.
Supervision in Art (2½ hrs.), Miss Thornton 2.

DIPLOMA COURSES

Same as College Courses and
Primary Drawing II. (2½ hrs.), Miss Patt 3-4-5, Miss Schuneman 2.

NORMAL COURSES

Drawing for Rural Schools, Miss Schuneman 1.

HOME ECONOMICS:

COLLEGE COURSES

Elementary Food Theory III. (2 hrs.) (Tu. Th.), Miss Young 1
and 2; 3 and 4; 5 and 6.

DIPLOMA COURSES

Household Management (1 hr.) (M. W.), Miss Young 1-3-4.
Methods, Home Economics (1 hr.) (Fri.), Miss Young 1-3-4.
Dietetics (1 hr.) (Tues.), Miss Roberts 3 and 4.
Demonstrations (M. W.) (1 hr.), Miss Young 5 and 6; 7 and 8.
Demonstrations (Tu. Th.) (1 hr.), Miss Young 5 and 6.
Third Term Sewing (Sub-collegiate):
Sections A and B (M. W. F. 1 and M. W. 2), Miss Roberts and
Miss Freer.
Section C (M. W. F. 3 and M. W. 4), Miss Roberts.
Section D (Tu. Th. 3 and Tu. Th. F. 4), Miss Freer.
Sections E and F (M. W. 5 and M. W. F. 6), Miss Roberts and
Miss Freer.

NORMAL COURSES

First Domestic Science:
.   Section A (Daily 1 and M. W. 2), Miss Osborne and Miss
Hurd.
Section B (Daily 3 and Tu. Th. 4), Miss Osborne and Miss
Hurd.
Section C (Daily 5 and Tu. Th. 6), Miss Osborne and Miss
Hurd.
Second Domestic Science:
Section A (Daily 2 and Tu. Th. 1), Miss Osborne and Miss
Hurd.
Section B (Daily 4 and M. W. 3), Miss Osborne and Miss
Hurd.

COMMERCIAL EDUCATION:

DIPLOMA COURSES

Accounting II., Mr. Cummins 1.
Commercial Law, Mr. Coffey 2.
Second Term Shorthand (Sub-collegiate), Mr. Coffey 1.
Third Term Shorthand (Sub-collegiate), Mr. Coffey 3.
Typewriting (Sub-collegiate), Mr. Coffey 4.

NORMAL COURSES

Elementary Bookkeeping, Mr. Cummins 2.
Second Term Shorthand, Mr. Coffey 1.
Third Term Shorthand, Mr. Coffey 3.

Typewriting, Mr. Coffey 4.
First Term Penmanship, Mr. Cummins 3-5-6.
Advanced Penmanship, Mr. Cummins 4.

MUSIC:

COLLEGE COURSES

Music II. (2½ hrs.), Mr. Fullerton 3.
History of Music I. (2 hrs.) (Tu. Th.), Miss Childs 1.
Harmony I. (3 hrs.) M. W. F.), Miss Thomson 1.
Harmony II. (2 hrs.) (Tu. Th.), Miss Thomson 4.
Harmony IV. (2 hrs.) (Tu. Th.), Miss Thomson 3.

DIPLOMA COURSES

Conducting (2½ hrs.) (M. W. F.), Mr. Fullerton 4.
Methods (Lower Grades) (2½ hrs.) (M. W. F.), Miss Barr 3.
Appreciation of Music (2½ hrs.) (M. W. F.), Miss Thomson 5.
Supervision (2 hrs), Mr. Fullerton 1.

NORMAL COURSES

First Term Music, Mr. Fullerton 2; Miss Hooper 1-4.
Second Term Music, Miss Barr 4-6.

PHYSICAL EDUCATION:

COLLEGE COURSES

Playground Methods II. (3 hrs.) (M. W. F.), Mr. Seymour 5.
Theory of Athletics II. (2 hrs.) (Tu. Th.), Mr. Seymour 5.

DIPLOMA COURSES

Same as College Courses and
Physiology of Exercise, Mr Seymour 2.
Medical Gymnastics and Massage (3 hrs.) (M. Tu. Th.), Mr. Seymour 3.
Medical Gymnastics and Massage (3 hrs.), Miss Hussey 6.
Physical Department Administration (2 hrs.) (W. Fri.), Mr. Seymour 3.

PRACTICAL WORK

Second Physical Training- (M. W.), Miss Nisbet 7.
Third Physical Training (M. W.), Miss Hussey 5; Miss Nisbet 6.
Third Physical Training (Tu. Th.), Miss Hussey 4; Miss Wild 4-6-7; Miss Nisbet 5.
Drills (Tu. Th.), Miss Hussey 5.
Drills (M. W.), Miss Grantham 5.
Gymnastics (M. W.), Miss Hussey 7.
Esthetic Dancing (Tu. Th.), Miss Hussey 7.
Athletics (Tu. Th.), Miss Hussey 8.
Tennis (M. W.), Miss Wild 4-8; Miss Nisbet 3-5.
Tennis (Tu. Th.), Miss Wild 3; Miss Nisbet 6-7; Mr. Berkstresser 5.
Swimming (Tu. Th.), Miss Hussey 8; Miss Nisbet 3; Miss Grantham 5-7; Mr. Berkstreser 4.
Swimming (M. W.), Miss Wild 6; Miss Nisbet 4; Miss Grantham 3-8; Mr. Berkstresser 5.
Plays and Games (Tu. Th.), Miss Wild 5; Mr. Berkstresser 6.
Plays and Games (M. W.), Mr. Berkstresser 4.

First Rhythm (M. W.), Miss Wild 7; Miss Grantham 3.
Second Rhythm (Tu. Th.), Miss Grantham 6.
Folk Dancing (Tu. Th.), Miss Nisbet 8; Miss Grantham 3.
Advanced Folk Dancing (M. W.), Miss Grantham 7.
Baseball (M. W.), Miss Grantham 6.
Baseball, Mr. Seymour 6.
Baseball Team, Mr. Seymour 7 and 8
Track Class (M. W.), Mr. Berkstresser 6.
Track Team, Mr. Berkstresser 7 and 8.
Corrective Work (M. W.), Miss Hussey 4; Miss Wild 5.
Corrective Work (Tu. Th.), Miss Nisbet 4; Miss Grantham 4.

Lightning Source UK Ltd.
Milton Keynes UK
UKHW011531191118
332599UK00012B/823/P